ISBN: 9781313360296

Published by:
HardPress Publishing
8345 NW 66TH ST #2561
MIAMI FL 33166-2626

Email: info@hardpress.net
Web: http://www.hardpress.net

COPTIC MANUSCRIPTS

BROUGHT FROM THE

FAYYUM

BY

W. M. FLINDERS PETRIE, ESQ., D.C.L.

TOGETHER WITH A PAPYRUS IN THE BODLEIAN LIBRARY

EDITED WITH COMMENTARIES AND INDICES

BY

W. E. CRUM, M.A.

Four Collotype Plates

LONDON

DAVID NUTT, 270-271 STRAND

1893

To

MONSIEUR ÉMILE CHÉDIEU

𝔍n gratitude and affection

PREFACE

A GENERAL account of these Manuscripts has already been given by me elsewhere.[1] The study of the texts, however, upon which it was based had been but superficial, and many of the statements there made require correction or modification.

The main collection is a result of Mr. Flinders Petrie's excavations in 1889, and was brought from Deir El-Hammam, three miles N. of Illahun. To it are added a few fragments (Nos. XX, XXVI, XLIX, and LIII), acquired at Hawara. Mr. Petrie writes to me: "The Deir has been rebuilt a few centuries ago, but there are outlines of a much larger Deir showing on the ground. Outside the older Deir are rubbish-mounds. Here we found plenty of scraps of papyrus," which the natives "brought and sold to me in scrap lots. I never had any occasion to suspect any outside admixture. Most of the Hammam pieces had evidently just been dug up; certainly they had never passed through a dealer's hands. The Hawara papyri were all found, scrap by scrap, by my own workmen. There were no circumstances to suggest in the least that these were found elsewhere or imported."[2]

The Oxford papyrus, given as an Appendix, was procured by the late Rev. G. J. Chester at Sheik Hammad, near Sohag. I publish it here on account of the recurrence in it of certain place-names found in the Petrie collection, as well as in order to allow of its comparison with No. XLV.

There are but two of the European collections of MSS. from Middle Egypt of which accounts have been given; those in the Museums of Berlin and Vienna. The former contained in 1885, some 300 fragments,[3] but it has since been increased. The number of Coptic fragments in the latter is estimated at 4000.[4] The Louvre is also said to contain a collection of some importance.[5] In the following pages are published all the texts of the Petrie collection from which it seemed possible that any positive results might be obtained. A number of small fragments have been passed

---

[1] In Flinders Petrie's "Medum," p. 48 ff.

[2] Mr. Petrie further suggests that the "Find" of a great quantity of fragments together may be due to the custom, prevalent at all events now in the district, of using a ruined building as a depository for all the rubbish of the neighbourhood.

[3] Stern in *Aeg. Zeits.*, 1885, 24.

[4] Krall in "Führer durch die Ausstellung" (Pap. Rainer), I. Th., s. 26.

[5] Stern *loc. cit.* I do not know if the above calculations pretend to include all the smaller fragments.

over, it being impossible, as yet, to utilise the few letters legible upon them, deprived as they are of all context.

The texts have been arranged on the basis of subject-matter; and within this (roughly) upon that of extent and actual preservation.

The subjects represented are (1) *Biblical texts:*—To the one example previously described, a second is now added. (II) *Patristic texts:*—I have placed among these some curious fragments which give, *inter alia*, the account of a dream, because I was at a loss more appropriately to class them. (III) *Liturgical texts:*—A small group, put together since I wrote my former description. (IV) *Letters:*—This section embraces (as in the other collections) a large proportion of the whole. (V) *Lists and accounts:*—Some very small scraps are included here. Of the so-called Legal documents, numerous in Vienna,[1] there are but three mutilated specimens (Nos. XXXV, XXXVI, XXXVII). These I have held it allowable to class with the letters.

Were this a collection of Greek instead of Coptic documents, the absence of all dated texts might not prove an insuperable obstacle to forming a chronological estimate. The palæographist would often be able, with tolerable assurance, to supply the want; so far, at least, as regards the strictly cursive MSS. But such are, in Coptic, a rarity, very few Fayyum texts being, in this respect, comparable with the Pap. Rainer, 1993.[2] "Where ligatures are almost or wholly absent, all merely 'graphic' dating rests upon a very weak footing."[3] It is, however, this practically ligatureless character[4] which these fragments display, and we are therefore forced to depend for chronological conclusions upon an occasional comparison with the dated plates of Hyvernat's "Album."[5] Beyond this, the language in which the texts are written and the materials used can serve, to some extent, as arguments. There is so little paper in the collection, that we may suppose it not to reach much beyond the end of the ninth century; while the comparative frequency of Arabic names, &c., point to about the beginning of the eighth century as a probable *terminus a quo.*[6] These circumstances, however, may be accidental. They do not, of course, affect the uncial texts, one of which (No. II) is perhaps the oldest Coptic document from the Fayyum.[7] The sizes, too, of the papyri point, as Karabacek has noticed, to a period when that material was already scarce. The largest sheet in the collection (No. XXIV), measured originally about 17 × 11 in., the smallest (No. XIX), $3\frac{7}{8}$ × $4\frac{1}{2}$ in.

---

[1] *Vide* "Führer"-Rainer, I. Th., s. 35.

[2] *Ibid.* s. 44. With the Djêmê Cartulary the case is different.

[3] Gardthausen, *Griech. Paläogr.*, s. 178.

[4] For this I have, in one or two cases, used the term "*semi-uncial*"; but have since noticed that Gardthausen already appropriates it otherwise.

[5] We are here shown an excellent series of texts for the middle and later periods, but could have wished for a larger selection from the earlier MSS. One misses, for instance, examples of the great Turin papyri and of those of Achmim.

[6] I am at a loss to draw any conclusion from the curious group here represented by No. XLIII. There are reasons for believing them to belong to the Arabic period. Can they be the work of Greeks, freshly immigrated?

[7] Yet Maspero has warned us (*Compt. Rend. Acad. des Inscr.*, XVI, 290), cf the uncertainty of the arguments from which even the so-called earliest uncial MSS. are dated.

I have, in the following descriptions, avoided any notice of the direction in which the lines of writing lie relatively to those of the fibre-layers. Wilcken has shown [1] the possibility of determining, in certain cases where a single papyrus bears a separate text upon each face, the relative ages of these. The present Coptic collection offers, however, little material of this kind; the only examples are Nos. IX and XVII, XII and XXIV, XIX (Arabic and Coptic), XXXVII (ditto), and as these consist, in each case, of but one σελίς, Wilcken's rules cannot be applied. Only the two larger papyri, Nos. XI and XLVI, show more than a single σελίς; and, in both cases, the text is upon that side whose fibres run at right-angles to the joining-line of the σελίδες. Yet it may be noted that, both in the Petrie collection and in that at Berlin, a very large majority of the texts are written, or at all events begun, at right-angles to the fibre-lines.

The already printed texts from the other Fayyum Papyri are Stern's selection from those in Berlin,[2] and those of the Vienna collection published entirely or in part by Krall.[3] The former publication has been here supplemented by my own copies (1891) of the remaining Berlin fragments.

I have made no attempt at a comprehensive treatment of the language of these texts. That will be a task possible only when the promised Rainer "Corpus" has appeared, together with editions of the other unpublished literature from Middle Egypt. For the present, Stern has sufficiently indicated the characteristic features of the various dialects. Of the 56 fragments here transcribed, the language of 22 may be called thoroughly Middle Egyptian; that of 7, Sahidic; 23 show both influences in varying proportions. Of Boheiric, there are 6 examples—yet none show this dialect in absolute purity. There is only one Achmimic text (No. II).

I have throughout used the term "Middle Egyptian" as including the dialects both of Memphis (Stern's "Untersahidisch") and of the Fayyum. It is not possible, with the few texts of any length at present known, to draw a satisfactory boundary between these two dialects. Not only are the majority of available documents short or imperfect; they often betray the work of very illiterate scribes, who wrote even their native dialect with little care or accuracy, and whose productions tend to an imitation now of southern, now of northern usage. A rough division may perhaps be made by classing as "Memphitic" those texts which, like Revillout's Passports, follow the Sahidic rule as to $r - l$, while showing, in their vocabulary, a distinct Boheiric influence; and as "Fayyumic," those which systematically replace r by l, have the characteristic vowel-scale $(a = o, e = a, \acute{e} = \breve{e}, \&c.)$, and show words unknown either in Sahidic or Boheiric. Confining ourselves to Nos. XI–XLIII, we might cite as typical examples—(a) of texts undoubtedly Sahidic, Nos. XXI or XXXIII; (b) of those in which Sahidic forms predominate, No. XVII; (c) in which Mid. Egyptian forms are in a

[1] "Recto od. Verso?" Hermes XXII, 487, ff.

[2] Aeg. Zeits., 1885, 23 ff.

[3] Mittheilungen a. d. Pap. Sammlg. Erzherz. Rainer, I–V. When the former description of the Petrie collection was written, I had not seen Bd. V, in which several texts are given in full with translations.

majority, No. XXIII; (*d*) which are wholly Mid. Egyptian, Nos. XXII or XXV; (*e*) of those with a decided Boheiric element, Nos. XIII or XXVII.

In explanation of this remarkable variety of dialect, no very satisfactory theory can be advanced. Although, as has been stated, the Petrie collection comes entirely from a district on the immediate borders of the Fayyum, the localities mentioned or implied in the texts are by no means confined to it. No. II points to Achmim, while Sahidic literary texts, such as Nos. III, IV, might have had their origin still farther south; and it is not impossible that some of the place-names found in No. XLV refer to the neighbourhood of the Natron Lakes. Still, the geographical data supplied cannot, for the most part, be utilised, since so many of the places named remain unidentified. All means, too, are absent by which to localise the writers of the various documents,—the single exception being No. XXXV,—though their movements and those of their correspondents can sometimes be traced (No. XXII). It is possible that Sahidic was, as Stern has suggested, at one time the universal literary language, at least, above the Delta; or perhaps the Sahidic fragments from the Fayyum may be merely traces of occasional passengers or residents from the south. Proximity of other clearly defined dialects and constant communication will sufficiently account for the heterogeneous and irregular character which marks so many of the Middle Egyptian texts.

As to the method followed in publishing the MSS.: I have given in each case (1) the material used, (2) the size of the sheet or fragment, stating the height and the breadth, measured always at the extremest remaining points, (3) the quality of the material and the style of the writing, (4) the text itself, followed by (5) a commentary and (6) an indication of the dialect.

The first attempt to extract their value from a body of fragments so varied and so dilapidated as those of the present collection, can seldom be productive of results more than partially satisfactory. A more prolonged study of the papyri would doubtless throw further light upon many points which still remain unclear. My chief aim, at present, has been to give reliable transcriptions of the texts; an adequate appreciation of their contents they may, I hope, receive at the hands of a future interpreter.

Finally, I have to express my best thanks to Mr. Flinders Petrie for his kindness in entrusting me with his collection; to Prof. Erman for permission to copy the unpublished papyri at Berlin, and to Mr. Nicholson for the use of those in the Bodleian; to Prof. Harnack, Prof. Wilcken and Prof. Karabacek, and especially to Dr. G. Steindorff and the Rev. G. Horner, for valuable help on certain points about which their opinions were of special weight.

LONDON, *December* 1892.

ABBREVIATIONS

The Abbreviations most frequently employed are :

Sah.	The Sahidic Dialect.
M.E.	The Middle Egyptian Dialect.
Boh.	The Boheiric Dialect.
R.	Mittheilungen aus der Papyrus Sammlung Erzherzog Rainer, I-V (Wien).
Ä.Z.	Zeitschrift für Ägyptische Sprache und Alterthumskunde.
Berl. P.	The unpublished Mid. Egyptian papyri in the Berlin Museum.
Stern.	Koptische Grammatik ; Ludwig Stern.
Peyr.	Lexicon Linguæ Copticæ ; A. Peyron.
Hyv., Alb.	Album de Palæographie copte ; H. Hyvernat.
Revill., A. et C.	Actes et Contrats des Musées égyptiens de Boulaq et du Louvre ; E. Revillout.

CONTENTS

BIBLICAL TEXTS.

I. *Parchment.*   about 4½ × 7 in.

S. Matthew, XI. 27, 28.
XII. 1−3, 6−10, 11.12.

The fragment is in so mutilated a condition, that the readings and restit-
-utions proposed are often very doubtful.
The M.S. is probably of no very early date. It has large, though plain
capitals, and uses the colon as a clause-divider. Δ is peculiar and
may be archaic; but Υ is distinctly young. Its chief peculiarity, however,
lies in the form, ᵡ, which it has in common only with a few other
M.E. parchments. (v. *Krall* in R.I, III; also a fragt. of S. John's Gospel in the
Berlin Museum, P. 5569.) *Gardthausen* has pointed out (Griech. Paläogr.,
s. 148,) that ʯ and ί, found here, occur already in very ancient texts.

Recto:

                           XII, 1. [ΑΥϩ]ΪΤΛΛΤΟΥ ΕΤ ?
                             ? Μ ΝϹΑ ΝΙϩΕ[ΜϹ]

XI, 27.
                          2. [Ε]ΟΥΩΜ ΝΙ[ΦΑΡ]ΙϹ
                             ΕΟϹ ΔΕ ΕΤΑΥΝΕΥ
              ΕϢ.?ΕΠ   ΠΕΧΕΥ ΝΗϤ ΧΕ ϩΕΙ
      [ϢΗΛΙ ΛΥ]Ω ΠΤΕϩ   ΝΕΚΜΛΘΕΤΗϹ ΕΙΡΙ
      [ΝΕ Π]ϢΗΛΙ ϢΛϤ   ΜΠΕΤΕϢϢΗ ΝΕ[ΡΙ]
         ? ί ΕΒΛΛ   ϩΜ ΠϹΛΒΒΛΤΟΝ
28.   [Ε]ΛΛΙ ΟΥΛΝ   3. Ṋ̇ΤΛϤ ΔΕ ΠΕΧΕϤ Ν[Η]
       [ΝΙΜ ΕΤϩΟϹ]ϊ ΛΥΩ ΕΤ   ΟΥ ΧΕ ό
             [ό]ΠΤ [ΛΥ]ω   ΕΙϤ ϩΟ
                            ΜΝ Ṅ
                            Δ̇Ε
                            ε

Verso:

              Λ̅Μ̅..Κ̅Β̅ ΕΤΒΕ ΠΕΤΕΛϹ ΤΕϤ6ΙΧ [ϢΟΥΩΟΥ]
XII, 6. [ΠΊ]ΕΛΠΗΙ ΜΠΕ[ΙΜ]
7.   [ε] ΛΛΤΕΤΕΝ Ϲ[Λ]
      ΟΥΝ ΧΕ ΟΥΝ ΠΕ
     Ο̇ΥΝΕΕΙ ΠΕΤΟΥΕϢ[ϥ]   XII, 12.
      ΛΥΩ ΝΝΟΥΘΥϹΙ[Λ]
      ΕΝ ΤΕ ΝΝΛΤΕΤΕⁿˢⁱᶜ   ΕϹΛΥ [ΝΛΥΗΡ]
                        Ċ̇ΩϹΔΕ Ϣ[ϢΗ ΕΕΛ]

NEϩI NIATNABI ΜΠ   ΜΠΠΕΤ[ΝΑΝΟΥΒ]

8.   ϩΕΠ ΕΝ Π⊙C ΓΑΡ ΜΠ   ϩΜ ΠCΑΒ[ΒΑΤΟΝ]

    CΑΒΒΑΤΟΝ ΠΕ ΠϢΗ   13. ΤΟΤΕ Π[ΕΧΕϥ ΜΠΙ]

    [λΙ ΜΠ]λΩϢΙ] (space)   λΩΜΙ[ΧΕ CΑΥΤΕΝ]

9.   [ΑΥΩ ΝΤΕλΕϥΟ]ΥΩΤΕΒ ΤΕΚ ϬΙ[Χ ΕΒΑλ &c.

    [ΕΒΑλ ΜΜΕ]Υ Αϥ Ε

    [ϩΟΥΝ ΕΤΕΥCΥΝΑΓΩ]

10. [ΓΗ ΑΥΩ ϩΕΙ Ο]Υ λΩ

    [ΜΙ ΕλΕ ΤΕϥϬΙΧ Ϣ]ΟΥ

    [ΩΟΥ &c.

A τίτλος written, as here, in the body of the text, is rare in Coptic M.S.S. Instances of it have been published Zoega, p. 150, (likewise M.E.,) and Palæograph. Society, Orient. Ser., pl. LXXX (Sah.) The example here is com-pleted from that corresponding in the Boh. prefatory lists of ΚΕΦΑλΕΟΝ ΝΟΥΕΙΝΙΝ ΝΝΙϢϮ (as e.g. in the Gospels, Br. Mm. M.S. de la Zouche 126, or Or. 1001.)

The dialect of these verses is similar to that of the Lower-Sah. texts published by Bouriant (Mém. de l'Instit. égypt. II, ii); that is, it stands near to the Sah. in its vocabulary, while in vocalisation, and in the use of λ for ρ, it is distinctly M.E., and in its use of –ι as the weak termination, of the article ΠΙ, ΤΙ, ΝΙ, and of ⊙C, shows Boh. influence. The versions of the other dialects will be found as follows;

        Sah., Woide, p. 15. (only ch. XI, 28.)

        Boh., Schwarze, p. 38.

        M.E., R.I, p. 69. (only ch. XI, 27.)

II. Parchment. (v. pl. I.)

        A. Epistle of S. James, IV. 12, 13.   4 × 3⅛ in.

        B.   „ S. Jude, 17–20 (paged CΙΗ, CΙϴ.)   ¾ × 3⅛ in.

        C.   ?   1¼ × 1 in.

The material and writing of the three fragts. are very fine. The text is in single column, and is the only remnant, as yet published, of the Achmimic New Testament.

I have elsewhere (in Flinders-Petrie's "Medum, p. 48) suggested the 6th cent. as a date for these texts; but I now feel clear that they are at least two centuries older, and would compare their character with that of the first scribe of the "Pistis Sophia". The letters Α, Ε, C, Ω, ϣ, ϥ, ϩ, are identical in the two M.S.S. The straight back in ε, c, — hardly so

marked here as in the "Pistis",— and the low central stroke in ω, ω,
separate our fragts. from the Berlin (Museum) Psalter, P. 3259, whose forms
of these letters are almost those of Hyvernat, Album, pl. II (Clarendon), but
whose grammatical peculiarities (v. A.Z. '90, 62,) throw it back to a very
early age. Is it possible that the above-mentioned palaeographical
features are characteristic of Middle Egypt? At any rate, they occur,
so far as I know, only in our Achmim fragts. and in the "Pistis", whose
language has a M.E. tendency. What does the presence of μ indicate?
It appears in the Cod. Sinaiticus, which Gardthausen (s. 148 and Taf. I,) places
"circa 400", but is unknown to any of the old Coptic M.S.S. in question.
Seeing, farther, that Harnack (Texte u. Untersuch. VII,² p. 94, ff.,) assigns the
"Pistis" from internal evidence, to the second half of the 3ᵈ cent., I would
propose to date these very valuable fragts. about A.D. 300–350.*

Fragment A. Recto:

Achmimic.	ογκριτης· ογε δε πε πνομοθετης λογ
Sah. (Woide).	ογκριτης· ογλ δε πε πνϫμοθετης λγω
Boh. (La Garde).	ογρεϥϯϩαπ·ογλι ϩαρ πε πινομοθετης ογοϩ
Cod. Sinaiticus.	κριτης εις εστιν ο νομοϑετης και
Cod. Alex. } variants	
Cod. Vatic. } only.	εις εστιν νομοϑετης

Verso:

a. πκριτης	Βωκ·αϩραϊ αϯπολις·τηρογραμπε
S. πεκριτης	Βωκ εϩογν (var. εϩραι) ετειπολις·ν̄τ̄ν̄ ρογρομπε
B. ν̄ρεϥϯϩαπ	ϣεναν εταιπολις ν̄τενιρι νογρομπι
C.S. κριτης	πορευσωμεϑα εις την δε την πολιν και ποιησωμεν ενιδυ—
C.A.	ενιδυτον
C.V.	πορευσομεϑα ποιησομεν

a. μ̄μ̄ο τ̄ηρε////	
S. μ̄ηλγ ν̄τ̄ν̄ρ	
B. μ̄ηλγ ν̄τενερ	
C.S. τον και	
C.A. ενα	
C.V. εκει	

*An inspection of the M.S. of the "Pistis" shows that pp. α—κβᵃ, ριαᵇ and ρϥϛ—τνλ,
were written by a very different hand from that which produced pp. κβᵃ, l. 30—ρϥε
and τνε. The contrast is greatest in the letters λ, ε, ο, c, γ, ϫ, (but p. 1ηᵃ
shows both forms,) ϩ, ϭ and the "paragraph" mark, to the left of the columns.
Schwarze (Coptic text, p. 124,) noted merely a new hand. The Palaeogr. Soc., Or.
Ser., pl. XLII shows the first, Hyvernat's Album, pl. II, the second scribe.

Fragment B. Recto: (ⲱ̄ⲧ̄ⲏ.)

ⲁ. ⲚⲚ̄ϢⲈϪⲈ ⲘⲠⲚ̄ϪⲀⲈⲒⲤ ⲒⲤ̄ ⲠⲬ̄Ⲥ ⲚⲈⲒ̈ ⲈⲦⲀ ⲚⲈϤⲀⲠⲞⲤⲦⲞⲖⲞⲤ ϪⲞⲞⲨ ⲈϪⲚ

Ⲋ. ⲚⲚ̄ϢⲀϪⲈ ⲘⲠⲈⲚϪⲞⲈⲒⲤ ⲒⲤ̄ ⲠⲈⲬ̄Ⲥ . ⲚⲀⲒ Ⲛ̄ⲦⲀ ⲚⲈϤⲀⲠⲞⲤⲦⲞⲖⲞⲤ ϪⲞⲞⲨ ϪⲒⲚ

Ⲃ. Ⲛ̄ⲚⲒⲤⲀⲬⲒ̀ ⲈⲦⲀⲨⲬⲞⲦⲞⲨ ⲒⲤϪⲈⲚ ϢⲞⲢⲠ ⲈⲂⲞⲖϦⲒⲦⲈⲚ ⲚⲒⲀⲠⲞⲤⲦⲞⲖⲞⲤ

C.S. τῶν ῥημάτων τῶν προειρημένων   ὑπὸ τῶν ἀποστόλων

C.A. τῶν προειρημένων ῥημάτων

C.V.   = C.S.

ⲁ. Ⲛ̄ϦⲀⲢⲠ̄ ⲀⲂⲀⲖ·ϪⲈ ⲀⲨϪⲞⲞⲤ ϪⲈ ϦⲚ ⲦϦⲀⲈⲒ Ⲛ̄ⲚⲞⲨⲀⲈⲒϢ ⲞⲨⲚ̄ ϦⲈⲚⲢⲈϤⲬⲢϪⲢⲈ

Ⲋ. ....Ⲛ̄ϢⲞⲢⲠ.ⲈⲂⲞⲖϪⲈ ⲀⲨϪⲞⲞⲤ ϪⲈ ϦⲚ ⲐⲀⲎ Ⲛ̄ⲚⲈⲞⲨⲞⲈⲒϢ ⲞⲨⲚ ϦⲈⲚⲢⲈϤⲬⲎⲢ

Ⲃ. Ⲛ̄ⲦⲈ ⲠⲈⲚϬ̄ⲞⲒⲤ ⲒⲎ̄Ⲥ ⲠⲬ̄Ⲥ ϪⲈ ⲚⲀⲨϪⲰ ⲘⲘⲞⲤ ⲚⲰⲦⲈⲚ ⲠⲈϪⲈ Ⲉ̀ⲠϦⲀⲈ̀ Ⲛ̄ⲦⲈ ⲚⲒ

C.S. τοῦ κ̄ῡ ἡμῶν ῑῡ χ̄ῡ . ὅτι ἔλεγον ὑμῖν ἐπ' ἐσχάτου τοῦ χρόνου ἔσονται

C.A.   ὅτι ἐπ' ἐσχάτου   ἐλεύσονται

C.V.   ἐπ' ἐσχάτου χρόνου   ἔσονται

Verso: (ⲱ̄ⲧ̄ⲑ)

ⲁ.   ⲚⲎⲨ ⲈⲨⲘⲀⲀϦⲈ ⲔⲀⲦⲀ ⲚⲈⲠⲒⲐⲨⲘⲒⲀ ⲚⲚⲞⲨⲘⲚ̄Ⲧ̄ϦⲈϤⲦ ⲚⲈⲒ̈ ⲚⲈⲦⲠⲰⲢϪ

Ⲋ.   ⲚⲎⲨ ⲈⲨⲘⲞⲞϢⲈ ⲔⲀⲦⲀ ⲚⲈⲠⲒⲐⲨⲘⲒⲀ ⲚⲚⲈⲨⲘⲚ̄ⲦϢⲀϤⲦⲈ . ⲚⲀⲒ ⲚⲈⲦⲠⲰⲢϪ

Ⲃ. ⲤⲚⲞⲨ ⲈⲨⲈⲒ̀ Ⲛ̄ϪⲈ ϦⲀⲚⲢⲈϤⲈⲢϦⲀⲖ ⲈⲨⲘⲞϢⲒ ⲔⲀⲦⲀ ⲚⲞⲨⲈ̀ⲠⲒⲐⲨⲘⲒⲀ Ⲛ̄ⲦⲈ ⲚⲞⲨⲘⲈⲦⲀ̀

C.S. ἐμπαῖκται κατὰ τὰς ἐπιθυμίας αὐτῶν πορευόμενοι τῶν ἀσεβειῶν.

C.A.

C.V.

ⲁ.   ⲀⲂⲀⲖ ⲈϦⲈⲚⲮⲨⲬⲒⲔⲞⲤ ⲚⲈ ⲈⲘⲚ̄ⲦⲈⲨ ⲠⲠⲚ̄Ⲁ Ⲙ̄ⲘⲞ̀   Ⲛ̄ⲦⲰⲦⲚⲈ

Ⲋ.   ⲈⲂⲞⲖ . ⲈϦⲈⲚⲮⲨⲬⲒⲔⲞⲚ ⲚⲈ . ⲈⲘⲚ̄ⲦⲞⲨ   ⲠⲚ̄Ⲁ Ⲙ̄ⲘⲀⲨ .   Ⲛ̄ⲦⲰⲦⲚ̄

Ⲃ. ⲤⲈⲂⲎⲤ . ⲚⲀⲒ ⲚⲈ ⲚⲎⲈⲦⲪⲰⲢϪ Ⲉ̀ⲂⲞⲖ Ⲙ̄ⲮⲨⲬⲒⲔⲞⲤ ⲚⲎ ⲈⲦⲈ Ⲙ̄ⲘⲞⲚ ⲠⲚ̄Ⲁ Ⲛ̄ϦⲎⲦⲞⲨ . ⲚⲐⲰⲦⲈⲚ

C.S. οὗτοι εἰσιν οἱ ἀποδιορίζοντες ψυχικοί πνα μὴ ἔχοντες   ὑμεῖς

C.A.

C.V.

ⲁ. ⲆⲈ ⲚⲀⲘⲢ̄ⲢⲈⲦⲈ ϦⲰⲠⲈ ⲈⲦⲈⲦⲚ̄ⲔⲰⲦ Ⲙ̄ⲘⲰⲦⲚⲈ ϦⲚ ⲦⲈⲦⲚ̄ⲠⲒⲤⲦⲒⲤ ⲈⲦⲞⲨⲀⲀⲂⲈ

Ⲋ. ⲆⲈ ⲚⲀⲘⲈⲢⲀⲦⲈ   ⲈⲦⲈⲦⲚ̄ⲔⲰⲦ Ⲙ̄ⲘⲰⲦⲚ . . . (deest) . . .

Ⲃ. ⲆⲈ ⲚⲀⲘⲈⲢⲀϯ   ⲔⲈⲦⲎⲚⲞⲨ   ϦⲈⲚ ⲠⲈⲦⲈⲚⲚⲀϦϯ ⲈⲐⲞⲨⲀⲂ

C.S. δὲ ἀγάπητοι   ἐποικοδομοῦντες ἑαυτοὺς τῇ ἁγιωτάτῃ ὑμῶν πίστει

C.A.

C.V.

ⲁ. Ⲙ̄ⲠϢⲀ̀ ⲈⲦⲈⲦⲚ̄ϢⲖⲎⲖ · ϦⲘ̄ ⲠⲠⲚ̄Ⲁ ⲈⲦⲞⲨⲀⲀⲂⲈ .

Ⲋ.

Ⲃ.   Ⲉ̀ⲢⲈⲦⲈⲚⲦⲰⲂϦ ϦⲈⲚ ⲠⲒⲠⲚ̄Ⲁ ⲈⲐⲞⲨⲀⲂ .

C.C.S.A.V. ἐν πν̄ι ἁγίω προσευχόμενοι

Fragment C. (from bottom of a page.)
Recto: ///ΥΠΕΤ///   Verso: /// ? ? ///
///ΥΕΜΠ///   /// ΑΛ ? ///
///ΟΠΕΤ///   /// ?ϨΕΝ ///

The language is that of the Achmim Papyri (_Miss. au Caire_, T.I, p. 243), the only additional forms being ϨΕϤΤ = ϢΑϤΤ, ΝΤΩΤΝΕ, and ΕΤΟΥΑΑΒΕ where the papyri use ΕΤΟΥΑΒΕ.
It will be remarked that the new texts agree throughout with the Sah. version, but that neither of these follow the Greek so closely as does the Boh. Stern (_Ä.Z. '86, 135_,) suggests that the two latter versions were made through the medium of the Achmimic.

PATRISTIC TEXTS

III. Papyrus. $4\frac{3}{4} \times 8\frac{5}{8}$ in.

Part of the page of a book. The papyrus is of light grey-brown colour; the ink brown and faded on Verso. There are wide margins at the top, on the right of the Recto and left of Verso. Between the columns of the Verso there are traces of a rectangular ornament.
The character is of the class represented by Ciasca, Sacr. Bibl. Frag., II, pl. xx, and the dialect is pure Sahidic.
Recto: (cf. S. Matthew, XXV, 18 ff.)

///C

ΠΟΝΗΡΙΑ ΝΝΑ[ϊ]   ΠΝΑΥ ΤΗΡΟΥ · ΑΥΩ
ΤΑϊ ΟΝ ΤΕ ΘΕ ΜΠΕΝ   ΝϤΤϨΑΠ [ΝΟΥΟΝ ΝΙΗ
ΤΑϤϪΙ ΜΠϬΙΝϬΩΡ   ΙΙΕΕΥΕ ϬΕ ΕΒΟΛ ΕΝΡΕ
ΕΛϤϢΙΚΕ ϨΜ ΠΚΑϨ   ϤῙΝΟΒ[Ε] ΜΠΝΑΥ Ε
ΑϤϨΟΠϤ · ΝΤΑϤϹΩ   ΤΜΜΑΥ ϪΕ ΕϢΑΥ
ΤΜ ΜΠΕΜΤΟ ΕΒΟΛ   ϢΩΠΕ ϨΝ ΛΥΠϹ
[Ν]ΟΥΟΝ ΝΙΜ · ΝΑϊ   ϹΜΟΤ · ΕΡΕ ΝΕΥϨΟΡ̄
ΝΤΑΥΕΙΝΕ ΜΠΚΕ   ΚΜ[ΟΜ] ΕΥΜΟΚ[Ϩ]
ΤΟΥ Ν[ϬΙ]ΝϬΩΡ · ΜΝ
ΠΚΕ[ϹΝΑΥ]

Verso:

(cf. S. Matthew, XXV, 31. ff.)

ΤΟΥ N̄NΒΑλ N̄Ν̄Ρω
ΜΕ ΕΚ[ο̄]Ν2ΟΤΕ 2Η
ΤΟΥ·[ο]ΥΚΟΥΝ̄†
ΝΑΤΡΕΚΧⲒ̄ Ν̄ΤΤⲒ̈
ΜωΡⲒⲀ̄ ΜΠΜΤΟ
ΕΒΟλ N̄ΝΕΚΒΑλ.
[†ΝΑΧΠⲒ̈ΟΚ Γ[Α]ρ ΠΕ
⌐Α̈Ϥ Αγω N̄·ⲦΑ̇Ο̇Υ

?ΔΕ 2̄Ν ΟΥΚλ̄ΧΕ
Αλλα Ε̇ωΑΥΤΑΥΟΟΥ
Μ̄ΠΝΑΥ ΕΤΕ ωΑΡΕ
ΠΚΡΙΤΗΟ ΕⲒ 2̄Μ
ΠΕϤΕΟΟΥ Μ̄Ν ΝΕϤ
ΑΓΓΕλΟΟ· N̄Ϥ̇Ϲω
ΟΥ2 Ε̄2ΟΥΝ̄ N̄Ν2ΕΘ
ΝΟΟ ΤΗΡΟΥ· Π̄ΝΑΥ
ΕΤΕ ωΑϤΠ[Ε̄]ΡⲜ ΝΑⲒ̈
ΕΒΟλ N̄ΝΗ N̄Ϥ†

Recto:– "…. wickedness of these(?). This was the way too of him that received the talent and, having digged in the earth, hid it, and heard in the presence of every one,— those that had brought also the other five talents and the other (two?)…" "… for them all, and judge every one. Consider also the evil-doers in that hour, what state they be in, while their countenances are darkened, being troubled (at heart?)"
Verso:– "…. for the eyes of men whilst thou art in fear. Shall I then have thee (or not have thee, ΟΥΚΟΥΝ N̄† ?) pay the penalty before thine eyes? For I will revile thee… and…" "…in a corner, but do bring them forth in the hour when the judge cometh in his glory with his angels and gathereth together all nations; the hour in which he parts thee one from the other and when he…"

IV. Parchment.

6 × 5⅛ in.

Part of the page of a book, in very bad condition. The text is in double column; the top lines of all, as well as the half of every line in two of the columns, are lost. Margins above col. b of Recto and below col. a of Verso, indicate the original length of the page. The character has some resemblance to Zoega, tab. II, n. VII (the smaller type.)

Recto:

	//Ϥ ΟΥΗΡ Ν̄	N	?	?
	//Ν ΝΕΝ̇	?··	?	?
	//ΟΥωΝΟΥ	ΠΕ	?	ı
	//Ε̇ΡΝΟϤΡΕ	ΝΑΟ	?	ΕλΝ
5.	//Ν̄ΤΟϤ ΑΝ	? ΠΟΥ2	? ΟΥΚΑΝ	5.
	//ΟΥΜΚΑ2 ΕϤ̇	Ε ? ϢΑΝ	?	ⲒλⲒ

	//ⲟⲧ ϣⲁⲣⲟϥ	ⲛ̄ϥⲛⲁϯⲙⲁⲧⲉ ⲛ̄ⲙ	
	//ⲓ̈ ⲙⲙⲟϥ	ⲙⲉ ⲁⲛ ϭⲉ ϫⲓⲛⲧⲉ	
	//ⲕⲟⲗⲁⲍⲉ	ⲛⲟⲩ ⲕⲁⲛ ⲉⲣϣⲁⲛ	
10.	//ϥⲛⲁⲧⲃ̄	ⲟⲩⲱⲛϩ ⲉⲃⲟⲗ ⲉ̄ⲣⲉ	10.
	//ⲃⲟⲗ ⲛ̄ⲟⲩ	ⲟ ⲛ̄ⲧⲉⲧⲉ ⲧⲱϥ ⲧⲉ	
	//ⲙⲁⲣⲓ ϩⲏⲃⲉ	ⲛ̄ϥⲛⲁⲁ̄ⲛⲉⲭⲉ ⲙ̄	
	//ⲛⲧⲉⲃⲉ ⲛ̄	ⲙⲟ ⲁⲛ ϭⲉ ⲕⲁⲛ	
	//ⲉ̄ⲛⲁⲣⲉⲓ̈ⲣⲉ	ⲉⲣϣⲁⲛ ϩⲣⲟⲕ ⲛ̄ϥ	
15.	//ⲟⲩⲡⲱϣⲧ̄	ⲛⲁⲡⲓⲥⲧⲉⲩⲉ ⲛⲉ	15.
	//ϯⲏⲣⲉ ⲉⲛ	ⲁⲛ ϭⲉ ⲕⲁⲛ ⲉⲣϣⲁⲛ	
	//ⲉϭⲉ ⲙ̄ⲙⲁⲩ	ⲟⲩⲱⲛϩ ⲉ̄ⲃⲟⲗ ⲉ̄	
	//ⲁ̄ϣⲧⲟⲣⲧ̄ⲣ	ⲣⲉ ⲟ ⲛ̄ϩⲏⲙⲉⲣⲟⲥ	
	//ϩⲁⲣⲟ ⲛ̄ⲧⲉ	ⲛ̄ϥⲛⲁⲣⲁϣⲉ ϭⲉ	
20.	//ⲙ̄ⲕ̄ ⲉϫⲱⲙ̄	ⲁⲛ ⲛ̄ⲙⲙⲉ ⲕⲁⲛ	20.
	//ⲁ̄ⲧⲉ ⲉⲧⲃⲉ	ⲉⲣϣⲁⲛ ⲧⲥⲁⲓ̈ⲉ	
	//ⲉϭⲟ ⲛ̄ⲧⲉ ⲡⲉ	ϣⲁϫⲉ ⲛ̄ϥⲛⲁⲥⲱ	
	//? ⲩⲉⲣⲉⲁ̄ⲛⲁ	ⲧⲙ̄ ϭⲉ ⲁⲛ ⲉ̄ⲛⲉⲧⲉ	
		ϣⲁⲣⲉ ϩⲟⲙⲓⲗⲓ	

Verso:

				ⲑⲉ ϩⲓⲧⲛ̄//		
				ⲛⲉⲙⲗⲁ̄//		
	ⲟ	?	ⲗⲓ	ⲱⲛⲉ ⲧⲏ//		
	ⲛⲁϥ	?	ⲉⲣⲉ	ⲛ̄ⲧⲉⲩⲉⲛ̄//		
5.	ⲕⲱⲣϣ	?	ⲥⲉⲙ̄	ⲛⲉⲥⲕⲟⲧ//	5.	
	ⲡⲉϥ	?	ⲧⲧⲏ ?	ⲛ̄ⲧⲉⲩⲁⲓ̈ⲟ̄//		
	ⲛ̄ⲙⲙⲉ ⲁⲛ ⲗⲟ̄ⲩ			ⲛ̄ⲧⲉⲩⲣⲉ//		
	ⲱⲛϩ ⲛⲁϥ ⲉⲃⲟⲗ			ⲉ̄ⲣⲉⲙⲉϩ//		
	ⲉⲣⲉⲛⲟⲧⲙ̄ ⲉ̄? ⲉ			ϩⲙⲧ//		
10.	ⲡⲁⲓ̈ ⲁ̄ϯⲙⲁⲧⲉ			ⲣⲓⲟⲛ ⲛ̄//	10.	
	ⲛ̄ⲙⲙⲁⲩ ⲉϥⲛⲁⲩ			ⲧⲉⲙⲁⲧⲉ̄//		
	ⲉ̄ⲡⲉⲓ̈ϩⲟ ⲛ̄ⲧⲉ ⲉ⳽			ⲉ̄ⲣⲉⲙⲉϩ//		
	ⲧⲟⲩⲟⲛϩ ⲉⲃⲟⲗ ⲉ			ⲕⲁⲙⲉ ⲉϥ//		
	ⲣⲉⲡⲟⲗⲉⲙⲓ ⲛ̄ⲙ			ϩⲣⲁⲓ̈ ϣⲁⲣⲟ̄//		
15.	ⲙⲁϥ ϩⲓⲧⲛ̄ ⲡⲉⲧⲉ			ⲉⲩⲅⲉⲛⲏⲥ̄//	15.	
	ⲛ̄ϥⲟⲩⲱⲛϩ ⲉⲃⲟⲗ			ⲏⲣⲛ̄ⲧⲉ ⲡⲉ̄//		
	ⲁⲛ ⲉϥϩⲟϭⲓ ϫⲉ			ⲧⲡ ⲉ̄ⲧⲃⲉ ⲏ̄//		
	ⲡⲟⲩⲥⲁⲓ̈ ⲡⲉⲛⲧⲁϥ			⳨ⲡⲕⲁⲑⲁⲣⲟ̄//		
	ⲛⲁⲩ ⲉ̄ⲣⲟϥ ⲁϥⲟⲩ			ⲟⲩⲟⲓ̈ⲛⲧⲏ//		
20.	ⲣⲟⲧ ⲉⲧⲃⲉ ⲡⲁⲓ̈ ⲁ⳽			ⲱⲛϩ ⲧⲏⲣ//	20.	
	ⲉϥϭⲙ̄ϭⲟⲙ ⲉϥ			ⲡⲧⲉⲣⲟⲕ//		
	ⲙⲉ ⲙ̄ⲡⲟⲩⲥⲁ ⲛ̄			ⲧⲁϥⲡⲱⲧ//		

ογοϊϣ ΝΙΜ ΔΥ
ϪⲰⲦⲈ ⲘⲘⲞⲤ Ⲛ
(margin.)

ⲣⲟⲕ̅ ϣⲟⲡ⫽   (as altered by a
ⲡⲉ⫽   later hand.)

Recto: (col. b.) "... If thou (κἄν)... yet will he not agree with thee. More-
-over, henceforth, shouldest thou show thyself as his own yet will he
not bear with thee. Also, shouldest thou be humble, yet will he not
believe in (πιστεύειν) thee. Also, shouldest thou show thyself gentle,
(ἥμερος), yet will he not rejoice with thee. Shouldest thou be eloquent,
yet will he not listen to that of which thou dost discourse" (ὁμιλεῖν).
Verso: (col. a.) "..... not with thee. Thou (?) showest thyself to him ..?....
Thou (?) hast pleasure in him, while he looks upon thy face, who show-
-est thyself, contending with him (πολεμεῖν) by means of that which
shows not itself, while he thinks, Thy beauty it is, (?) which he has
seen; he rejoiced at it. Thou (?) hadest power while he loved thy
beauty, at all times. He has been struck (col. b.) like ...."

The translation of these two columns is of considerable difficulty,
chiefly, no doubt, because of the absence of all explanatory content.
Besides this, not only is the construction here and there obscure,
but at Verso, ll. 5, 8, 18, appears an otherwise unknown verbal-
-prefix, ⲁ, which one is inclined to regard as of the 2ᵈ Sing. fem.
The forms ογοϊϣ, ⲡⲟⲗⲉⲙⲓ, ⲇⲟⲃⲓ, the pointing e.g. of ϩⲁⲣⲟⲛ̅, ⲉ̄ⲃⲟⲗ, ⲉ̄ⲣⲉ,
and the use of ϊ in ⲥⲁ̈ⲓ, ⲡⲁ̈ⲓ, ογοϊϣ, seem to deny the purity of
language which might be expected to accompany so archaic a
script.
The dialect is strictly Sahidic.

———————

V. Papyrus.   9¾ × 6 in.
Of tough, dark-brown material, upon which the ink shows but faint-
-ly. The character is of the class of semi-uncials, illustrated
by Hyvernat's Album, pl. IX and X, both of which are dated in the
beginning of the 11ᵗʰ cent.
There is no proof that the two sides of the fragment bear a contin-
-uous text. If they do so, Prof. Harnack's suggestion that the papyrus
contained episodes of the Athanasius-Arsenius story (v. Hefele,
Conciliengesch.², I, 458, 464,) is probably appropriate. If not, the reference
(Recto, l. 16,) to Southern Egypt, and soon afterwords, to "Arsenius,"

may possibly point to S. Arsenius the Great (v. Act. SS. Boland., Jul. IV, 605 and Makrizi ed. Wüstenf., 92, 112,) though his hermitage in the desert of Schihêt (near the Natron lakes,) can scarcely be referred to the "South." The final paragraph of the Verso seems to apostrophise S. Athanasius and to refer also to other prominent bishoprics.*

It is impossible to determine which was in reality Recto and which Verso in this fragt.; each face shows the termination at least of a sentence. At Recto, l.l. 10–12, the original margin remains.

Recto:

```
    Ξ̅ΝΕϬΟ ΝΚΟΥ[Ι] ΕΡΕ ΝΕϥΕΙΟ
    ΏΛΟΝ . Δ ΤΕϥΜΛΛΥ ϪΙΤϥ ⲉ̀
    [ϣ]ΩΠΕ Ν̅Χ̅ΡΗ[ⳅΤ]ΙΛΝΟⳅ//
    ⲟⲥ ϪΕ ΧΙΝ ΕϥϪ[ⲟ]ΝΛΝΛΓΝΩⳅⲧ[Ηⳅ]
5.  ΝΝΟϬ ΕΜΛΕΙΝ · ΕΥΤΕΝΤΩΝ ΕΝ
    ⲟⳅ · ΠΕΤΡΟⳅ ΜΝ Ι̅Ω̅ · Ν̅ΤΕΡΕϥϪΙ
    ΧΗ · Λϥ ΕΙΡΕ ΝϬΕΝΝΟϬ ΝϬⲟ[Ν]
    ⲉ ΝΙΜ ΝΛΕϣϣΛϪΕ ⲉ̀ΠΕΚΤΛ̣ⲓ̀
    ⲉ ΝΛΓΓΕΛΙΚΟΝ · ΛΚΕΙΜΕ ΕΤⲉ̀
10. Μ̅ΠΝΟΥΤΕ · ΛΚΕΙΜΕ ⲉ̀ΤΛ ΝΚΕΡⲱ̀
    ΛΥϬΛΗ ⲉⲓ̀ ΕϥΠΛΡΛΓΕ Μ̅ΜΟΚ ΝΟΥϩ
    Εϥϣ̀ΙΝΕ Ν̅ⳅⲁ ΟΥΜΕΤΝΛΗΤ Ν̅ΤΟⲟ[ΤΚ]
    Ν̅ΤΕΡΕ ΝΕΚϬΟΪΤΕ ϪΩϩ ⲉ̀ΝΕϥΟⲩ̀
    ϥ̣ⲡⲓ̀ⲑⲉ ΕϣϪΕ Μ̅ΠΕϥϣΩΝΕ ΕΝΕϩ
15. ⲟⲕⲣⲁϥ̀ϯ ΝⲀΝ Ν̅ΤΕΚϬΙⳅΤⲱⲣ
    ΤΕΚϬΙΝΒΩΚ ΕΠΜΛΡΗⳅ ⲉⲕⲏⲙ
    Ϫⲉ ⲀΚⲀΠⲀΝΤⲀ ⲉⲩⲣⲱⲙⲉ Νⲉⲩϣ
    ϥⲣⲁⲛ Πⲉ ⲀⲣⳅΗΝΙΟⳅ · Ν̅Τⲉⲣⲉⲕⲛ̅
    Ϭⲟⲓⲗⲓ ⲉⲣⲟϥ : Ⲁⲡⲛ[ⲟⲩ]ⲧⲉ ⳅⲙⲟⲩ ⲉⲣ[ⲟϥ]
20. (space)  ΜⲚ̅ ΠⲉϥΗⲓ // (space)
```

Verso:

```
    ⲉ̀ΝΕΙΩΤ Ⲁϥⲓ̀ⳅⲀΙⲉ ΝΟΥⳅⲟ[Π]
    ⲉ ⳅΝⲀΥ ΟΥΗϩ Ν̅ⳅⲱϥ · Ⲁϥ
    ⲉⲣⲠⲉ · ⲉⲩϣ[ⲉⲙ]ϣⲉ ⲉⲓⲇⲱⲗ
    Ν̅ΤⲉⲣⲉϥΒⲱⲕ ⲉϥϪⲱϩ ⲉ̀Ⲡⲉⲓ
5.  ϣⲟⲣϣⲉⲣ Ⲁϥⲉⲓ ⲉ̀Ⲡⲉⳅⲏⲧ //         5.
    ⲧⲉⲛ Ν̅ⲧⲉⲓⲕⲉⲛⲟϬ Ν̅ϣⲡⲏⲣⲉ · Μⲉ
    ϯⲱⲛ ⲉⲣⲟⳅ · ⲛⲭⲓ ⲛⲉⲣⲉⲀⲑⲀⲛⲀⳅ
    Ηⲃⲉⲛ · ⲉϥⳅⲱ[ⲧ]Πⲉⲙ ⲉⲛⲉϣⲏⲣⲉ
    Ν̅ ϩⲟⲓⲛⲉ Ν̅ⲇⲓⲀⲕⲟⲛⲟⳅ · ϩⲉⲛⲕⲉⲕⲟ̀ⲩ̀
10. ⲩⲧⲉⲣⲟⳅ · ΠⲉϫⲀϥ ϫⲉ ΠⲉⲛⲧⲀ ΠⲟⲩⲀ
    ϫⲓⲧϥ ⲉ̀ϥⲟ Ν̅[ⲕⲟ]ⲅ̀ⲓ̀ · ⲱⲁϥⲕⲗⲏⲣⲟⲛⲟ
    ϥ Μ̅ΠⲀⲧⲉϥⲙⲟⲩ ///-----
    -----------------
    -----------------
    Ⲁ Ν̅ⲕⲀⲑⲉⲇⲣⲀ Ν̅ⲧⲕⲟⲩⲙⲉⲛⲏ · ⳅⲉⲉⲠ
    ⲓ Ν̅ⲛⲀⲩ ⲉ̀ⲣⲟⲕ · Πⲱ̀ⳅ ⲉⲙⲉ ⲧⲱⲗ̀
15. ⲧⲩ̀ · ⲀⲑⲀⲛⲀⳅⲓⲟⳅ ⲡⲀⲣⲀⲕⲟⲧⲉ · ⲧ 15.
    ⲧⲀⲣⲀⲕⲟⲧⲉ ⲧⲀϩⲣⲱⲙⲏ · ⲧⲀⲧ
    ⲭⲓⲀ · ⳅⲉϫⲱ [Μ̅]ΠⲉⲕⲧⲀⲓ̈ⲟ · ϫⲉ Μ
    (space) ⲉϥⲧ[ⲉⲛ]ⲧⲱⲛ ⲉ̀ⲣⲟⲕ :⁓
    -----------------
```

Recto: "— while he was young, his fathers(?) being — his mother placed him in — become Christian. — while he was (v Stern, §.621,) Reader — great signs like to — [Apostles?] Peter and John. After he had — he did great deeds of power — every man shall be able to speak of thy glory— angelic. Thou knowest the — of God. Thou knowest what the men(?) too — there came a cripple, introducing thee(?) — seeking compassion of thee(?) — after thy raiment had touched his [feet?] — believe if he had not been in pain — write for us thy story — thy journey to

*The Arian Deacon, Arsenius, expelled from the Church by the partizans of Athanasius (Zoega, 272,) may perhaps be the same person as the notorious Melitian bishop.

— thou hast met a ..... man — named Arsenius. After thou hast —
dwell with him — God blessed him(?) — and his house".
Verso: "— father, he ?... (*not* ⲧⲟⲗⲓⲉ) — two men(?) follow him, he — temple,
serving idols — after he had come, touching the — overthrown, he (it?)
fell down. — us(?) this great marvel also — it .... Athanasius being (is?) —
hearing the children — certain deacons, some few(?) other — presbyters. He
said that which each(?) — place him while he was young(?). He doth
inherit — before he die.
— the (episcopal) thrones of the world (ὀικουμένη) — they behold thee,
the true(?) shepherd — Athanasius of Alexandria — the (throne) of
Alexandria, that of Rome, that of — ...chia(?). They tell thine honour
that — he being like(?) to them."

The dialect here is a somewhat faulty Sahidic; cf. e.g., *Recto*, 5, 8, ὲ =
ⲙ; 12, ⲙⲉⲧ = ⲙⲛⲧ; *Verso*, 14, ὲ = ⲙ. But these are possibly signs of M.E. influen-
-ce. The pointing is sometimes irregular; e.g. ϣⲓⲛⲉ, ⲁⲑⲁⲛⲁⲥⲓ̈ⲟⲥ, ⲉⲣⲟϥ,
ⲁϥⲉⲓ.

VI. Papyrus.

Fragt. A, 5 × 4 in.
" B, 6¼ × 5 in.
" C, 1¾ × 8¼ in.

Three mutilated fragts. of brittle, brown papyrus, the remnants of whose
very coarsely and untidily written texts are hardly anywhere to be read
with certainty. Fragt. C can not now be joined to the others; but from
its margin, it evidently formed the bottom of the papyrus. Nor is it
possible to tell howmuch from the middle of the lines on Fragts. A, B
has been lost. The side-margins remain, however, both to right and
left; while the width of Fragt. C must be approximately that of the
whole.

Recto: Fragt. A.

```
//. ⲁⲓⲛⲁⲩ ⲉⲟⲩⲣⲁ[ⲥⲟⲩ]
    ϫⲉ ⲡⲱⲧ ⲉⲡⲉⲥⲏⲧ ⲱ̀
    ⲟⲁⲣⲉⲭ ⲉⲣⲁ ⲁⲓⲡⲱⲧ ⲉⲡⲉ
    ⲱⲛ ⲡⲱϩ ⲉⲛⲁⲙⲉϩⲧ
5. ⲣⲁⲥⲟⲩ ⲛⲧⲁ ⲡⲉⲑⲏⲣⲓⲱⲛ ⲡⲱ
    ⲕⲗⲁⲩⲧⲓⲱⲥ ⲡⲁⲙⲉⲣⲏⲧ ⲛⲥ[ⲁⲛ]
    ⲟⲩⲙⲉⲧⲁⲧⲟⲁⲙ ⲁⲥϣⲱⲡⲓ ⲙⲁⲕ
```

Fragt. B.

```
⁈ⲉⲣⲉ ⲟⲩⲣⲱⲙⲉ ⲁϧⲓⲣⲁ̣ϥ ⲉⲣⲁ̀ⲓ  sic ⁈
ⲁⲙⲁⲛ ⲉⲣⲉ ⲡⲉⲑⲏⲣⲓⲱⲛ
ⲧⲉϣⲧⲁⲙ ⲉⲡⲁⲣⲁ ⲁ ⲡⲉⲑⲏⲣⲓ
⁈ⲉⲡⲉⲟⲩⲁⲉⲓϣ ⲛⲧⲁⲓⲛⲉⲩ ⲉⲧ
ⲟ̣ϧ ⲓⲧ ⲙⲡⲉ ⲛⲉⲕⲣⲉⲙⲓⲁⲩⲓ ⲗⲁϧ ⲛⲁⲃⲉⲗ  5⁈
ⲱⲡⲓ ⲛⲟⲩⲡⲱⲗⲓⲙⲟⲥ ⲧⲱⲟⲩⲛ ⲉⲃⲱⲕ
    ⲧⲟⲩ ⲉⲣⲁϥ ⲉⲃⲉⲧⲁⲙⲁⲓ ⲉⲡⲉⲕϧⲁ
```

ⲙⲡⲛⲉⲩ ⲉⲩⲥⲱⲛⲓ ⲉⲥⲣⲏⲙⲏⲉ   ⲛⲓ ⲕⲗⲁⲩⲧⲓⲱⲥ ⲙⲡⲛⲉⲩ ⲧⲁⲥⲓ
ⲉⲣⲟⲩⲛ ⲉⲡⲉⲱⲧⲉⲕⲁ//ⲭⲉ ⲱ ⲗⲣⲏⲓⲁ   ⲉ̇ⲁⲛ ⲱⲉⲡⲉⲣⲟⲩ̇ⲭ?ⲛ?ⲁ?

10.   ?   ?   ⲧⲗⲁⲧⲉ ⲭⲉ ⲙⲡⲟⲩⲥⲁ   ⲭ̇ⲗⲓ ϩⲓ ⲡⲉϥⲗⲁⲥ ⲉⲣⲉ ⲡⲥ̄ⲱ̇ⲣ   10.

ⲟⲩⲛⲁⲓ ⲛⲉⲙⲏϥ⌐ ?   ?   ?   ⲙ̄ⲉⲥⲓ ⲛⲟⲩⲥⲁⲛ
ⲙⲛ ⲟⲩⲥⲱⲛⲓ   ⲱⲥ ⲁⲩⲉⲙⲧⲁⲛ ⲙⲁϥ̇
ⲉ̇ⲛⲱ ⲕⲟⲩⲓ ⲁⲩ   ?ⲃⲱⲕ ⲉⲡⲱⲗⲉ ?
                      ⲟⲩⲛⲁⲓ ⲛⲉⲙⲏⲃ
                      ⲱⲡⲓ̄ⲧⲁϥ ⲉⲣⲟⲩⲛ   15.
                      ⲥⲉⲩⲡⲣⲉⲡⲏ ⲉⲡⲁⲃⲏ
                      ⲗ̇ⲟ̇ⲧ ⲉⲣⲟⲕ ⲙⲡⲉⲣ

Fragt. C.

ⲣⲁϩⲁⲙ ⲁⲙⲁϩⲧⲓ?ⲛⲭ ⲙⲉⲛ ⲓⲥⲁⲕ ⲡⲉϥⲱⲏⲣⲓ ⲉϥⲟⲩⲱ
ⲭ ? ϥ?ⲛⲧⲛⲃⲉⲃⲉⲗ ⲉⲗⲁⲃ ⲁϥⲥⲱⲧⲉⲙ ⲉⲛⲥⲁ ⲡ̄ ? ⲓ̇
ⲛⲉⲙⲁ̇ ? ⲧⲃⲉⲧⲉϥ ⲡ̄ⲥ̄ⲧⲉⲥ ⲉϩⲟⲩⲛ ⲉⲣⲁϥ : ⲁⲡ̄ⲟ̄ⲥ ⲛⲟⲩϩⲉⲙⲁ̇ⲃ

Verso: *Fragt. B.*   *Fragt. A.*

ⲑⲉⲱⲥ⁽ˢⁱᶜ⁾ ⲧⲱⲟⲩⲛ ⲉϩⲣⲁⲓ   ⲱ̇ⲥ ⲡⲉϯⲙⲉ ⲙⲁⲃ ⲟⲩ
ⲁϩⲕⲉⲥ̇ⲥⲱⲓ ⲧⲁⲓⲁⲕ ⲉⲃⲁⲗ   ⲙⲉⲛⲉϩⲣⲉⲧⲓⲕⲱⲥ
ⲥⲟⲩⲱⲛⲧ ⲛⲏⲕ ⲉⲓⲙⲏ ⲛⲁⲕ   ⲕ̇ ⲡⲉ ⲡⲱⲏⲣⲏ ⲉⲛⲧⲟⲣⲑⲱ
ⲧⲱⲕⲝ̄ⲏⲓⲁ ⲉⲕⲧⲁⲭⲣⲁ ⲡⲏⲥⲧ   ⲉⲧⲥⲟⲩⲧⲱⲛ ⲧⲉ ⲡ̇ⲉⲕⲣⲁⲛ   4.

5. ⲥϥⲓⲙⲏ ⲛⲓⲙ ⲉⲧϩⲓⲭⲉⲛ ⲡⲕ   ⲡⲟⲩⲉϩ ⲭⲓⲛ⸗ ⲭⲓ ⲧⲁⲓⲁⲓ⸗ⲁ//ⲓ   4.
ⲉⲧⲁϩⲏ ⲟⲩⲱⲏⲣⲓ ⲉⲛⲟⲩⲱⲧ ⲁⲓⲙ⁽ˢⁱᶜ⁾   ⲟⲁⲛⲥ ⲃⲟⲩⲁⲛ   5.
ⲁⲩⲥⲧⲁⲩⲣⲟⲩ ⲙⲁⲃⲍ̄ ⲉⲛⲧⲟⲃ   ⲁⲃ ⲁ ⲛⲓⲟⲩⲇⲁⲓ ⲭⲏϥ̇ⲧ
ⲉⲥⲁ ⲡⲉⲧⲛⲁⲛⲟⲩⲃ ⲛ   ⲉⲙⲡⲕⲁϩ ⲙⲡⲉⲃⲉⲣ ⲡⲉⲑⲁⲩ
   (no space in original)   ⲁⲕⲁⲑⲱⲥ ⲧⲉⲛⲛⲁⲟⲩⲃ
                      ⲉⲧⲓ ⲡⲟⲩⲭⲁⲓ ⲛⲁⲇⲁⲙ
10. ⲗⲓⲛⲁⲛ̇ ? ⲉ̇ⲣⲁⲱ   ?ⲧⲛⲉⲩ ⲉⲛⲁⲥⲛ   10.
ⲓⲱⲥⲏⲫ ⲉⲫⲁⲣⲁ̇[ⲱ]   ⲙ̇ⲧⲁⲛ ⲉⲣⲁⲓ ⲭⲁⲓⲛ̇ⲉⲩ ⲉⲃⲉⲛ
ⲓⲁⲙⲏⲛ ⲡⲁⲕⲟⲩ[ⲓ]   ⲗⲁⲓ ⲡⲛⲟⲩϯ
ⲉⲅⲉⲧⲉ ⲧⲁⲛ   ⲭⲱⲕ ⲉⲃⲁⲗ
ⲟⲩⲑⲏⲣⲓⲱ
15. ⲉⲛⲓⲟⲩⲧⲁⲓ ϩ
ⲉⲛ̇ⲧⲁⲃⲧ

Fragt. C. 5 lines, of which

1.   ⲧⲙⲁⲛ̇ⲙⲏⲕ ? ⲉ̇ⲁⲕⲉ ⲕⲉⲥⲁⲡ
4. ⲭⲓⲙ̇ ? ⲟⲩⲕⲁϩ ⲉⲱ ?   ⲟⲩⲭ   ?   ⲧⲓⲥ ?   ⲙⲁⲥ
5. ⲛⲉⲕⲱⲏⲗ ⲉⲣⲛⲁⲱⲧ ?   ϩⲓⲙⲁⲛⲁ̇ⲙⲉⲡ̄ⲛ̄ⲧⲉ   ?

From such débris one can only gather vague notions as to the original
contents of the text. The dividing lines seem sometimes to separate
disconnected paragraphs.

On the Recto, the 1st section has the story of a dream, (related apparent-
-ly to a second person by a woman; cf. l.3, εργ.) in which the narrator
had been bidden to encounter a monster. Among other intelligible words
and phrases, are mentioned; "Claudius, my beloved brother," a war,
and in the 2d sect, a sister weeping, a prison, the name Areia (cf.
Ἀρεία f., Pape, p.121), and the phrase, "the Saviour(?) show mercy to him." This
last occurs also in the 3d sect., which is otherwise unintelligible. In the
4th sect. occurs the Greek ЄΥΠΡЄΠΗ (?= εὐπρέπεια or πρέπει). Fragt C. seems
to contain a separate section, dealing with Abraham and "his
son, Isaak."

The 1st section of the Verso seems to contrast in some way Orthodoxy and
Heresy and to give the name of the person now addressed as Taiaia
(cf. Brit. Mm. Pap. n° XL, †ΔΙΔ masc.) The 2d sect. has some general statement
as to women who have but one son, and then refers, perhaps, to the
eagerness of the Jews for Christ's(?) crucifiction, who had done no wrong,
but had come? for the "salvation of Adam." The 3d sect. relates to Joseph
and Benjamin, "my youngest [son]." In the 4th sect, the Jews are again
mentioned. From the Verso of Fragt. C nothing can be learned.

The language of this Papyrus is very irregular, the vowels especially
being treated with great freedom. Its M.E. character is evident.
Punctuation (above letters) is wholly absent. Clauses or paragraphs are
occassionally divided by peculiar marks (Recto, A.9, Verso, A.4, B.7.)
The text can not properly be called "patristic"; yet it seems even less
suited to appear in either of the other groups into which the present
collection divides itself.

LITURGICAL TEXTS

VII. Papyrus.

Fragt. A,	4 × 7 in.
" B,	5½ × 2¼ in.
" C,	5½ × 5 in.
" D,	4¼ × 4½ in.

These fragts. (put together from several smaller pieces,) are brown in
colour and somewhat coarse in texture. The two texts which they

bore may be the work of a single scribe and are written in a clear, semi-uncial character, probably of the 10ᵗʰ or 11ᵗʰ cent.

They show versions of two of the nine "Odes", — on the Recto, the "Song of Moses"; on the Verso, the "Song of the three Children", both originally in their entirety.

The original width of the M.S. can be gathered from Recto, ll.3 and 4.

Recto: Fragt. A.   (margin)

v. 1   [Ⲧⲟⲧ]ⲉ ⲀϤ̣ϨⲰⲤ Ⲛ̀ⲬⲈ ⲘⲰⲨⲤⲎⲤ ⲚⲈⲘ ⲚⲒ
        [ϢⲎ]ⲢⲒ ⲘⲠⲒⲤⲖ ⲚⲦⲀⲒ ϨⲰⲆⲎ ⲘⲠⲞ̅Ⲥ̅ ⲈϤⲬ[Ⲱ]
        [Ⲙ̀]ⲘⲞⲤ : ⲬⲈ ⲘⲀⲢⲈⲚϨⲰⲤ̀ ⲈⲠⲞ̅Ⲥ̅ ϨⲈⲚⲚ ⲞⲨⲰⲞⲨ ⲄⲀ[Ⲣ]
        [ⲀϤ̣]ⲬⲒ ⲈⲰⲞⲨ :// ⲞⲨϨⲐⲞ ⲚⲈⲘ ⲞⲨⲬⲀⲤⲒ

5. v. 2   [Ϩ̣]ⲐⲞ ⲀϤⲂⲈⲢⲂⲰⲢⲞⲨ ϨⲈⲚ ⲪⲒⲞⲘ // ⲞⲨⲂⲞⲎ
        [ⲐⲞⲤ] ⲚⲈⲘ ⲞⲨⲢⲈ[ϤϨⲰ̀]ⲂⲈⲤ ⲈⲂ[Ⲟ]Ⲗ ⲈⲬⲰⲒ ⲀϤϢⲰⲠⲒ
        [ⲚⲎⲒ ⲈⲨⲤⲰⲦⲎⲢⲒⲀ ⲪⲀⲒ ⲠⲈ] ⲠⲀⲚⲞⲨ†

    Fragt. B.

                ... ⲠⲞ̅Ⲥ̅ Ⲡ̀Ⲉ ⲠⲈϤ

v. 4   [ⲢⲀⲚ // ⲚⲒⲂⲈⲢⲈϬⲰⲞⲨⲦⲤ Ⲛ̀ⲦⲈ Ⲫ̀]ⲀⲢⲀⲰ ⲚⲈⲘ ⲦⲈϤ
10.   [ϬⲀⲘ ⲀϤⲂⲈⲢⲂⲰⲢⲞⲨ ⲈⲪⲒⲞ]Ⲙ : ϨⲀⲚⲤⲞⲠⲦ
        [ⲚⲀⲚⲀⲂⲀⲦⲎⲤ ⲚⲦⲢⲒⲤⲦⲀⲦⲎⲤ] ⲀϤϬⲞⲖⲔⲞⲨ

v. 5   [ϨⲈⲚ ⲪⲒⲞⲘ ⲚϢⲀⲢⲒ // ⲀϤ̣]Ϩ̣ⲰⲂⲤ ⲈϨⲢⲎⲒ
        [ⲈⲬⲰⲞⲨ Ⲛ̀ⲬⲈ ⲠⲒⲘⲰⲞⲨ ⲀⲨ]ⲰⲘⲤ ⲈϨⲢⲎⲒ

v. 6   [ⲈⲠⲈϢⲎⲔ Ⲙ̀ⲪⲢⲎ† ⲚⲞⲨⲰ]ⲚⲒ //. ⲦⲈⲔ
15.   [ⲞⲨ ⲒⲚⲀⲘ ⲠⲞ̅Ⲥ̅ ⲀⲤⲬⲒⲰⲞⲨ Ϩ̣ⲈⲚ]ⲞⲨϬⲀⲘ [ⲦⲈ]Ⲕ
        [ϬⲒⲬ ⲚⲞⲨ ⲒⲚⲀⲘ ⲠⲞ̅Ⲥ̅ ⲀⲤⲦⲀ̈Ⲕ[ó]ⲚⲈⲔ[ⲬⲀ]ⲬⲒ //

v. 7   [ϨⲈⲚ ⲠⲀϢⲀⲒ ⲚⲦⲈ ⲠⲈⲔⲰⲞⲨ ⲀⲔϨ̣Ⲁ̣Ⲙ̣Ϩ̣ⲈⲘ]
        [ⲚⲚⲎ ⲈⲦ†ⲞⲨⲂⲎⲚ : ⲀⲔⲞⲨⲰⲢ]Ⲡ ⲘⲠ[ⲈⲔϬⲰⲚⲦ]

v. 8   [ⲀϤⲞⲨⲞⲘⲞⲨ Ⲙ̀ⲪⲢⲎ† ⲚϨⲀⲚⲢⲰ]ⲞⲨ // [ⲞⲨⲞϨ]

    Fragt. C.
20.   [ⲈⲂⲞⲖ ϨⲒⲦⲈⲚ ⲠⲒⲠ̅Ⲛ̅Ⲁ̅ Ⲛ̀ⲦⲈ ⲠⲈⲔⲘ]ⲂⲞⲚ : ⲀϤⲞϨⲒ
        [ⲈⲢⲀⲦϤ Ⲛ̀ⲬⲈ ⲠⲒⲘⲰⲞⲨ ⲀⲨ̂ϬⲰⲤ Ⲛ̀ⲬⲈ] ⲚⲒⲘⲰⲞⲨ Ⲙ̀ⲪⲢⲎ†
        [ⲚⲞⲨⲤⲞⲂⲦ ⲀⲨ̂ϬⲰⲤ Ⲛ̀ⲬⲈ Ⲛ]ⲒϬⲂⲖ ϨⲈⲚ ⲐⲘⲎ

v. 9   [† Ⲙ̀ⲪⲒⲞⲘ // ⲀϤⲬⲞⲤ ⲄⲀⲢ Ⲛ̀ϫⲬⲈ ⲠⲒⲬⲀⲬⲒ : ⲬⲈ †
        [ⲚⲀϬⲞⲬⲒ ⲚⲦⲀⲦⲀϨⲞ ⲚⲦ]ⲀⲪⲰϢ ⲚⲦⲀϢⲰⲖ
25.   [ⲚⲦⲀⲦⲤⲒⲞ ⲚⲦⲀⲮⲨⲬⲎ Ⲛ̀]ⲦⲀϨⲰⲦⲈⲂ ϨⲈⲚ

v. 10   [ⲦⲀⲤⲎϤⲒ Ⲛ̀ⲦⲈ ⲦⲀϬⲒⲬ] ⲈⲢⲞ̅Ⲥ̅ // ⲀⲔⲞⲨⲰⲢⲠ
        [ⲘⲠⲈⲔⲠ̅Ⲛ̅Ⲁ̅ ⲀϤϨⲞⲂⲤⲞⲨ Ⲛ̀]ⲬⲈ ⲪⲒⲞⲘ : ⲀⲨⲰⲘⲤ ⲈⲠⲈⲤⲎⲦ
        [Ⲙ̀ⲪⲢⲎ† ⲚⲞⲨⲦⲀϨ ϨⲈⲚ ϨⲀ]ⲚⲘⲰⲞⲨ ⲈϤⲞ̈Ϣ //

v. 11   [ⲚⲒⲘ ⲈⲦⲞⲚⲒ ⲘⲘⲞ]Ⲕ ϨⲈⲚ ⲚⲒⲚⲞⲨ† ⲠⲞ̅Ⲥ̅ ⲚⲒⲘ ⲈⲦⲞ

30.
      [ΝΙ ΜΜΟΚ ΕΥ†]ϢΟΥ ΝΑϤ^sic [ΕϤ]ΡϢΠΗΡΕ ΜΜΟϤ:

v. 12   [ϦΕΝ ϦΑΝΝϢΟΥ Ε]ϤΙΡΙ ΝϦΑΝ[ϢΠΗΡΕ⫽ ΑΚ

      [ⲤΟΥΤΕΝ ΤΕΚ]ΟΥΙΝΑΜ Ε[Β·ΟⲖ] ΑϤϢΜΚΟΥ Ν

Fragt. D.

v. 13   [ϪΕ ΠΚΑϦ ⫽ ΑΚⳈΙΜϢΙΤ ϦΑϪϢϤ ΜΠΕΚ]ⲖΑΟⳠ

      [ϦΕΝΝ ΟΥΜΕΘΜΗΙ ΦΑΙ ΕΤ]ΑΚ[ⳤϢΠ∩[Τ[Ε]Ϥ ΑΚ†

35.   [ϬΑΜ ϦΕΝ ΤΕΚΝΟΜ]† Ε̄Μ̄Μ[Ⲁ]Ν̄ΜΤΟΝ^sic

v. 14   [ΕϤΟΥΑΒ ΝΑΚ⫽] ΑῩⲤϢΤΕΜ ΝϪΕ ϦΑΝΝΕΘ

      [ΝΟϬ ΟΥΟϦ ΑΥⳠϢ]ΝⲦ ϦΑΝΝΑΚϦΙ ΑΥϬΙ

v. 15   [ΝΝΗ ΕΤϢΟΠ ϦΕΝ] ΝΙΦΥⲖΙ^sicⲘⳤΤΙΜ ⫽ ΤΟΤΕ

      [ΑΥΙⲎⳠ ΝϪΕ ΝΙϦΗⲄΕ]ΜϢΝ · ⲚⲦΕ ΕⲆϢΜ : ΝΙⲆⲢ

40.   [ϪϢΝ ⲚⲦΕ ΝΙΜϢⲀΒΙ]ΤΗ[Ⳡ] ΟΥⳤⲦΕⲢⲦΕⲢ ⲠΕ

      [ΤⲀϤϪΙΤΟΥ ⲀΥΒϢⲖ]ΕΒΟⲖ ⲚϪΕ ΟΥΟΝ ΝΙΒΕ^Ν·

v. 16   [ΕΤϢΟΠ ϦΕΝ ϢΑΝⲆⲀⲚ⫽] ΕϤΕϦΕΙ ΕϦ]ΡΗΙ ΕϪϢΟΥ

      [ⲚϪΕ ΟΥⳤⲦΕⲢⲦΕⲢ ΝΕΜ ΟΥϦΟ†] Ϧ]ΕΝⲠⲀ

      [ϢⲖΙ &ⲥ.

The dialect of this text is of considerable interest. Its basis is Boh., i.e. its vocabulary is substantially that of Lagarde's version (*Der Pentateuch*, p. 162), showing, as well as the characteristic use of aspirated letters, such distinguishing forms as ΒΕⲢⲈϬΟΥΤⳤ, [Ⲙ]ΒΟΝ, ϢΟΥ, ΟΥΙΝΑΜ, ΝΕⲘ, ⲚϪΕ. Yet the guttural ϧ is absent and the employment of ϫ–ϭ follows the Sah. law,[*] while M.E. influence also is visible in ⲤⲞⲠⲦ, ϦⲀⲚⲚ, ϦⲈⲚⲚ, ϦⲀ[ⲘϦⲈⲘ], ϬⲀⲘ, ϬⲀⲖ. I can not recall any other text in which the three dialects are combined in these proportions, — the counterpart of the frequent Sah. texts with a northern tendency.

The new forms ⳤⲦⲈⲢⲦⲈⲢ (40) and ϬⲀⲖ (22) are to be noted; also l. 2, ΕϤϪ[Ϣ] ΜⲘΟⳤ for Boh. ΟΥΟϦ ΑϤϪΟⳤ ΕΘⲢΟΥϪΟⳤ.

_____

Verso: A fresh line is begun with every verse (as in Bardelli's edition.) There is just space, to the left of the fragts. preserved, for the formula ⲤΜΟΥ (or ⲤⲘ̄Ο̄) ΕⲠⳠⳠ. The opening verses are lost.

    Fragt. D.

    [ⲤΜΟΥ ΕⲠ̄Ⳡ̄ⳠⳠ ΝΙΜΟΥΝϦϢΟΥ ΝΕ]Μ ΝΙΙϢ† ⫽

    [ⲤΜΟΥ ΕⲠ̄Ⳡ̄Ⳡ ΝΙϬΗⲠΙ ΝΕΜ ΝΙΘΗⲆⲨ· ⫽

    [ⲤΜΟΥ ΕⲠ̄Ⳡ̄Ⳡ Π̄Ν̄Ⲁ] ΤΗΡΟΥ ⫽

    [ⲤΜΟΥ ΕⲠ̄Ⳡ̄Ⳡ ΠΙϢⲦⲈϤ] ΝΕΜ ΠΙⲔⲀⲨⳤϢΝ ⫽

_____

[*] The lack of Sah. correspondants for ϬϢⳤ (22) and ϬⲀϪΙ (24), causes uncertainty as to the forms to be here supplied. If the former had its origin in the hieroglyphic ⟠, the form here should be ϪϢⳤ.

5.   [ⲤⲘⲞⲨ ⲈⲠ⳪ ⲚⲒ]ⲰⲦ ⲚⲈⲘ ⲚⲒⲚⲒϤ//

   [ⲤⲘⲞⲨ ⲈⲠ⳪ ⲚⲒⲈ]ⲬⲰⲢⲈϦ ⲚⲈⲘ ⲚⲒⲈϨⲞⲞⲨ//

   [ⲤⲘⲞⲨ ⲈⲠ⳪ ⲠⲒⲞⲨ]ⲰⲒ[Ⲛ]Ⲓ: ⲚⲈⲘ ⲠⲒⲬⲀⲔⲒ//

   [ⲤⲘⲞⲨ ⲈⲠ⳪ ⲠⲒⲬⲀϤ ⲚⲈⲘ] ⲠⲒⲰ[Ⲝ]ⲈϤ//

Fragt. C.

   [ⲤⲘⲞⲨ ⲈⲠ⳪ ⲠⲒⲠⲀⲬⲚⲎ ⲚⲈⲘ]ⲠⲒⲬⲒⲰⲚ//

10.   [ⲤⲘⲞⲨ ⲈⲠ⳪ ⲚⲒϭ]ⲈⲦⲈϤⲢⲎⲬ ⲚⲈⲘ ⲚⲒϬⲎⲠⲒ//

   [ⲤⲘⲞⲨ ⲈⲠ⳪ ⲠⲒ]ⲔⲀϨⲒ//

   [ⲤⲘⲞⲨ ⲈⲠ⳪ ⲚⲒ]ⲦⲰⲞⲨ ⲚⲈⲘ ⲚⲒⲔⲀⲖⲀⲘⲪⲞ//

   [ⲤⲘⲞⲨ ⲈⲠ⳪ ⲚⲎ ⲦⲎⲢⲞⲨ Ⲉ]ⲦⲢⲎⲦ ϨⲒⲬⲈⲚ ⲠⲔⲀϨⲒ//

   [ⲤⲘⲞⲨ ⲈⲠ⳪ ⲚⲒⲘⲞⲨ]ⲘⲒ//

15.   [ⲤⲘⲞⲨ ⲈⲠ⳪ ⲚⲒⲀⲘⲀⲒⲞ]Ⲩ: ⲚⲈⲘ ⲚⲒⲒⲀⲢⲰⲞⲨ//

   [ⲤⲘⲞⲨ ⲈⲠ⳪ ⲚⲒⲔⲎⲦⲞⲤ Ⲛ]ⲈⲘ ⲈⲚⲬⲀⲒ ⲚⲒⲂⲈⲚ

   [ⲈⲦⲔⲒⲘ ϧⲈⲚ ⲚⲒⲘⲰⲞⲨ//]

   [ⲤⲘⲞⲨ ⲈⲠ⳪ ⲚⲒϨⲀⲖⲀⲦ ⲦⲎ]ⲢⲞⲨ ⲚⲦⲈ ⲦⲪⲈ//

   [ⲤⲘⲞⲨ ⲈⲠ⳪ ⲚⲒⲐⲎⲢⲒⲞⲚ ⲚⲈⲘ] ⲚⲒⲦⲈϤⲚⲰⲞⲨⲒ ⲦⲎⲢⲞⲨ//

20.   [ⲤⲘⲞⲨ ⲈⲠ⳪ ⲚⲒϢⲎⲢⲒ ⲚⲦⲈ ⲚⲒ]ⲢⲰⲘⲒ//

      (lacuna)

Fragt. B.

   [ⲤⲘⲞⲨ ⲈⲠ⳪ ⲚⲒⲠⲚⲀ ⲚⲈⲘ ⲚⲒⲮⲨⲬⲎ ⲚⲦⲈ ⲚⲒⲐ Ⲙ]Ⲏ̣Ⲓ ^{??sic}

     (space for 2 lines)

   [ⲤⲘⲞⲨ ⲈⲠ⳪ ⲀⲚⲀⲚⲒⲀⲤ Ⲁ]ⲌⲀⲢⲒⲀⲤ ⲘⲒⲤⲀⲎⲖ ^{sic}

   [ⲔⲈⲆⲀⲚⲒⲎⲖ//]

             [Ⲧ]ⲎⲢⲞⲨ ⲚⲦⲈ Ⲡ⳪

25.   ⲢⲞϤ//

               [Ⲡ]ⲢⲰⲪⲎⲦⲎⲤ

           (traces of letters here.)

Fragt. A.

               ⲚⲈⲚⲒⲰⲦ ^{sic}

   ⲘⲀⲔⲀⲢ *(about 6 letters)* ⲈⲚⲒⲰⲦ ⲀⲠⲀ ⲠⲒⲤⲈⲚⲦ

30.   [ⲚⲈ]Ⲙ ⲠⲬⲰⲢⲞⲤ ⲦⲎⲢϤ ⲚⲦⲈ ⲚⲎⲈⲐⲞⲨⲀⲂ

   [Ⲛ]ⲦⲈ ⲚⲈⲨⲤⲘⲞⲨ ϢⲰⲠⲒ ⲚⲈⲘⲀⲚ ϨⲰⲤ ⲈⲢⲞϤ

   ✝   *(margin)*

<u>l.2</u>: This verse, absent in the Greek versions, is found in Tattam and in Bardelli. Also, the sections omitted by Theodotion (H. and P.), are pre-sent in the Coptic (l.l. 2, 5, 8.)

<u>l.l. 3-6</u>: follow the order of the LXX. Otherwise the sequence is that of Tatt. and Bard., differing both from Theod. and the LXX. The opening verses of the Ode, (lost here,) are shown in Sah. by Ciasca, (Sacr. Bibl. Frag., II, 317,) and follow the order of Theod., with which the Boh. version —so far—

agrees.

l.4: This line appears to represent two verses of the other Boh. versions (vv. 42,43 of _Tatt_., 66,67 of _Bard_.), and to correspond to the ψυχος και κανουν of Theod. (_H._ and _P._; but Tischend., ψυχος και καυμα.)

l.10: ⲤⲈⲦⲈⳓ︦ⲣ︦ⲏ︦ⲭ is uncertain. The space would allow of –ⲈⳓⲣⲏⲞ̄Ⲉ.

l.23: There is space here for a line, and the absence of // after ⲘⲓⲤⲀⲎⲖ suggests the name of _Daniel_, which stands thus in some Boh. liturgical versions.

ll.24,25: I cannot fill these lacunæ. The words remaining plainly are no part of the verse, ⲤⲘⲞⳙ ⲈⲠⲞⲤ ⲚⲎ ⲈⲦⲈⲣⲤⲈⲂⲈⲤⲐⲈ ⲠⲞⲤ ⲫⲦ ⲚⲦⲈ ⲚⲈⲚ–10✝ ⳘⲰⲤ ✠., which follows *l.22* in other M.S.S. (e.g. _Bodl_., M.S. _Hunt_. 605, M.S. _Copt_. e.1), or terminates the Ode in others (edd. Tatt., Bard.)

l.26: Perhaps some amplified form of the verse which stands after *l.22* in the _Horologium_, Ευλογειτε αποστολοι προφηται και μαρτυρες κυριον.

l.28: These words are very uncertain. They seem to be connected with the lines following.

It chances that there are, in this text, none of those test-words preserved which displayed the dialectal peculiarities of the foregoing Ode. The only form distinctly diverging from the Boh. is ⲚⲈⳙⲤⲘⲞⳙ (Sah., or M.E., pace Stern, Gr. §.252; cf. Quatremère, Rech⁵ 242, ⲚⲈⳙⲀⲖⲎⲞⳙ; 234, ⲦⲈⳙⳅⲎ; 237, ⲠⲈⳙⳗⲎⲓⳙ.) One may be tempted to find in this and in the significant, though not decisive ⲀⲠⲀ, an indication of the native dialect of the scribe.

VIII. Parchment. $8\frac{2}{8} \times 1\frac{6}{8}$ in.

A narrow strip of coarse parchment, bearing texts on both sides, and written (across the width of the strip,) by two very unskilled scribes, whose work is easily to be distinguished by the ink used and by the form of the letters. The texts are divided into sections by horizontal lines.

I give the sections side-by-side, separated as by the dividing-lines. Scribe *a* wrote on "Recto"

(1)	(2)	(3)	(4)
ⲠⲢⲞⲈ	ⲔⲀⲦⲀⲜⲒ	ᵍⁱᶜ ⲦⲆⲈⳙⲦⲈ	ⲈⲠⲀⲔ
ⲫⲐⲀⲤⲀⲚ	ⲞⲚⲤⲞⲚⲔ	ⲠⲢⲞⲤⲔ	ⲞⲤⲞⲚ
	ⳙⲢⲒⲈ	ⲎⲚⲤⲞⲘ	ⲎⲘⲞⲚ
		ⲈⲚ	

Scribe a, upon "Verso"

(7) ЄГЄΙΡЄС	(8) КΥΡΙЄ	(9) ΝΑΤΟΥⲀϩΗ	(10) ϚΔЄΥΤЄ	(11) СΥΚΥΡ
ΘΛΙΥΙΟΙФ	ΙΔΟΥΔΗ		ΠΡΟСΚΗ	ΙЄ
ωτος	ЄΥΛΟΓЄ		ΝСΟΜЄΝ	
	ΙΤЄΤΟΝ			
	ΚΥΡΙΟΝ			

Scribe b, upon "Recto"

(5) ϯοΙЄΛ	(6) ΝΤЄ
ΠΙСΤ	ΛЄΠⲞⲤ
ωΝΠ	ΚωϯΝ
ЄΡΑΤ	ΤЄΧΜ
ωΝΤ	ΛΛΟСΙΑ
ΗСΓ	
ΗС	

Scribe b, upon "Verso"

(12) ϯΝЄΤ
ΚωΝϩ
ΤΗΟΥ
ЄΠⲞⲤΝ
ΤϩΗΜ
ΠΤΑΥ
ΝСΙωΝ

The distribution of these sections upon the original is as follows;

"Recto" | 1 | 2 | 3 | 4 | 5 | 6 |

"Verso" | 7 | 8 | 9 | 10 | 11 | 12 |

The Greek portions of the text (1–5, 7, 8, 10, 11,) seem intended for

Προσεφθαϲὰν κατάξιον σου(?) κυριε

δευτε προσκυνησωμεν επακουσον ημων

ω η ελπις των περάτων της γης

Εγειρεσθε υιοι φωτος

κυριε ιδου δε ευλογεσετε τον κυριον

δευτ προσκυνησωμεν σε(?σου) κυριε

Since I have found 7 (above), as ΤΩΟΥΝΟΥ επιφωι ΝΙϢΗΡΙ ΝΤЄ ΠΟΥωΙΝΙ, at the beginning of the opening hymn of the Midnight Office in various Boheiric collections,* perhaps those less ignorant than myself in liturgical matters will be able to identify the other sections also. № 3 has the initial words of the "Invitatorium".

The Coptic (M.E.) portions (6, 12) are;

ΝΤЄΛЄ ΠⲞⲤ Κωϯ ΝΤЄΧΜΑΛΟСΙΑ (αἰχμαλωσία) ΝΝЄΤΚω ΝϩΤΗΟΥ ЄΠⲞⲤ ΝΘΗ (?=ЄΘΗ) ΜΠΤΑΥ ΝСΙωΝ, "After that the Lord has relieved (= turned away) the captivity of them that trust in the Lord, before the hill of Sion." I do not know the value here of the indication (9), "Those of (? for) the Evening." The marks at the commencement of 3 and 10 are perhaps initial signs, similar to those used in Hyv. Alb. XXVII, 22 and XXVIII, 19, 30.

This parchment had one fold at the middle, and may have served as an

* e.g. Bodl. M.S. Hunt. 603, do., Maresc. 49 and 100.

amulet.

IX. Papyrus.   5 × 5¾ in.

Upon one side of this leaf is a Coptic letter, (Nº XVII below,) and upon the other, the following Greek Benediction, which differs considerably from any of those in the published Oriental Liturgies. Similar forms are found in the Liturgies of S. Gregory (Renaudot, Lit. Or. Collect. I, 98,) and S. Mark (ib., 164.)

✝ Η ΑΓΑΠΗ ΤΟΥ ΘΥ ΚΑΙ ΠΑΤΡΟΣ

ΚΑΙ Η ΧΑΡΙϹ ΤΟΥ ΜΟΝΟΓΕΝΟΥϹ ΥΙΟΥ

ΤΟΥ ΜΕΓΑΛΟΥ ΘΥ ΚΑΙ ϹΩΤΗΡΟϹ

ΗΜΩΝ ΙΥ ΧΥ ΚΑΙ Η ΚΟΙΝΩΝΙΑ

ΤΟΥ ΑΓΙΟΥ ΚΑΙ ΠΡΟϹΚΥΝΗΤΟΥ ΑΓΙ

ΟΥ ΠΝΑΤΟϹ Η(sic) ΜΕΤΑ ΠΑΝΤΩΝ ΗΜΝ ω sic

The only peculiarity of the Greek here is Η for εἴη.

This text and the letter which accompanies it (Nº XVII), are possibly by the same hand. Both are clearly written.

The Address of the letter, which is also upon this face, will be found under Nº XVII.

X. Papyrus (from Hawara.)   3⅜ × 2¼ in.

A fragment similar in appearance to Nº VII (above). It contains parts of a narrative (?) and of a doxology, neither of which I have succeeded in identifying.

Recto: ΔΥΝΕΫ ΝΟΫ

ΚΕ ΜΕΗΤΕΒ̇

Χ̇ // ΔΙΗΫ ΩΕΧΙ

ΠΕΙΩΕΧΙ ΕΡΕ ΤΕ

ΙΜ ΠΕ ΠΕΚ[Ρ]ΑΝ //

Υ ΕϹΟΤΜ ΝΕΙΩΕ

ˀΔ͘ϤΒΤΙΗ͘ΠΕΒΟΥ

ϤΟ͘ΗΠΗ ΑΒΕΛ

ΝΕΡ̅Ρ̅ˀ[Ω̇]ΗΝΕΥ

Verso: ⲉ́ⲥ

ⲭⲉⲣⲉ ⲛⲁⲡⲟⲥⲧ
†ⲍⲉ ⲛⲟⲩⲁⲛ

ⲭⲉⲣⲉ ⲡⲁⲡⲣⲉⲛⲱⲟ̀
ⲛⲁⲣ[ⲭ]ⲏⲥⲧⲣⲁⲧⲓⲕⲟ
ⲉⲥⲁ ⲡⲉⲟⲁⲡ ⲕⲉⲛ

ⲥⲟⲧⲙ ⲉⲡⲁⲣ̄ⲧⲓⲙ
ⲁⲩ ⲙⲛ ⲡⲧⲁⲓⲁ ⲙ
? ⲃ ? ?

The dialect is clearly M.E.

LETTERS

XI. *Papyrus.* (*v. pl. 2.*) $8\frac{3}{8}$ × $13\frac{7}{8}$ in.

The material is tolerably fine and of a light yellow-brown colour. The text is in a clear character, free from ligatures. Some of the lines, however, have completely lost half their letters, while smaller lacunæ and uncertainties are frequent. In such cases, I represent the probable number of letters to be supplied by dots.

Recto:

1. †ⲁⲓ̈ⲭⲓⲛⲉⲥⲟⲁⲓ̈ ⲛ̄ⲧⲉⲧⲛⲙⲛⲧⲱⲏⲣⲉ ⲙⲁⲓ̈ⲛⲟⲩⲧⲉ ⲁⲩⲱ ⲁⲛⲓⲙⲉ ⲉⲛⲉⲧⲛ̄ⲟⲏⲧⲟⲩ ⲉⲧⲉ
   ⲛⲉⲧⲛ̄ⲁⲣⲓⲕⲉ

2. ⲛⲉ ⲉⲡⲭⲓⲛⲭⲏ ⲉⲧⲉⲧⲛ̄ⲡⲣⲟⲕⲣⲏⲙⲁⲧⲓⲍⲉ ⲙⲟⲛ ⲟⲁⲃⲉ ⲣⲱ ⲙ̄ⲡⲁⲧⲉⲧⲛ̄ⲥⲁⲧⲙ̄ ⲗⲁⲁⲩ
   ⲛ̄ⲱⲗⲭⲉ ⲛ̄

3. ⲧⲏⲛ ⲉⲱⲱⲡⲓ ⲁⲓⲥⲟⲁⲓ̈ ⲛⲏⲧⲛ̄ ⲕⲁⲕⲟⲥ ⲉⲓ̇ⲥ †ⲁⲉⲡⲓⲥⲧⲟⲗⲏ ⲛ̄ⲧⲉⲧⲉⲩⲧⲛ̄ ⲗⲙ[ⲗ]ⲟⲉ
   ⲙⲙⲟⲥ ⲱⲁⲛⲧⲉⲧⲛ̄

4. ⲛⲧⲥ ⲛⲁⲓ̈......ⲙ̄ⲡⲁⲧⲉⲣⲥⲁⲟ̀ ⲧⲁⲕⲣⲓⲛⲉ ⲛⲟⲩⲟⲱⲃ ⲙ̄ⲡⲓⲉⲓⲙⲉ ⲉⲧⲉⲟⲁⲕⲣⲓⲃⲓⲁ
   ⲡⲗⲏⲛ ⲧⲁⲓ̈ⲥⲟⲁⲓ̈

5. ⲛⲏⲧⲛ̄ ⲭⲉ ⲱⲓⲛⲉ[ⲛ̄ⲟⲩ]ⲣ̄ⲱⲙⲉ ⲛⲏⲧⲛ̄ ⲉⲭ[ⲓ] ⲛ̄ⲟⲉⲣⲱⲁⲩ ⲛⲏⲧⲛ̄ ⲁⲛ ⲁⲩⲱ ⲟⲁⲃⲉ ⲉⲧⲣⲁ
   ⲥⲟⲁⲓ̈ ⲁⲓⲟⲩⲱ ⲉⲓ̇ⲭⲱ ⲙⲁⲥ

6. ....ⲛ̄..ⲣⲱⲙ...ⲁⲕ ⲟⲩⲇⲉ ⲅⲁⲣ ⲙ̄ⲡⲉⲧⲛ̄ⲧⲁⲙⲁⲓ̈ ⲉⲡⲉⲧⲛ̄ⲟⲱⲃ
   ⲭⲉ ⲟⲩⲛ ⲡⲉ ⲡⲗⲏⲛ ⲉⲱⲱ·

7. ⲡⲓ ⲁⲟⲉⲣⲛⲁⲃⲉ ⲙⲁⲛ †ⲥⲟⲟⲩⲛ ⲙⲡⲉⲟ[ⲟⲱ]ⲃ ⲁⲛ ⲁ̀ⲩⲧⲁⲙⲁⲓ̈ ⲭⲉ ⲁⲕⲉⲛⲡⲉⲟⲟⲱⲃ
   ⲉⲡⲉⲛⲭⲟⲉⲓⲥ ⲛⲓⲱⲧ

8. ⲡⲉⲡⲓⲥⲕⲟⲡⲟⲥ ⲁⲩⲱ ⲁϥⲧⲛⲉⲡⲁⲣⲁⲃⲗⲁⳝⲉⲛ ⲛⲏⲕ ⲭⲉ ⲟⲩⲛ ⲙ̄ⲡⲉⲕⲧⲣⲉⲩϥⲓⲧϥ
   ⲉⲡϭⲓⲗⲁⲥⲧⲏⲣⲓ......?

9. ϣⲏ ⲙ̄ⲡⲉⲗⲙⲁ ⲛⲁϥ ⲛ̄ⲥⲉⳝⲥⲃⲱ ⲛⲏϥ ⲡⲣⲟⲥ ⲡⲉϥⲛⲁⲃⲉ ⲛ̄ⲧⲁϥⲁⲗⲁϥ ⲁⲩⲱ ⲉϣⲱⲡⲓ
   ⲙ̄ⲡⲉⲕⲟ̄ⲛⲙⲟⲩⲥⲑⲁⲣⲓ

10. ⲥⲉⲧⲧⲉϥϭϭⲓⲙⲉ ⲉⲡϭⲓⲗⲁⲥⲧⲏⲣⲓ ϣⲁⲛⲧⲉⲕⲟ̄ⲛⲧϥ ⲁⲩⲱ ⲙⲁⲕⲟ̄ⲛⲧϥ ⲙⲁⲗⲉⲩ†ⲕⲁⲕⲏ
    ⲛⲛⲉⲥⲭⲁ† ⲛⲁϥ   [-ⲟⲩ

11. ....···ⲓ̈ⲛⲁⲓ̈ ⲭⲉ ⲛⲧⲉⲧⲛ̄†ⲣⲱⲙⲉ ⲛⲁⲓ̈ ⲁⲛ ⲧⲁ†ⲁⲗⲁ ⲛⲉⲥⲁⲩⲃ-
    ⲁⲛⲁⲕⲁⲥⲉ ⲛⲉⲩⲗⲓⲉ ⲛ̄ⲥⲉ

12. ⲧⲁϣⲣⲱⲙ[ⲉ̈] ⲓⲉ ⲛⲥⲉⲧⲱϣ ⲉ̂ⲡ̂ⲱϩⲥ̄ ⲓⲉ̈ ⲛⲉϭⲣⲏ ⲉⲧⲣⲉⲛⲁⲁⲩ ⲧⲁⲗⲉⲩⲓ̈ ϩⲁⲃⲁⲗ ⲙⲁⲛ
    ⲁⲗⲉ ⲡⲣⲱϣⲉ ⲛϧⲱⲃ ϩⲓ̈

13. ⲭⲱⲟⲩ ⲁⲛⲓⲕⲁⲧⲁⲫⲣⲟⲛⲓ ⲛ̄ϩⲱⲃ ⲛⲓ̈ⲙ ⲁⲛⲧⲁⲩⲁⲩ ⲛⲏⲧⲛ̄ ⲁⲩⲱ ⲉϣⲱⲡⲓ ⲡⲕⲟⲩⲓ̈
    ⲛⲁⲗⲟⲩ ⲙⲟⲩⲥⲑⲁⲣⲓ ϣⲁϥϣⲉⲣⲡ̄ϩⲱⲃ

14. ⲕⲁ̈· ⲁ̈ⲛⲙⲡ...........ⲟ̈ϥ ⲉⲡ̂ⲛⲟⲩⲛ ⲙ........ϩⲁⲧⲛ̄·· ⲕⲉⲥⲟⲡ ⲁⲩⲱ † ⲟⲩ
    ⲕⲟⲩϩ ⲇⲱ ⲛⲏⲣⲡ ⲛⲉⲃ ⲁ

15. ϩ̈ⲁ·ϩ·ⲉ[ϣ]ⲱ̈ⲡⲓ ⲙ̄ⲡⲁⲧⲉⲛ†ⲛⲁⲩ ⲁⲩⲱ ⲁⲛⲁⲕⲁⲥ[ⲉ̈] ⲙⲁⲛ ϩⲁⲕⲡⲉⲩ ⲓ̄ ⲛⲓⲱ ⲙⲏⲛ
    ⲉⲙⲁⲛ ⲁⲩⲧⲁⲙⲁⲓ̈

16. ⲭⲉ̈ ⲛⲥⲁ ⲱ̈ⲙⲟⲩⲛ ⲛⲥⲉϩⲱⲕ ⲁⲛ ⲧⲁⲣⲉϥⲧⲁⲗⲁⲩ ⲧⲁ̈ⲗⲏ ⲛ̄ϭⲉⲓ ⲉⲡⲙⲟⲛⲁⲥⲧⲏⲣⲓ
    ⲡϫⲟⲉⲓⲥ ⲉϥⲉϩⲁⲣⲉϩ ⲉⲣⲱⲧⲛ̄

17. ϩⲓⲟⲩⲥⲟⲡ ⲉⲧⲉⲧ̄ⲛ̄ⲟⲩⲁⲭ ⲥⲱⲙⲁ ⲯⲩⲭⲏ ⲡ̄ⲛ̄ⲁ

Verso:

† ⲧⲁⲁⲥ ⲛⲉⲛϣⲏⲣⲉ ⲙ̄ⲙⲁ̈ⲛ̈ⲟⲩⲧⲉ ⲉⲧⲧⲁⲓ̈ⲏⲟⲩ(sic) ⲕⲁⲧⲁ ⲥⲙⲁⲧ ⲛⲓⲙ ϩⲓⲧⲛ
  ⲅⲉⲱⲣⲅⲓⲟⲥ ⲡⲓⲉⲗⲁⲭⲓϣ

This letter is addressed to some congregation (ⲛⲉⲛϣⲏⲣⲉ,—yet ll. 7-11, the 2ᵈ
sing. is employed;) presumably to a monastery. The writer appears to be in a
position of authority, though not of episcopal rank (l.7.)*

Recto: ll.1-4. "I have received the letters of your pious Sonships and we
have acquainted ourselves with what is in them, namely, your complaints.
In vain do ye prejudge us before that ye have heard any word of ours.
If I have written ill to you, then keep my letter—? until ye (?can) bring it
to me."

ⲭⲓⲥϩⲁⲓ, "receive a letter"; v. A.Z., '85,32; also Berl., P.5553, ⲛ̄ⲧⲉⲧⲛⲟⲩⲁϩⲙ̄ ⲭⲓⲥϩⲁⲓ̈
ⲉⲡⲱⲛ ⲁⲛ ⲡⲉ; and R.V, 37,46.

ⲡⲣⲟⲕⲣⲏⲙⲁⲧⲓⲍⲉ = προκριματίζειν, "prajudicare"(Du Fresne.)

ϩⲁⲑⲉ for ϩⲁⲑⲏ, with ⲙ̄ⲡⲁⲧⲉ-, v. Stern, §.621.

ⲛ̄ⲧⲏⲛ, because the substantive has no Article; v. Stern, §.299,1.

ⲉϥϣⲱⲡⲓ ⲁⲓⲥϩⲁⲓ is written over an erasure.

ⲉⲓⲥ ⲧⲁⲉⲡⲓⲥⲧⲟⲗⲏ ⲛⲧⲉⲧⲉⲩⲧⲛ̄ (=ⲛⲧⲉⲧⲏⲩⲧⲛ̄,) "See, here is my letter to you." Yet
    one would expect ⲛⲏⲧⲛ̄ or a prepositional equivalent, and ⲉⲓⲉ is

*The epithet ⲉⲗⲁⲭⲓⲥⲧⲟⲥ, applied by a writer to himself, is no indication of posit-
-ion. It is used as here by bishops, A.Z.'92,38, R.V,34.

perhaps a better reading.

ll. 4, 5. "I have not been so foolish as to judge a matter whose details I did not know. However, I wrote to you (saying), Seek you a man."

ΠΛΗΝ ΤΑΪ- for ΠΛΗΝ ΝΤΑΪ-.

ΕΧΙ for ΕΧΙΝ, a M.E. form of ΧΙΝ; v. Stern, §.567. It is followed by the participle,— probably negative;— though, if instead of ΕΧΙ Ν̄ϥΕϢ-, we read ΕΧΙΝ ϥΕϢ-, the following ΑΝ might = Sah. ΟΝ:

ΡΩΜΕ "servant"; v. R. V, 42 (ΝΕΚΡΩΜΕ ΤΗΡΟΥ.)

l. 5. "And before I wrote, I had already said—"

ϨΑΘΕ = ϨΑΘΗ with ΕΤΡΑ· is noticeable.

ll. 6–8. "— nor have ye told me your matter, what it is. However, if he has offended against us, I have knowledge of his matter also(?). (And) I have been told that thou hast brought his affair to our lord and father, the Bishop, and he has—"

†ⲤΟΟΥΝ ΑΝ. I take ΑΝ here as = Sah. ΟΝ. If it be the negative, ΜΑΝ must stand for ΜΑΝ Ν·

ΝΕΠΑΡΑΒΛΑ?ΕΝ. The uncertain letters seem most like ΑΛ. I am at a loss to explain the group. It has the appearance of a Greek word, used nom- -inally. Be it even of verbal origin, the usage of the present text makes a final (infin.) Ν improbable, and tempts one to read the following word ΝΝΗΚ.

l. 8. "— what it is. Thou hast not had him taken to the seat of Pardon (or Altar.)"

ϦΙΤϤ is corrected from ϥΤϥ(?)

ϦΙΛΑΣΤΗΡΙ = Ἱλαστήριον (Suidas, = Θυσιαστήριον,) a word apparently well known to the Copts; v. Tuki, Rud. 37, المُغْران ϩ̄ⲱⲙ, "place of pardon", and Kircher, Scal., 245, المَذْبَح, "altar." I do not know if it has here any narrower, technical meaning.

ll. 9, 10. "— they instruct him as to the evil which he has done. And if thou hast not found Musthation, place his wife at the seat of Pardon until thou find him. And if thou (still) continue not to find him, let him be punished (?) to the uttermost (?)."

ΜΟΥΣΘΑΡΙ = *Μουσθαρίων (or Μωσθαρίων), rather than *Μουσθάριον, a fem. form. v. Pape, XXI, XXII.

†ΚΑΚΗ is, I suppose, (†ΚΑΚΕ =) κακὸν ποιεῖν, and ΝΝΕΣΧΑ† an imitation of ἐπ᾽ ἔσχατον.

ll. 11, 12. "— ye do not (?) give me a man, that I may (?) — the — Compel (?) the husbandmen either that they fix upon a man or that they fix (?) the harvest or the provisions, so that we may make them, (and) that they depart from us." This translation is very uncertain.

ΑΝΑΚΑΣΕ I take as Imperat. of ἀναγκάζειν, and

NEYλIE *for* (NEOYλIE =) Sah. NOYOEIE. (*cf.?* Rev. égypt., V, pl. 21, ⲣ̄ⲙⲟⲩⲁⲉⲓ, Berl. P. 5653, ⲣⲟⲙⲟⲩⲁ̈ⲓ.)

ⲉⲡⲱ̄ⲅⲥ. Perhaps ⲉ-=ⲙ-? The group might be read ⲏⲱⲅⲉ (*for* ⲉⲓⲱⲅⲉ); but *cf.* the form of ⲡ *in* (2) ⲡⲣⲟⲕⲣⲏⲙⲁⲧⲓⲍⲉ, (7) ⲡⲉ̄ⲩⲅ̄ⲱⲃ, (14) ⲏⲣⲡ.

ⲘⲀⲚ "*from us*"; *v.* Stern, §.298, 2.

ll. 12, 13. "Give heed to the matters that concern them. We are not troubled about (take no thought for) any of the matters and have entrusted them to you. And should the youth Mustharion—?"

ⲩⲉⲣⲡⲅⲱⲃ reminds of verbal formations like ⲩⲣ̄ⲡⲥⲅⲁⲓ, ⲩⲣ̄ⲡⲧⲁⲩⲟ, ⲩⲣ̄ⲡⲟⲛⲟⲙ-ⲁⲍⲉ in the Djēmē Papyri. But here the second element is a noun.

l. 14. "and give him one Kor of wine." The Greek κόυρς, κόρος, χός, Heb. בֹּר, is a frequent liquid-measure.

l. 15. "Ten asses" and, apparently, their "harness" are here spoken of. There was nothing between ϯⲚⲀⲨ and ⲀⲨⲱ.

ⲘⲎⲚⲈⲘⲀⲚ ? = Sah. Ⲙ̄ⲘⲓⲚ Ⲙ̄ⲘⲟⲚ.

l. 16. Schmûn seems to be mentioned, but the letters are half erased. Farther on, "—they go to the Monastry." "The Lord shall keep you, one and all, sound in body, soul and spirit." A similar formula terminates Brit. Mᵐ. Ostrak. 5854, ⲧⲚⲟⲩⲟⲬ [Ⲥⲱ]ⲙⲀ ⲯⲨⲬⲎ ⲡ̄ⲚⲀ †; and N° XXIII; *v.* also R.V, 27, ⲈⲔⲟⲩⲟⲬ.

Verso: "For (lit, Give it to) our god-loving right-reverend Sons; from Georgios, the most humble."

ⲚⲈⲚⲩⲎⲣⲉ = Ⲛ̄ⲡⲈⲚⲩⲎⲣⲉ.

The M.E. element predominates over the Sah. in this text; but the usage is, in many cases, inconsequent; *cf.* ⲚⲀⲒ (4, 11) ⲚⲀⲨ (9, 10) with ⲚⲎⲔ (8) ⲚⲎⲩ (9), ⲘⲀλⲈⲨ-(10) ⲧⲀλⲈⲨ-(12) with ⲧⲀⲣⲈⲩ-(16). The weak ending is throughout −ⲉ (excepting, of course, ⲈⲩⲱⲡⲒ). The forms ⲒⲘⲈ (1), Ⲓⲱⲧ (7), ⲒⲈ (12), ⲓ verb (12, 16), ⲔⲀⲧⲀ-ⲫⲣⲟⲚⲒ (13) may be noted.

XII. Papyrus. (*v.* N° XXIV.)　　　　　　　　　　17 × 5¾ in.

A thin papyrus, of dark-brown colour, which, owing to its having been folded throughout (width) at intervals of ¾ in., is in a very fragile condit-ion. It is an opisthograph, the original text being N° XXIV, as is evident at ll. 26–28 here and from the present condition of the text of N° XXIV. The character on this face (which might be classed with Hyv., Alb. X, dated A.D. 1003,) is large and clear. ⲀⲒ is the only real ligature. In the *reverse direction* from the following text, but by the *same scribe*;

✝ ⲕ̅ⲩ̅ ⲡⲓ⳿ϩⲏⲩ   S ⲙ̅ⲛ̅✝ⲅⲁⲃⲣ
ⲉⲛ ⲁ̅ⲣ̅   3'

"(For) Master Pihêw, most eminent Archon, and —; (from) Gabriel."

✝ⲥⲩⲛⲑⲱ̅ ⲧⲓⲱ[ⲓ]ⲛⲓ ⲁ̅ⲱ ⲧⲓⲁⲥ
ⲡⲁⲍⲉ ⲙ̅ⲡⲟⲩϣⲁⲓ ⲙ̅ⲡⲁⲙⲁⲓ
5. ⲛⲟ̅ⲩ̅ ⲛ̅ϣⲁⲓⲥ ⲛⲥⲁⲛ ⲉⲧ^ ⲙ̅ⲡ̅ⲕ̅
ⲁ̅ⲱ ⲧⲓⲱⲓⲛⲓ ⲉⲡⲉⲕⲥⲱⲟⲩϩ
ⲧⲏⲣϥ ⲛϩⲟⲩⲁⲧⲉ ⲛⲉ ⲧⲓⲉⲙ
ⲧⲁⲛ ⲙⲡⲉⲕⲁⲅⲓⲱⲛ
ⲙ̅ⲡ̅ⲛ̅ⲁ̅ ϩ̅ⲙ ⲡⲟ̅ⲥ̅ ⲓ̅ⲥ̅ ⲡⲉⲭ̅ⲥ̅
10. [ⲧ̅ⲏ̅ⲣ̅ⲏ̅ⲛ]ⲓ ⲛⲁⲕ ⲉⲃⲁⲗ ϩⲓ ⲡⲛⲟ̅ⲩ̅
ⲙⲉⲛⲉⲥⲁ ⲛⲁⲓ ⲡⲁϣⲁⲓⲥ ⲛⲥⲁⲛ
ϩⲉⲓ ⲡⲁ̂ⲓ ⲁⲡⲁ ⲕⲩⲣⲱ ⲁⲓⲟⲩⲁⲁ
ⲧⲉⲩ ⲛⲁⲕ ⲛⲉϩⲏⲙⲉⲭ ⲉⲛ
ϣⲁⲕⲉⲣⲛⲁ ⲛⲉⲙⲁⲓ ⲙⲙⲟⲟⲩ
15. ⲧⲁⲟⲩ ⲙ̅ⲡⲁ̂ⲓ ⲁⲡⲁ ⲕⲩⲣⲱ
ⲉⲛⲃⲟⲩⲉϩⲟⲩ ϩⲁⲑⲏ ⲁⲡⲁ ⲓⲁ
ⲕⲱⲃ ϣⲁⲛⲧⲉ ⲡⲁ̂ⲓ ⲡⲓ
[ⲥ]ⲩⲛⲧⲓ ⲉⲓ ⲉⲛϥϭⲁⲡⲟⲩ
ⲁ̅ⲱ ⲡⲁⲟⲩϣⲁⲓ ⲉⲣⲁⲕ ⲟⲩ
20. ⲁⲡⲱⲕⲣⲉⲥⲓⲥ ⲉⲕ[ⲉ]ⲣⲭⲣⲓⲁ
[ⲙ̅]ⲁⲥ ϩⲉ ⲡⲁϩⲁⲩ ⲧⲟⲩⲥϭⲁⲓ
ⲛⲁⲓ ⲧⲁⲁⲥ ⲉⲓⲉⲩⲭⲁⲣⲓ̅ⲥ̅
ⲉⲛⲑⲏ ⲉⲕⲓⲣⲓ ⲛⲁⲁⲡⲱⲕ
ⲣⲉⲥⲓⲥ ⲧⲁⲉⲣⲛⲱⲓ̀ ϩⲱⲱⲧ
25. ⲉⲓⲉⲩⲭⲁⲣⲓ̅ⲥ̅ ⲧⲓⲱⲓⲛⲓ ⲉⲡⲁ
ϣⲁⲓⲥ ⲛⲥⲁⲛ ⲕⲁⲗⲟⲥ ϩⲙ ⲡⲟⲩ
ⲱϣ ⲙ̅ⲡⲛⲟ̅ⲩ̅ ⲟⲩⲭⲁⲓ ϩⲙ ⲡⲟ̅ⲥ̅
[ⲁ]ⲩⲱ ⲙⲡⲉⲣⲁⲣⲓⲕⲉ ⲙⲁⲛ ⲙⲡⲓⲟⲙ

The following line, by the *scribe of*
N⁰ XXIV, is in the *reverse direction*;
ⲁⲣ̅ⲁ̅ⲕ̅✝ ϥⲓⲗⲱ̅ ⲁⲣ̅ⲡ̅ⲣⲣ ✝ⲅⲉⲱ̅ⲧ̅ ⲉⲛⲕⲱ̅

Then, by the *scribe of the above letter,*
as before;
30. ⲭⲱⲱⲙⲉ ⲛⲕⲁⲑⲁⲣⲱⲛ ⲕⲁⲧⲁ
ⲡⲉⲕⲧⲁⲓⲁ ✝

"In God's Name! I greet and embrace the wellfare of my God-loving, rev-erend Lord Brother in the Spirit, and I greet thy whole congregation, that is, the foremost (members). Repose thy holy Spirit in the Lord Jesus Christ. Peace (be) to thee from God! And now (lit., thereafter), my Lord Brother, lo, I have sent the Deacon, Apa Kyros, to thee. Give the vinegars with which thou art used to favour me, to the Deacon, Apa Kyros, that he place them with Apa Jakob, until the Deacon Pisynthius go and take them, together with my greeting for thee (?) If thou desirest an answer in return and they write to me, I will give it. I am obliged for the manner in which thou hast answered me, so that I too might be informed (?) I am obliged. I greet my Lord Brother fairly, ac-cording to the will of God. Farewell in the Lord! And blame us not (because) I have not been able to

find a clean papyrus, worthy of thine honour."

Of the two addresses, the *first (ll. 1, 2,)* is that belonging to the above text. The name of the scribe, Gabriel, occurs in N⁰ XXIV²⁴, possibly as that of the bearer of the letter. Yet it can not be proved that the same person is meant; we do not even know if the two texts are contemporaneous. For the second address (l. 29), v. N° XXIV.

ll. 1, 2. K͞Y = κύριος. v. also Versos (Addresses) of N°ˢ XX, XXII, and XXIII.
ΠΙϨΗΥ. This name occurs R. V, 27, 31; A.Z. '84, 159.
ЄN ᾱρ̄ = ἐνδοξότατος ἄρχων, or ἀρχιμανδρίτης. The first is the more likely, since this epithet usually is found with civil titles (v. R. I, 6, II; V, 31; A.Z. '91, 5.) and that of ἄρχων can be quite definite, e.g. Revil., Ac. & Contr., ō͞N. Yet ΠΑΡΧ, for ἀρχιμανδρίτης, is a reading assured by variants (A.Z. '85, 147.)
What follows Ϥ, "and", must be another title, — not ΜΑΝΤϤΡΙΤΗϹ.
ΝΟῩ. The T superscript has, throughout this text, the form ⅃.
ЄΤᔕ = ЄΤΤΑΙΗΟΥΤ. The same abbreviation, N°ˢ XX, XXIII.
Π͞Ϛ = πνευματικός. v. Hyv., Alb. XXIV, ϹΑΡΚΙΚ° ϱι Π͞ΝΙϚ (? cf. N° XXIII, Verso), ib. XXVII, Π͞ΝΑΤΙΚΟΝ, A.Z. '92, 39, ΠΝΑΚ. v. also N°ˢ XVII, XXIII².
l. 6. ϹΩΟΥϨ ΤΗΡϤ. For this phrase, v. the variants R. V, 25, 26, 27 and N° XIII.
l. 7. ΝϨΟΥΑΤЄ ΝЄ. v. N°ˢ XXIII² and, presumably, XX. cf. Boh. ϨΟΥΑϮ (Peyr. 368.)
ΤΙЄΜΤΑΝ ϥ̄c. v. N°ˢ XX and XXXIII.
l. 10. ΤᎪΡΗΝΙ. One only of the missing letters was prolonged below and ι is certain. cf. Berl., P. 5559, ΤΙΡΗΝΗ ΝΑΚ ЄΒΟ⅃ ϨΙΤ͞Ν ΠΝΟΥΤЄ, and R. V, 31; variants, R. II, 56; V, 26, 35, and N° XIX.
l. 12. ϨЄΙ. This M.E. interjection occurs Isaiah, XXX, 27 (Mém. de l'Instit. égypt. II, ii), corresponding to Boh. ϨΗΠЄ ΙϹ; also in N°ˢ XVI, XIX, XXVI. It has the forms ϨЄЄΙ R. II, 47, ϨЄ N° XXIV²⁴.
ΚΥΡΩ = ΚΥΡΟϹ. v. Berl., P. 3251, A.Z. '68, 65. A fem. form, ΚΥΡᎪ, R. V, 32, seems, at A.Z. '78, 26, to be a title, not a name, as is the masc. sometimes.
ΟΥ⅃ΑΤЄϨ occurs A.Z. '85, 32; R. V, 53; N°ˢ XIV, XVI, XXIII⁷, XXVI. cf. Sah. ΟΥΩΩΤЄ, ΟΥΟΤ⸗, Ciasca, Levit., XVI, 8, 10.
l. 13. ϨΗΜЄΧ, more probable than ϨΗΜЄ (ναύλον) Χ[Є] ЄΝϢΑΚ⸗ ϥ̄c.
l. 14. ΝЄΜΑΙ after ЄΡΝΑ, v. Zoega, 7, Ν̄ΤЄ Π͞Ο͞Ϲ ЄΡΠΙΝΑΙ ΝЄΜΑΙ; also S.B.A., Proc. VIII, 185, A.Z. '78, 25 (Anm.)
l. 15. Τ⅃ΟΥ = Sah. ΤΑ⅃Υ.
l. 16. ЄΝΒΟΥЄϨΟΥ. Final Conjunctive after Imperat., v. Stern, §. 448.
ϨΑΘΗ ΑΠΑ = ϨΑΘΗ ΝΑΠΑ ϥ̄c.
l. 18. ϬΑΠ⸗ = Sah. ϬΟΠ⸗, the usual word in these letters for "receive, take over". The same form A.Z. '85, 39; R. II, 60, V, 53, N° XVI and Berl., P. 5559, ΜΑΡЄ ΤЄΚ͞ΜΤΜΑΪΝΟΥΤЄ ΚЄ⅃ЄΥ ΤΟΥϬΑΠ ΝЄΪ ΚΟΥΝΤΑΡΗΧΗ ЄΠ⅃ΟΓΟϹ Ν̄ΠϢΑΠΗΪ.
l. 19. My translation here is unsatisfactory, for it implies, I think, ΜΝ rather than ΑΥΩ and ΝΑΚ than ЄΡΑΚ. I have supposed an idea like that of B[ор]Π ΠЄΚϢΙΝΙ ΝΗΙ, R. V, 42.
l. 20. I do not know if Conjunct. Τ⅃ΑϹ (= Ν̄ΤΑ⅃ΑϹ) for Fut., is admissible.

To regard ⲧⲟⲩⲥⲅⲁⲓ as ruled by ⲅⲉⲡⲁⲅⲁⲩ is still more to increase the difficulty of translation. For examples of ἀπόκρισις, v. <u>R</u>.V, 47 and <u>Ä.Z.</u> '85, 30.

l.21. ⲅⲉⲡⲁⲅⲁⲩ = Sah. ⲅⲓⲡⲁⲅⲟⲩ. (M.E. also ⲅⲓⲡⲉⲅⲟⲩ, <u>Peyr.</u>)
ⲧⲟⲩⲥⲅⲁⲓ. This prefix is found (M.E.) N⁰ XXIII ⁹; <u>R</u>.V, 35, ⲧⲟⲩⲉⲗⲡⲣⲟⲥⲕⲩ; <u>Berl.</u>, P. 5559 (v. ad *l.18*, above.) *

l.22. ⲉⲩⲭⲁⲣⲓⲥⲧ = εὐχαριστεῖν. The translation is again uncertain.
l.23. ⲓⲣⲓ = ⲉⲓⲣⲉ. ⲛⲁⲁⲡⲱⲕⲣ⁻ for ⲛⲛⲁⲁⲡⲱⲕⲣ⁻.
l.24. ⲉⲣⲛⲱ? A small lacuna here, with remnants of ⲕ rather than ⲓ.
l.25. ⲙⲡⲉⲣⲁⲣⲓⲕⲉ =? ⲙⲡⲉⲣⲣⲁⲣⲓⲕⲉ.
ⲟⲙⲭⲱⲱⲙⲉ could be read ⲟⲏ⁻ (not ⲟⲛ⁻). For ⲟⲙ⁻, v. Quatrem., Rech., 245, ⲃⲉⲙⲅⲏⲟⲩ, and <u>Stern</u>, §.66. For ⲟⲏ⁻, v. N⁰ XVI. ⲭⲱⲱⲙⲉ is the form, "roll", rather than the *material*, ⲭⲁⲣⲧⲏⲥ. (cf. N⁰ XLIV.) The word recurs in Fayyum M.S.S., <u>R</u>. II. 44, 48, V. 24; <u>Ä.Z.</u> '85, 35.
l.29. v. N⁰ XXIV.

XIII. Papyrus. $4\frac{5}{8}$ × 12 in.

The material is somewhat coarse-fibred; the colour, light brown. The text is written in a small, very neat hand, greatly resembling that of the colophon, Hyv., Alb. XX.
<u>Note</u>:— The inconsistent word-division, given below, is that of the original.
All lines, except *l.8*, are broken off at the end. Lost letters are represented by a corresponding number of dots.
Recto: † sic
1. †ⲥⲩⲙ ϣⲟⲣⲡⲙⲉⲛ ⲧϣⲓⲛⲓ ⲁⲩⲱ ⲧⲁⲥⲡⲁⲍⲉⲉⲛⲟⲩ[ⲙ]ⲏ ϣⲉⲉⲛ[ⲥⲟ]ⲡ . . . .
 [ⲛⲁⲥ]ⲛⲏ ⲩⲁⲩⲱⲡ[ⲁⲓⲱⲧ]
2. ⲡⲁⲓⲁⲕ̇ ⲙⲱⲛⲉ ⲡⲁⲓⲱⲧ ⲡⲁⲓⲁⲕ̇ ⲅⲉⲱⲣⲅⲓ ⲡⲁⲓⲱⲧ ⲡⲁⲡⲁⲓ ⲱ[ⲁ]ⲛⲛ[ⲏ]ⲥ ⲡⲁⲓⲱⲧ
 [ⲡⲁⲡ[ⲁ] ⲃⲓⲕⲧⲱⲣ ⲡⲁⲓ[ⲱⲧ ⲡⲁⲡⲁⲇⲁ]
3. ⲙⲏⲁⲛⲉ ⲡⲁⲓⲱⲧ ⲡⲁⲡⲁ ⲡⲉⲧⲣ[ⲟⲥ ⲡ]ⲁⲓⲱⲧ ⲡⲁⲡⲁⲁⲑⲁⲛⲁⲥⲓ ⲡⲁⲓⲱⲧ ⲡⲇⲓⲁⲕ̇ ⲡⲉⲧⲣ
 [ⲟⲥ] ⲡⲁⲓⲱⲧ ⲡⲁⲓⲁⲕ̇ ⲑⲱⲙ[ⲁⲥ]
4. ⲡⲁⲓⲱⲧ ⲡⲁⲡⲁ ⲡⲉⲧⲣⲟⲥ ⲡⲁⲓⲱⲧ [ⲡⲁⲡ]ⲁ ⲡⲟⲓⲙⲏⲛ †ⲧϣⲓⲛⲓⲉⲡⲥⲱⲟⲩⲁⲅ ⲉⲅⲟⲩⲛ
 ⲉⲛⲛⲁⲥⲛⲏⲩ ⲧⲏⲣⲟⲩ ⲡⲟⲩ[ⲁ ⲡⲟⲩⲁ ⲕⲁ]
5. ⲧⲁⲡⲉⲅⲣⲁⲛ ⲟ̅ⲓⲛⲉⲟⲩⲛⲟⲥⲱⲗⲉⲩ̇ⲕⲟⲩⲓ̇ †ⲧϣⲓⲛⲓ ⲉⲣⲱⲧⲉⲛ ⲕⲁⲗⲟⲥ ϣⲁⲧⲉⲛⲛⲁⲩ sic
 ⲉⲛⲉⲛⲉⲣⲏⲩ ⲅⲉⲛⲡⲕⲉⲗⲓⲱ[ⲛ ⲉ̄ⲣ]
6. ⲡⲉⲛⲙⲉⲩⲉ ⲅⲉⲛⲛⲉⲧⲉⲛⲱⲗⲏⲗⲉⲑⲟⲩⲁⲃ ⲧⲉⲫ†ⲭⲟⲕ ⲧⲉⲛ ϩ̅ⲁⲓⲏ ⲉⲃⲟⲗ [ⲕⲁ̅ⲗⲟⲥ sic
 ⲡⲉⲅⲙⲟⲧ ⲉⲛⲡⲛⲟⲩⲧⲉ

---

* <u>Sah.</u>, <u>Guidi</u>, Fram., 22, ⲁⲙⲱⲓⲛⲓ---ⲛⲧⲟⲩⲥⲟⲡⲥ; <u>Revill.</u>, <u>A. et C.</u>, ⲝⲑ̅, ⲛⲧⲟⲩⲭⲛⲟⲩⲓ.

7. ⲁⲫ︦ϯ ϯⲉⲙⲧⲟⲛ ⲛⲁⲛ̇..ⲉ....ⲛⲓ[ⲃ]ⲉⲛ ⲋ ⲡⲉⲛϩⲏⲧ ⲑⲏⲧ ⲉⲭⲉⲛⲡⲟⲩⲭⲁⲓ ⲉⲛⲧⲉⲛ ⲯⲩⲭ.ⲫ..

8. ⲥⲁⲡⲱⲱⲓ ⲉⲛⲉⲙⲧⲟⲛ̇.......ⲛϩⲉⲛⲡ̅ⲟ̅ⲥ̅ ⲛⲁⲓⲟⲧⲉ ⲉ̇ⲑ̇ⲟ̇ⲩ̇ⲁⲁⲃ ⲉⲥⲙ̇..ⲛ̇ⲙ̇ⲉⲉ ⲛⲁⲟⲅⲙⲁⲧⲓⲟⲛⲁⲓ

9. ⲟⲩⲟⲣⲡⲉϥ ⲉⲧⲉⲕⲕⲗⲏⲥⲓⲁ [ⲧⲉ̇ⲓⲣ]ⲏⲛⲏⲛⲱⲧⲉⲛ ϩⲓⲧⲉⲛⲛⲓⲥϧⲁⲓ ✝ ⲁⲛⲟⲕ ⲡⲓⲉⲗⲁ̅ⲭ̅ ⲉⲩⲥⲧⲁⲑⲓⲟⲥ ϯϩⲟ [ⲉ̇ⲣ]

10. ⲡⲁⲙⲉⲩⲓ ϧⲉⲛ ⲛⲉⲧⲉ[ⲛ ˢⁱᶜ ⲱ]ⲗⲏ[ⲗ]ⲉⲑⲟⲩⲁⲃ ⲛⲁ ⲟ̅ⲥ̅ ⲉⲛⲓⲟⲧⲉ ✝

Vertically, along the left side;

11. ⲁⲩⲱ ⲡⲁⲓⲱⲧ ⲡⲁⲡⲁⲭⲁⲏⲗ ⲱⲓⲛⲉ ⲉⲣⲟⲧⲉⲛ

12. ⲕⲁⲗⲟⲥⲙⲉⲛⲛⲉⲥⲛⲏⲩ ⲧⲏⲣⲟⲩ ✝

Verso;

$$\overline{\Xi}\text{ⲘⲈ́ⲚⲚⲀⲤⲚⲎⲨ}^{???} \overline{\text{ⲦⲎⲢⲞⲨ}}^{???} ✝ \text{ⲠⲀⲠⲀⲪⲞⲒⲖⲞ́}^\theta \text{ⲡⲉ̇[ⲧⲉ]}$$

ⲛ̇[ⲕ]ⲟⲛ ✝

Recto; "With God! Firstly, I greet and embrace many times ___? my brethren and my father, the Deacon Môné, my father, the Deacon Georgios, my father, Apa Johannes, my father, Apa Victor, my father, Apa Damianos, my father, Apa Petros, my father, Apa Athanasios, my father, the Deacon Petros, my father, the Deacon Thomas, my father, Apa Petros (sic), my father, Apa Poimen. I greet thee congregation of all my brethren, each according to his name, from great to small. I greet you fairly, until we see eachother in the other age. Our memory (be) in your holy prayers, (and) God complete prosperously our end-of-life! The Grace of God (be with us)! God hath given rest to us(?) ___? and our heart is turned toward the welfare of our soul ___? above ___? of the Lord, my saintly Fathers ___? dogmatical(?) I have sent it (?him) to the Church. Peace be to you through this letter! I, Eustathios, the most humble, I pray you, my Lords Fathers, have mind of me in your holy prayers. And my father, Apa Chael, greets you fairly, and all the brethren."

Verso; ["For ___?] and all my brethren; (from) Apa Philotheos, your(?) brother."

Recto;

A cross above l.1 is found in N°ˢ XXIII, XXV, and is comparable with the ornamented crosses, similarly placed, in uncial codices; e.g. *Hyv., Album* XLII.

l.1. A similar introductory formula in N° XIV. Other variants, *R. V,* 24 ff.

l.4. ⲡⲥⲱⲟⲩϩ ⲉϧⲟⲩⲛ; v. ad N° XIIᵇ. There is scarcely space for the second ⲡⲟⲩⲗ. The phrase occurs *R. V,* 25, 27.

l.5. The form ϭⲓⲛ, *Berl. P.* 3260, ⲉϭⲏⲛ, *R. V,* 55, ⲉϭⲛ, = ⲉⲭⲓⲛ, ⲉⲭⲉⲛ, N° XXX, *R. II, III; V,* 26, = ⲭⲓⲛ, ⲭⲉⲛ, *R. V,* 25, 27, 32, *Berl. P.* 5553, = ⲉⲓⲥϫϧⲉⲛ (ⲓⲥⲭⲉⲛ),

R. II, 56. Of these, the first and second are in M.E., the third in Sah., and the last in Boh. contexts. The same ϭⲓⲛ occurs also R. 1, 20 (M.E.) The prosthetic ⲉ- in these variants (and Ä.Z. 92, 41) speaks against Stern's (§. 567) condemnation of such forms. An example of ⲱⲁ ⲉ- (M.E.) is found Quatrem.; op. cit., 231. If the etymology; Sah. (ⲉ)ϭⲓⲛ = ⌒ 𝔛𝔛 ⌣ (Steindorff) be accepted, it follows that (ⲉ)ϭⲓⲛ is the regular Boh. form, borrowed in M.E., and that ⲓⲥϫⲉⲛ has some different origin.

l.6. [ⲉⲣ]ⲡⲉⲛⲙⲉⲩⲉ---ⲧⲉ ⲫ̅ⲧ̅ &c. There is not space for ⲁⲣⲓ. Similar exhortations with Conjunctive, Hyv., Alb. XXIV, XXVII, XXVIII (no conjunction), XXX, XXXI, XXXII (with ϩⲟⲡⲱⲥ, ϩⲓⲛⲁ.)

ϫⲟⲕ = either ϫⲉⲕⲧⲉⲛϩⲁⲓⲏ ⲉⲃⲟⲗ or ϫⲱⲕ ⲛ̅ⲧⲉⲛ-

l.7. For †ⲙⲧⲟⲛ with Dative, v. Zoega, 65, Hyv., Alb., XXXIX (similar phrases.)

l.8. Here formula are apparently relinquished and some piece of information given; but lacunæ make the text illegible.

ⲁⲟⲅⲙⲁⲧⲓⲟⲛ ? for ⲁⲟⲅⲙⲁⲧⲓⲕⲟⲛ.

l.9. ϧⲓⲧⲉⲛ ⲛⲓⲥϧⲁⲓ. For this phrase v. R. V, 35. †ϩⲟ = ††ϩⲟ.

Verso; The Chrysmon (twice) seems to replace ϧⲓⲧⲉⲛ here and in Nᵒˢ XII, XVII, XIX, XX, XXIII, XXIV, XXV(?), XXVII ; likewise ⲧⲁⲁⲥ in Nᵒˢ XII, XIV, XVII.

ⲫⲟⲓⲗⲟⲑ occurs R. II, 262 (Wessely). Cf. ⲫⲟⲓⲃⲁⲙⲙⲱⲛ, ⲫⲓⲃⲁⲙⲙⲱⲛ &c. Note that the name is not Eustathios, as would be expected (l.9). Was Philotheos the bearer, Eustathius the writer of the letter?

The titles of the 12 persons named (l.l. 2-4, 11) have no sequence of rank. Of the proper names, ⲙⲱⲛⲉ alone is uncommon. It is found R. II, 64; ⲙ̇ⲟⲛⲉ. Cf. Zoega, 116, ⲙⲟⲛⲁ masc.

The dialect of this text is of special interest. It is one of those, so rare in the Fayyum collections, which show the letter ϧ (once only in Vienna, and that on paper; R. V, 41.) The other examples here are Nᵒˢ XXXI, XXXII, XXXIX*. The Boh. element is the strongest and gives the forms ϧⲁⲓⲏ, ⲫ̅ⲧ̅; ⲉⲑⲟⲩⲁⲃ, ⲑⲏⲧ, ⲟⲩⲟⲣⲡ-, ⲱⲁⲧⲉ-, ⲥⲁⲡⲱϣⲓ, ⲛⲱⲧⲉⲛ, as well as a tendency to insert the helping-vowel. To the Sah. belong ⲥϧⲁⲓ, ⲥⲱⲟⲩⲁϩ, ⲙⲏϣⲉ, ⲛⲟϭ, ⲕⲟⲩⲓ, ϩⲉⲛ ; while ⲛⲟⲩⲧⲉ-ⲫ̅ⲧ̅, ⲙⲉⲩⲉ-ⲙⲉⲩⲓ, ⲱⲓⲛⲉ-ⲱⲓⲛⲓ, ⲉⲑⲟⲩⲗⲁⲃ-ⲉⲑⲟⲩⲁⲃ show both influences.

XIV. Papyrus. (v. pl. 3.)   5⅝ × 10¼ in.
The material is fine and, owing to the folding, brittle. The colour, a

* The forms (traced) are; Nᵒ XIII ϩ, XXXI ϩ, XXXII ϩ, XXXIX ϩ

light, warm brown. The character is not far removed from that of the preceding M.S. Yet it is more cursive and shows the ligatures ΔΥ (l.2 &c.), ϵⲧ, ϵι (l.7), ΔΙ, ϵρ (l.10), ΤΙ (passim.) A comma-like mark is placed above an initial 'ⲛ and the ends of several words. The use of initial ⲧⲓ, for ⲧ, is the common fashion of the Fayyum texts. This letter too observes an inconsistent word-division, which is ignored in the following transcript.

Missing letters are represented (approximately) by dots.

Recto;

1. ϯ ⲥⲩⲛ̄ ⲛⲱⲁⲣⲡ ⲙⲉⲛ̄ ⲧⲓϣⲓⲛⲉ ⲁⲩⲱ ⲧⲓⲁⲥⲡⲁⲍⲉ ⲙⲡⲟⲩϫⲁⲓ ⲙⲡⲁⲙⲉⲣⲓⲧ
    ⲛⲓⲱⲧ ⲉⲧ̣ⲧ̣, ⲁⲩⲱ ⲧⲓϣⲓⲛⲉ

2. [ⲉⲡⲁ]ⲥⲟⲛ ⲃⲓⲕⲧⲱⲣ̄ ⲁⲩⲱ ⲧⲓϣⲓⲛⲉ ⲉⲣⲟⲕ ⲛⲟⲩⲙⲏⲛϣⲉ ⲛⲥⲁⲡ ⲁⲩⲱ ⲙⲡⲉⲕ-
    ⲟⲩⲁⲧⲉ ⲡⲉⲕ

3. [ⲟⲩϫⲁⲓ] ⲛⲟⲩⲥⲁⲡ ⲁⲩⲱ ⲡⲁⲓⲕⲁⲓⲟⲛ̄ ⲡⲉ ⲛⲕⲟⲩⲁⲧⲉ ⲡⲉⲕϣⲓⲛⲉ ⲛⲏⲓ ⲧⲁⲉⲓ-
    ⲙⲉ ⲉⲣⲟϥ̄

4. ⲗⲟⲓⲡⲟⲛ ⲁⲛ̣ⲁ̣ⲩ ⲉⲧⲃⲉ ⲫⲱⲃ̄ ⲛⲉⲃⲱⲟⲓ ⲉⲧⲅⲁⲧⲏⲕ⸱ ⲙ̣ⲁⲫⲗⲟⲩ ⲉϣⲱⲡⲉ
    ⲙⲡⲉⲕϫⲓⲧⲟ̆

5. ⲛ̄ⲧⲁⲁⲧ . . ⲝ̣ⲓ̇ⲧ[ⲟ]ⲩ ⲛ̄ⲧⲁⲁⲧⲃ ⲧⲉⲓⲧⲟ̆ⲩ ⲛ̄ⲧⲟⲩϭⲁⲛ ⲛⲁⲡⲉ̇ⲧⲣⲉ̇ⲙⲁⲍ̇ ⲙⲁⲛ̄
    ϩⲁⲓⲛⲉ

6. ⲁⲩⲉ̄ⲛⲁ̆ⲩ̄ⲉⲛ̄ⲧⲟⲩ ^(sic) ⲁⲅⲁ ⲡⲕⲟⲩⲡⲗ̈ⲓ ⲙⲁⲣⲟⲩϭⲁⲛ ⲛⲁⲃ ⲁⲅⲁ ⲙⲡⲉⲣⲕⲁⲧⲉⲭⲉ
    ⲙⲁⲃ ⲙⲁⲛ̄ ϣⲁⲛⲧⲓ

7. ⲡⲉⲙ̣·ⲁ̣ⲛ̣ ⲉⲧⲛⲏⲟⲩ ⲁⲩⲱ ⲙⲡⲉⲣϭⲱ ⲛ̄ⲁⲧⲟⲩⲁⲧⲉ ⲡⲉⲕϣⲓⲛⲉ ⲛⲏⲓ ⲧⲁⲉⲓⲙⲉ
    ⲉⲣⲟϥ̄ ⲙⲁ ⲛⲉⲛ̄

8. . . ϭⲉ . . ⲗⲁⲟⲩ ⲛⲥⲉⲕ ϣⲗⲉⲓ ⲉⲫⲓⲣ ⲙⲡⲉϩⲁⲟⲩ ⲛ̄ⲁⲡⲟⲥⲧⲟⲗⲟⲥ ⲁⲩⲱ ⲧⲓϣⲓ-
    ⲛⲉ ⲉⲣⲟⲕ

9. ⲕⲁⲗⲟⲥ ⲧⲓϣⲓⲛⲉ ⲉⲡⲇⲓⲁⲕ̆ ⲇⲁⲙⲓⲁⲛ̄ ⲙⲛ̄ ⲡⲁⲥⲟⲛ ⲥⲧⲉⲫⲁⲛ̄ ⲙⲛ̄ ⲡⲁⲥⲟⲛ
    ⲑⲉⲟⲇⲱⲣⲟⲥ

10. ⲙⲛ̄ ⲡⲥⲏⲏⲡⲉ ⲛⲉⲥⲛⲏⲩ ⲧⲏⲣⲟⲩ ⲕⲁⲧⲁ ⲛⲉⲩⲣⲁⲛ ⲟⲩϫⲁⲓ ⲡⲁⲙⲉⲣⲓⲧ ⲛⲓⲱ̄
    ϩⲙ ⲡϭ̄ⲥ̄ ϯ

Verso;

   ϯ ⲡⲁⲙⲉⲣⲓⲧ ⲛ̄ϩⲟⲉⲓⲥ ⲛⲓⲱⲧ ⲉⲧ̣ⲧ̣, [   ] ⲡⲁ̄ⲓⲱⲧ ⲉⲧ̣ⲧ̣, (sic) ϯⲅⲉⲱ[ⲣⲅⲓⲟⲥ]

Recto;

ll. 1–3. "With god! Firstly I greet and embrace the well-being of my beloved, reverend father, and I greet my brother Victor, and thee I greet, many times. And thou hast not sent me (news of) thy health once. But (= and) it is right that thou send thy greeting to me, so that I may know it."

ⲉⲧ̣ⲧ̣, for ⲉⲧⲧⲁⲓⲏⲩ, is found R.V, 49 and N° XXII, XXVI, XXXVIII.

ⲟⲩϫⲁⲓ, suggested by the tail of the letter preceding. ⲛ. Cf. R. V, 37, ⲥϩⲏ ⲡⲉⲕⲟⲩϫⲉⲓ ⲛⲏⲓ ⲧⲁⲉⲓⲙⲓ ⲗⲁϥ.

ⲟⲩⲁⲧⲉ. v. ad N° XIIᵃ.

ⲡⲁⲓⲕⲁⲓⲟⲛ ⲡⲉ. Cf. this expression Revill., a. et C., ⲟⲍ.

<u>l.4.</u> "For the rest, see to the matter of the —? that are by thee —?"
ⲀⲚⲀⲨ is uncertain. ⲀⲘⲞⲨ is possible, though less probable.
ⲚⲈⲂⲰⲰⲒ, perhaps plur. of ⳝⲱ (for ⲂⲰⲞⲨⲒ = Sah.* ϥⲟⲟⲨⲈ.) Camel's and
goat's hair were presumably articles of commerce.

<u>ll.4.5.</u> "If thou hast not received them from him(?), receive them
from him (and) give them to (? place them in) —?"
But few letters of l.5 are sufficiently certain to justify discussion. A second
ⲭⲒⲦⲞⲨ ⲚⲦⲀⲀⲦⲂ is perhaps a scribe's error, for the Imperative
ⲦⲈⲒⲦⲞⲨ seems sufficient. Following this, one might read ⲚⲦⲞⲨ-
as 3ᵈ pl. Conjunctive (v. ad Nᵒ XII.²¹.)

<u>ll.5–7.</u> "Some they have (already) brought. And let them —? the —?,
and do not withhold it(?) from us until the approaching —?
ⲔⲞⲨⲠⲖⲒ. I can suggest nothing here. The word is probably Greek.
ⲔⲞⲨⲔⲖⲒ can not be read.
ⲞⲀⲚ? The same word as in the preceding line. It is obviously a verb.
ⲔⲀⲦⲈⲬⲈ = ⲕⲁⲧⲉⲭⲉⲓⲛ; similarly used in Nᵒ XXVI and R.V,43.

<u>l.7.</u> "And do not continue not sending thy greeting to me, that I
may know it," i.e., that I may have the satisfaction of
receiving it.
ⲚⲀⲦⲞⲨⲀⲦⲈ. A somewhat curious use of ⲁⲧ-. Cf. also R.V,42, (Ⲛ)ⲀⲦⲠⲈⲔ-
ⲂⲒⲞⲨⲤ, ib. 47, ⲚⲀⲦⳘⲰⲂ.

<u>l.8.</u> "—? any —? I go to the street of the Apostle daily" or, "to the
street on the day of the Apostles" (for ⲚⲚⲀⲠⲞⲤⲦⲞⲖⲞⲤ), i.e., of
S.S. Peter and Paul, June 29ᵗʰ (v. Ludolf, Ad Hist. Æth. Com., and
Malan, Calender). Perhaps ϩⲓⲣ has a restricted, local meaning
cf. R.V,54, (M.E.) ⲦⲀⲈⲒ ⲈϥⲒⲖ.

<u>ll.8–10.</u> "And I greet thee fairly. I greet the Deacon, Damianos and
my brother, Stephanos and my brother, Theodoros and the rest
of the brethren, according to their names. Farewell, my beloved father, in the Lord!"
ⲆⲀⲘⲒⲀⲚ̄, ⲤⲦⲈⲪⲀⲚ̄. An unusual mode of abbreviation.

<u>Verso:</u> "For my beloved, reverend Lord Father, my reverend Father ⁻⁻ˢⁱᶜ;
from Georgios."
An ornament stands, in Berl., P.5560, between the names of the writer
and recipient. But here it does not separate these, nor is
its use clear to me. That it should be a cipher, peculiar
to the recipient and substituted for his name,—the space
for which is notably void,—seems improbable. After ⲄⲈⲰⲢ-
ⲄⲒⲞⲤ, there was room, at most, for ⲠⲒⲈⲖⲀⲭ.

The Sah. and M.E. appear here mixed, the former preponderating.
Both ⳜⲞⲈⲒⲤ and ⲟ̄ⲥ̄ are employed, as, e.g., R.V,49.

XV. *Paper.* (v. pl. 3.) 5¾ × 4⅜ in.

With the exception of two or three Arabic and Syriac fragts., this is the only paper M.S. in the collection. For its character, cf. *Hyv., Alb.*, XV (A.D. 1014), XXVIII (A.D. 962), and XXX (colophon A.D. 1025). The use of the double colon is quite unsystematic. The letter has had two folds in height, five in width. On the back are remnants of a few lines in Arabic *, but there is no address.

$$\dagger \overline{\text{CYN}}\ \text{ЄM ПРАN ЄПNОY}\dagger : \text{АNАК ПП БАІΛ}$$

         MN : $\overline{\text{IШП}}$? ПП МАРКОYРI : ЄNШIN[I]

         ЄПОYЖАI NПЄNМЄРI : NСАN · КIРШ

         ПАІ РМIНΛ : ПŌС КΛАЧ : ЄЧ†ЖАРI

5.   NАК ЄI ПАРЄСIА : NПМTА ЄВАΛ

         ЄПNОY† МN NЄЧАNГЄΛОС : ЄTTО^{sic}

         ΛАВ : ΛIПI ЄIС ПЄNСАN ΛОYКАС

         АВЄI : ШАРАК ЖIПЄСМОY NАК

         ШАП : ОYΛЄКШTСI : NНРП : NАN

10.   NСАIН : КАТАРАК NНРП NАΛЄY

         NШΛОYЄСΛШЄ : ЄПЄNIШ ПŌС К

         ΛАЧ : ΛIПI ЄIС †ЙITАNI : NШ

         АКОYАЖНР ММАY †ШINI ЄРАК

         КАΛШС : ОYЖАI ЄM ПŌС

ll. 1–7. "With God! In God's name! I, Apa Kail and Johannes, the son of (?) Apa Mercurios, we enquire after the health of our beloved brother, Master Deacon Remiel,— may the Lord be gracious to him! giving thee (sic) grace and freedom (παῤῥησ-ία) in the presence of God and his holy angels.

CYN $\overline{\text{ӨШ}}$ and ЄM ПРАN &c. are rarely found together; e.g., Nº XXXII.

ПП = ПП = ПАПА. Cf. *Hyv., Alb.* XXVII, XXVIII with *ib.* XXIII, XXV, also *Berl., P. 3285.* Titles similarly abbreviated are Nº XII²⁹, ПŖŖ, *Revill., A. et C.* ЧА, ΔIАКК.

БАIΛ. The same, I suppose, as ЖАНΛ. Cf. *R. I, 3; II, 171* خليل , with the usual خالل .

$\overline{\text{IШП}}$? Very indistinct. I incline to Υ, for Ч; although the article would then be exceptional.

МАРКОYРI. v. *R. V, 55*, МЄРКОYРЄ, *ib.* II, 171 and the note below, مرقورة, Μερκύριος. КIРШ, standing where it does, can hardly be but the title, κύριος.

* From a tracing of these very faded lines *Prof. Karabacek* has recognised a note as to the taxation (land), in the month Burmoodeh, of مرقوره الفراش, presum-ably the joint author of the above letter.

ΡΜΙΗΛ. An angel has the name ΕΡΕΜΙΗΛ (Syr., Ramiel; Mém. de la Miss. 1,262
   cf. Stern, Ä.Z.'86,118.)
ΠΟΟ ΚΛΛϤ &c.; also in R. V, 28, 46.
ll. 7-12. "For the rest, lo, our brother Lukas has gone to thee. Take a
   blessing for thyself (and) buy a solidus-worth of good (?) wine
   for us, according to thy (judgment ?), white wine, such as they
   are used to ___? our father, — to whom the Lord be gracious!"
ϪΙΣΜΟΥ. v. Ä.Z.'85,68. Here the verb can hardly be final, since ("take a blessing
   from thee" would require rather ΝΤΑΛΤΚ.
ΛΕΚΩΤϹΙ. The only example I have seen with Ε. ΟΥ· must be the article.
   These M.S.S. show also No XVIII (M.E.) ΛΟΥΚΤ, No XXV (M.E.) ϩΟΛΟΚΩΤϹΙ,
   No XXXV (Sah.) ϩΟΛΟΚΟΤΤΙΝΟϹ.
ϣΑΠ, for (ϣΟΠ=) ϣΩΠ ΝΟΥΛΕΚΩΤϹΙ. The same form as Imperative, R. V, 32.
ΝϹΑΙΗ. "Good" in a similar context (cheese), R. V, 32, is ΝΑΝΟΥϤ. Yet cf.
   Ä.Z.'85,106, ΠΝΟΥϤ ΝϹΑΗ, and perhaps Denkschr. (Wien), XXXVII, 246,
   οἶνον καλλ(ίστου), ib., 203, συαρϲοτου.
ΑΛΕΥ, λευκός; Sah (Peyr.) ΑΛΗΥ. Cf. Bodl., M.S. Copt. (P.) a.1 and R. II, 46, ΑΛΑΥ.
ΝϣΛΟΥΕϹΛΩϥ apparently a verb, 3d plur. Aorist. Otherwise, ΝϣΛΟΥ a 2d
   epithet of ΗΡΠ and ΕϹΛΩϥ, a verb (Stern's Cl. VII), with prefix. Ε.
ll. 12-14. ΕΙϹϮΝΙΤΑΝΙ =? ΕΙϹ ϮϮΝΙΤΑΝΙ, δάνειον ἀποδιδόναι. ΕΙϹ with Imperat.
   ϯ, is improbable.
   "I greet thee fairly. Farewell in the Lord!"
ΟΥΑΧΗΡ. A noun, ΧΗΡ masc., seems to occur Ä.Z.'78,14. The first element
   may be the verb ΟΥΑϩ.

The Dialect here is M.E., with several Sah. forms interspersed.

_____

XVI. Papyrus. (v. pl. 4.)   6¾ × 4¼ in.
The M.S. is so discoloured and the fibre so frequently split, that many
points must remain doubtful.
Recto;   ϮϹΥΝ ΤΙϣΙΝΙ ΕΠΟΥΧΕΙ ΝΤΕ
                  ΚΜΕΤΜΑΙΝΟΥΤΙ ΕΤΑΕΙ
                  ΟΥΤ ΤΙΤΑΜΑ ΜΑΚ ΧΕ
                  ΑΙΧΙ α ΝϩΕΝΚΑΝ
         5.   ΠΑΡϹΛ..ΑΝ ϩΕΙ ΝΙΧΕ
                  ΝΤΗΙ ΑΙΟΑΤΟΥ ΝΕΚ
                  ϬΑΠ ϤϤ ΝΤΕΡϭΑΜ
                  ΝΤΛΟΥ ΧΙΤΟΥ ΜΠΑΡ
                  ϹΝΕΥ ΤΑΟΥΛΟΥ ΝΕΙ ΝΟΥ

10. ΛΕΟΙ ΑΜΑ ΤΑΧΡΙΑ
ΛΑΥ ΤΙΝΑΝΑϬΙϬΗ
ΠϢΙΝΙ ΝΤΕΚΨ͞Χ͞Η *sic*
ϨΑΛΑΙ ΚΑΛΩϹ
ΟΥϪΕΙ ϨΕ Π͞ΟϹ +

Verso;

Ϯ ΤΕΙϹ Ν͞Τ? *(space)* ϨΙΤΕΝ ΕΙϹΑΚ
? ΠΙϹ   ΠΕΒϹΑΝ

Recto;

ll. 1–5. *After the usual greeting, the writer states that he owes one*
(or eleven?) —? to his correspondent.

ΔΙΧ Α *(or* ΔΙΧ ΙΑ*), for* ΧΡΕΩϹΤΕ͞Ι. *But* A̱.Ẕ. '78, 18 [ΧΡ]ΕΩϹΤΕΙ *takes a dative.*
ΚΑΝΠΑΡϹ? *I take* ΚΑΝ⸱ *to be the* **form** *discussed* A̱.Ẕ. '85, 28, *and would*
offer the following as a possible etymology.

     (1.) ΚΟΥΙ Ν⸱, *passim.*
     (2.) ΚΟΥΝϢΗΗΛΙ, *sg. f.,* N͞o *XXIX; M.E.*
         ΚΟΥΝΤΑΡΗΧΗ, *pl.,* Berl., P. 5559; Sah.–M.E.
         ΚΟΥ͞ΝϪΑΚ, *sg. m.,* Brit. M͞m., Ostr. 5854; Sah.
         (ΕΛ)ΚΟΥΝΨΙΧΗ, *verb,* R.V, 49; M.E. (cf. Peyr., 60, P̄ΚΟΥΙ
         Ν̄ϨΗΤ.)
     (3.) ΚΟΝϹΑΒΤΙ, *pl.,* N͞o *XVII; Sah.–M.E.*
     (4.) ΚΑΝΠΑΡϹ, *pl.,* N͞o *XVI; M.E.*
         ΚΑΝϢΗΛΙ, *sg. m.,* A̱.Ẕ. '85, 28; M.E.
         ΚΑΝΛΩΜΙ, *pl.,* ib. , 38; M.E.
         ΚΑΝΝΗΙ, *sg. m.,* ib. , ib; M.E.
         ΚΑΝϹΑΧΑ, *sg. m.,* R.V, 52; M.E.
         ΚΑΝΑΛΑΛΙ, *pl.,* N͞o *XX; M.E.*

The last of these would make Stern's *proposed derivation from* ϬΑΥΟΝ
impossible. Perhaps N͞o *XLV, Ver.*[2] ΠΚΑΝϢΑΡΕ, *ib.*[23], ΠΚΟΥΝϢΑΡΕ *are to*
be included here. N͞o *XLIV,* ΝΕΚΑΝΚΟΥΙ ΝϪΩΩΜΙ, *would thus be a*
reduplication.

ll. 5–11. *"See, I have sent thee my own —?, and take thou* $6\frac{1}{3}$ *drach-*
-mas-worth of them (?). Receive them as —?"

    The novelty or illegibility of the principal words makes a
translation impossible. It is plain merely that, in the first
clause the object is some divisible material, spoken of in the
plural. Instructions follow as to its employment. ΝΕΙ *is perhaps*
"on my behalf". The succeeding word-division is unsatisfactory.

ΛΕϹΙ *seems to occur* Append., P. Bodl., ΚΟΛΛΑΘΙ ΝΛΕϹΙ, *which shows it to*
be a liquid. *

---

* *Du Fresne gives* ΛΙϹΕΥ ΕΛΧΑΜΕΛ το υδωρ του αρνογλωϲϲον = Forsk., Mater. Med. 160,
ما لسان الحمل ; *but a comparison of the two words is hazardous.*

ΔΜΔ ? = ἄμα.

ΤΔΧΡΙΔ ΛΔΥ ? = Sah. ΝΤΔΡΧΡΙΔ ΝΛΔΔΥ.

l.l. 11–14. lit., "I will make enquiries after thy soul fairly on my part. Farewell in the Lord!" The scribe intended apparently ΤΙΝΔ-ϬΗΠϢΙΝΙ. For this ϬΗ (also B. V, 47 twice, ib. 49, Nᵒ XXII thrice,) the variants ϬЄ (Nᵒ XXX, XLI,) and ϬΙ (Nᵒ XL, twice,) are found. They all occur in M.E. contexts and appear to correspond to ϬΜ : ϢЄΜ, while suggesting a confusion of the verbs ϬΜ and ϢΙ (Cf. Berl., P. 3285, M.E., ΔΙϬΙ·Β̄ ΝΟΛΟΚΞ̄, and ib., ϢΙΜΟΙΤ.) Indeed there may be a difference of meaning; "take news of," rather than "visit."

ϨΔΛΔΙ, in this frequent formula, represents a sort of Ethic Dative.

Verso: All very faint and uncertain.

The Dialect here is purely M.E.

XVII. Papyrus. (v. Nᵒ IX.)   5 × 5¾ in.

Written upon the same leaf as the Benediction, p. 18, and possibly by the same scribe, though in a character slightly smaller, belonging to the class of Nᵒ XIV (pl. 3) and Hyv., Alb. XX.

Recto:

 ✝ ϹΥΝΘⲰ ΝϢΟΡΠ ΜΝ ΤΙϢΙΝЄ ЄΤΚΜΝΤ
 ΜΔΙΝΟΫ ΝϢΗΡЄ ΜΠΝΙΚ̄, ΜΝΝϹΔ ΝΔΪ ΤΔΟΥΔ
 ΠΕΙΜΟΝΟΧΟϹ ϪЄ ΠΔϹΟΝ ΙⲰ ΠϹΔΝϢϪⲰΤ
 ЄϤЄΤ ΤЄΒ?. ΔΡ ϨΝΚΟΝϹΔΒΤΙ ЄΝЄΙ
5. ΤЄϤΝΟΟΥЄ ΝΤΝ ϨΜ ΠΟΥⲰϢ ЄΠΝΟΫ ΔΥⲰ
 ΤΔΟΥΔ ΠЄΙϹΔΧΔ ΝЄΚⲰ ΝΤЄΚ ΤЄΒΚΔΤ
 ΝЄΙΚΔΝΔϨΙ ΝΤЄ ΝЄΤЄϤΝΔΥЄΙ ϨΜΠΟΥ
 ϢϢ ЄΠΝΟΫ ΟΥϪΔΙ ϨΜ Π̄Ο̄Ϲ̄ ✝

Verso:

✝ ΠЄΝΜΔΙΝΟΫ ΝϢΗΡ ΠΝΙΚ̄ (space) ΠЄΤΡ ΠЄ ✝ ΜΗΝΔ ЄΝΚⲰ

Recto: "With God! In the first place, I greet thy God-loving Sonship in the Spirit. Next, send this (? the) monk, my brother Johannes, the mason (?), to —?, that he may —? some —? for these cattle of ours, according to God's will. And send this —?, the builder of thine(?), that he may build the stables for the cattle, according to God's will. Farewell in the Lord!"

Verso: "(For) our God-loving son, in the Spirit, Petros, presbyter; (from) Mena, in the Lord."

l.1. ϭⲨⲚⲰⲰ, a form associated usually with Boh. texts, but found also in these letters; e.g., Nᵒˢ XII, XV.

l.2. ⲠⲚⲒⲔ . v. ad Nᵒ XII⁵.

ⲦⲀⲞⲨⲀ, "send", frequently in Fayyum texts; (v. *Stern*, Ä.Z. '85, 29.) Also *R.*II, 60, V, 37; *Berl.*, P. 5558, ib., 5567 and Nᵒ XVI.

l.3. ⲠⲈⲒ- and ⲚⲈⲒ- (below) are perhaps for the Art., ⲠⲒ-, ⲚⲒ-, denoting persons or things of which the writer expects his correspondent already to have knowledge. (v. *Stern*, §.228 and cf. Nᵒ XVIII, ⲠⲒϹⲈⲀ, also Nᵒ XXII, Rec.", Ver.¹) This is the more probable from the use of ⲚⲦⲈ, l.7 (v. *Stern*, §.294.)

ϹⲀⲚϢϪⲰⲦ. A new combination, but presumably connected with the verb ⲰϪⲰⲦ. If our form (for ⲰϪⲞⲦ) be correct, we should expect an intransitive sense (as in *Stern's* "Class VII".) Yet in *Peyron's* two instances, ⲰϪⲰⲦ can not be a Qualitative. The radical meaning appears to be "to work upon a hard material, metal or stone."

l.4. ⲈⲪⲈⲦⲈ; the name of the place where or of the object upon which Johannes is to be employed. It seems to have the directive Ⲉ- prefixed.

ⲦⲈⲂ?ⲀⲢ. The missing letter may be ⲙ. A space between ⲣ and ⲅ may indicate that the words divide there.

ⲔⲞⲚϹⲀⲂⲦⲒ. For ⲔⲞⲚ-, v. ad Nᵒ XVI⁴. But it should be noted that here both ⲔⲞⲚ- and ⲔⲀⲚ- occur together.

l.5. ⲦⲈⲒⲚⲞⲞⲨⲈ. Whether this and also l.7, ⲦⲈⲒⲚⲀⲨⲈⲒ (cf. *Lemm*, *Apokr. Apostelacten*, 560, ⲦⲈⲒⲚⲀⲨⲒ,) can, in the same text, = Sah. ⲦⲂⲚⲞⲞⲨⲈ, seems questionable.

Ⲛ·ⲦⲚ̄ ? for Ⲛ̄ⲦⲎⲚ; and, l.6, ⲚⲦⲈⲔ for Ⲛ̄ⲦⲎⲔ. Cf. *Berl.*, P. 5558, ⲚⲈⲒⲗⲰⲘⲒ ⲚⲦⲈⲔ.

l.6. ϹⲀⲬⲀ . Cf. *R.* V, 52, (M.E.) ⲠⲔⲀⲚϹⲀⲬⲀ, and perhaps Z.Ä. VI, 103, 36, ⲠϹⲀⲬⲞ, which are likewise titles or nomina agentis.

ⲈⲔⲰⲦ, "builder," with attributive Ⲛ-. Cf. *Mém. de la Miss.* I, 384, where, among the officials of a monastery, ⲈⲔⲰⲦ occurs (between ⲔⲰ- -ⲘⲀⲠⲈ and Archimandrite). v. also Ä.Z. '68, 66; '75, 59, and '78, 25.

ⲔⲀⲚⲀϨⲒ. For ⲔⲀⲚ-, v. ad Nᵒ XVI⁴. ⲀϨⲒ is probably that word which stands for Boh. ⲀϨⲞ, ἀυλή, in Isaiah XXXIV, 13 (*Mém. de l'Inst. égypt.* II, ii.) Perhaps Ä.Z. '84, 146, Sah. ⲀϨⲞⲨ is plur. of this (for ⲀϨⲰⲞⲨ.)

Verso: ⲈⲚⲔⲰ = ἐν κυρίω., as in Greek N.T. MSS. (e.g., *Cod. Sinait.*, *Philipp.* I, 14; Col. IV, 7.) It recurs in the addresses of Nᵒˢ XXIV and XXVII, in each case after the writer's name.

The text has a Sah. basis and comparatively few M.E. forms.

XVIII. Papyrus. (v. pl. 4.) $5\frac{1}{4} \times 6\frac{1}{2}$ in.

This sheet has been cut from a larger, traces of whose artificially erased text are discernable upon the Verso. The letters H, M are of very ambiguous forms which impede certainty of reading.

†ΜΕΝΕϹΑ ΝΤΑΙϹϨΑΙ ΠΙϹϨΑΙ ΝΑΚ ΑΠ
ΝΟῩ ΤΙΤΑΑΤΝ ΑΝΒΑΛ ΠΑΛΚΕΝͲΩ̇
ΕΒΑΛ ΝΕΒΙ ΝΑΚ ϨΑ ΟΥΛΟΥΚ̄ ΜΕ
ΟΥΚΡΑΜΜΑ ΛΟΙΠ̄ ΟΥΛΑΤΟΥ ΝΑΝ
5. ϨΙΧΟ ΚΕϹΑΠ ΑΝ ΛΥΩ ΟΥΛΑΤΕ ΤΚΕ
Δ̄ Ν̄ΤΕΡϨΑΜ ΜΠΙϨΛΟΥ ΝΑΝ ΑΝ
ΜΑΝΜ̇ Λ ΠΑΛΚΗΠ̄Ⲱ ΕΙ ΝΑΚ̇
ΜΕ·ϛ̄ ΒΑΛΚ +

"After I had written that (= the) letter to thee, God helped us. We dis-missed the ___?, that he might go to thee concerning (or, in return for) a solidus and a gram. For the rest, send them to us once more also, and send us the four drachmas today too ___? The ___? is gone to thee, with six (? drachmas) ___? thee."

One of the few letters free from the usual formulæ. We may conclude that the correspondents were in specially intimate relations. The writers (? or writer) were the superiors or equals of the recipient. As it has no address (like e.g. R. V, 54 or N° XXVI,) it was either destined for someone near at hand or was entrusted to a confidential bearer.

l. 1. ΠΙϹϨΑΙ. v. ad N° XVII³.

l. 2. ΝΟΥΤ. The Τ has the form Λ.

ΠΑΛΚΕΝⲰ. The 6th letter could be Ν. v. ad N° XXIII¹².

ΛΟΥΚΤ. v. ad N° XV⁹.

l. 4. ΚΡΑΜΜΑ = γράμμα. New, I think, in Coptic texts, at least as a coin. Its value seems to be ¼ dinar or ϨΟΛΟΚΟΤϹΙ; v. Du Fresne and Stephanus, s.v., and Hultsch, Metrol.², 134. Its use here may be com-pared with that of ΟΥϹΙΑ; v. A.Z. '84, 150.

ΟΥΛΑΤΟΥ. The suffix was altered from -ΕϹ.

l. 5. ϨΙΧΟ lacks a suffix, as R. V, 49, ϨΙΧⲰ, Berl. P. 3267, ϨΙΧⲰ ΤΚΟΥ⫯⫯, and N° XXIII¹⁹.

l. 6. ΤΕΡϨΑΜ; always femin.; v. A.Z. '70, 134, R. V, 29, 53.

ll. 7.8. The reading is doubtful.

The Dialect is M.E., with the exception of the forms ϹϨΑΙ, ΝΑΝ, ΝΑΚ.

XIX. *Papyrus.* $3\frac{7}{8} \times 4\frac{1}{2}$ in.

Cut from a larger sheet of very thin, light brown material, bearing on the back, the remains of an Arabic text.* The character is regular and clear, but blotted and eaten away in several places.

Recto:

⳨ ⲤⲨⲚ ⲦⲒⲢⲎⲚⲎ ⲚⲈⲔ ⲘⲚ

ⲚⲈⲤⲀ ⲚⲈⲒ ϨⲈⲒ ⲠⲈⲦⲒ ⲀⲒⲦⲀ

ⲞⲨⲀⲂ ⲚⲂⲤⲈⲦ ⲚⲈⲎⲢⲠ ⲈϨⲞⲨⲚ

ⲠⲈ ⲦⲀϨⲢⲈ ⲦⲚⲈⲢ..ⲨⲚ ⲦⲚ

5. ⲦⲈⲤ ⲈⲦⲞⲨϨⲞⲨ ⲀϨⲀ ⲘⲀⲔ

ⲤϨⲈ ⲦⲞⲨϨⲞⲨⲚ ⲀⲘⲞⲨ ⲚⲈⲒ

ⲘⲈⲚⲈⲂ ϨⲈ ⲠⲞⲨⲱϢ ⲈⲠⲚⲨ

ⲞⲨⳈⲀⲒ ϨⲘ ⲠⲞ̄Ⲥ ✝

Verso: ✝ ⲠⲈ̄Ⲧ̄Ⲣ̄ⲞⲤ Δ⳨

One of the least intelligible M.S.S. in the collection.

Recto: l.1. For variants, v. ad Nº XII¹⁰.

ll.2,3. "See, (here is) he whom(?) I have sent that he may deposit(?) the wine." ⲠⲈⲦⲒ ⲀⲒ-; neither this (for ⲠⲈⲚⲦⲀⲒ- or ⲠⲈϮ-), nor ⲠⲈⲦⲒ, for ⲠⲈⲀ[ⲔⲱⲚ], are satisfactory. ⲤⲀⲦ ⲈϨⲞⲨⲚ, in both Peyron's e.g.g, = "to throw something at someone"; while if ⲤⲈⲦ be the stat. cons. of ⲤⲱⲦⲈ, I can not explain ⲈϨⲞⲨⲚ.

ll.4,5. ⲠⲈ ? explicative. The missing letters might be read Ⲥⲟ or Ϩⲟ. Adopting the former of these and supposing the second ⲚⲦ to be superfluous, I would translate; "(As to) my provisions, we are selling them(??) at Touhou." There is a town, in Mid. Egypt, ⲦⲞⲨϨⲟ, ⲦⲞⲨϨⲱ; v. Quatrem., Méms. I, 367.

ⲤϨⲈ, for ⲤϨⲀⲒ, R. II, 48; V. 52.

ll.5,6. ⲘⲀⲔⲤϨⲈ(Ⲉ)ⲦⲞⲨⲞⲨ, "If thou dost not write to T." But what of the following Ⲛ? Or, ⲘⲀⲔⲤϨⲈⲦⲞⲨ(Ⲉ)ϨⲞⲨⲚ, as in l.3, but with an erroneous Ϩ.

ll.6,7. "Come to me with him", i.e., with the person mentioned in l.2.

ⲘⲈⲚⲈⲂ for (ⲚⲈⲘⲎⲂ =) Ⲛ̄ⲘⲘⲀϤ. Cf. R. V, 34, ⲘⲈⲚⲎⲒ, Nº XX¹¹, XXII, Rec.?, Ver.¹,⁵,⁹.

Verso: I take Petros to be the recipient. Or is he the bearer? (v. l.2.) All names being avoided in the letter, we may suppose the writer to have purposely omitted here his own.

Δ, for ⲀⲒⲀⲔⲱⲚ, R. V, 33.

The Dialect is M.E.

---

* Profr. Karabacek dates this in the 9ᵗʰ cent. and notes the name زكرى = زكريا, and the title الشمّاس, Deacon.

XX. *Papyrus. (from Hawara.)* 7 × 3½ in.

Coarse fibre and rough penmanship, which has some resemblance to that of Ä.Z.'85, taf. 1, N.º I, and R. V, 51. There was a line below l.16.

Recto:
ϯ ⲥⲩⲛ̄ ⲧⲓϣⲓⲛⲓ ⲁⲩⲱ ⲧⲓ
ⲁⲥⲡⲁⲍⲉ ⲡⲟⲩⲭⲉⲓ ⲧⲉⲕ
ⲙⲉⲧⲙⲁⲓⲛⲟⲩ ⲓⲱ ⲉⲧ
ⲁⲩⲱ ⲧⲓϣⲓⲛⲓ ⲛⲉⲧⲛⲉ
5. ⲙⲁⲕ ⲧⲏⲣⲟⲩ ϩⲟⲩⲁ ⲛⲉ ⲧⲓⲙ
ⲧⲁⲛ ⲡⲉⲕⲡⲛⲉⲩⲙ[ⲁ]
ⲙⲉⲛⲉⲥⲁ ⲛⲉⲓ ⲁⲩⲧⲁⲙⲁⲓ
ⲭⲉ ⲁ ⲡⲟ̄ⲥ̄ ⲧⲏ. [ⲛ̄]ⲁⲕ ⲁⲕ
ⲭⲁⲗⲉ ⲛⲉⲕⲁⲛⲁⲗⲁⲗⲓ
10. ⲁ ⲡⲁϩⲏ ⲧⲱ ⲧⲁ ⲡⲟ̄ⲥ̄ ⲙⲉϩⲓ
ⲙⲉⲛⲉⲕ ⲗⲓⲡ. ϯⲁⲙⲁ
ⲭⲉ ⲁⲕⲟⲩⲱ ⲗⲓ
ϩⲏⲧ ⲧⲱⲧ
ⲁ ⲡⲟ̄ⲥ̄ ⲉⲗⲁⲕ
15. ⲁⲛⲁⲕ ⲁⲓⲟⲩⲱ
ⲛⲁⲓ ⲉⲧϩⲉⲙ

Vertically, at the side of the above; ⲙⲁⲥ ϩⲉ ⲡⲟⲩ[ⲱ]ϣ ⲡⲛ[ⲟⲩ]ᵀ[ⲟⲩ]ⲭ[ⲁ]ⲓ &c.

Verso: ⲁⲥⲟⲛ ⲙⲁ / ? ⲓⲱ ⲉⲧ (space) Ⲕⲩⲣ ⲡⲁⲡ̄ ⲅⲉⲟⲣ / ϯⲭⲁⲏⲗ ⲫⲓⲗⲟ +

ll. 1–6. Salutations very similar to those of N.º XII, where the present phrases can be seen under more correct forms.

ϩⲟⲩⲁ ⲛⲉ ? for ϩⲟⲩⲁⲧⲉ ⲛⲉ; v. ad N.ºs XII 7, XXIII 3.

After ⲡⲛⲉⲩⲙⲁ there has not been space for ϩⲉ ⲡⲟ̄ⲥ̄.

ll. 7–11. "Now I have been told that the Lord has —? to thee and that thou hast harvested thy grapes. I am persuaded that the Lord has repaid thee."

ⲁⲗⲁⲗⲓ, presumably = Sah. ⲉⲗⲟⲟⲗⲉ. v. Lemm, Apokr. Apostelac. 514, R. II, 61, ⲁⲗⲁⲁⲗⲓ.

ⲧⲁ ⲡⲟ̄ⲥ̄. The M.S. would hardly allow ⲧⲉ.

ⲙⲉϩⲓ. Also Berl. P. 3260, R. V, 50. Cf. ⲙⲟⲩϩ, Ä.Z.'85, 150.

ⲙⲉⲛⲉⲕ ? for (ⲛⲉⲙⲏⲕ =) Sah. ⲛ̄ⲙⲙⲁⲕ, as in N.º XIX 7.

Verso: The first half of the Address could be read; ⲡⲉⲛⲙⲁ[ⲓ]ⲛⲟⲩ ⲓⲱ ⲉⲧ.
Ⲕⲩⲣ. v. ad N.º XII 1.

Apa Georgios is the recipient, Chael-Philotheos the writer.

The Dialect is M.E.

XXI. *Papyrus. (v. N.º XLVII.)* 4¼ × 5½ in.

Thin papyrus, of light yellow-brown colour. The character is bold and clear and to be classed with that of N.º XIV (pl. 3.) That of N.º XLVII (which occupies the bottom of this and fills the other side of the leaf,) is finer, but probably by the same hand. Indeed the present text, contain-

-ing merely formula, was perhaps to serve as a preamble to the list which follows it.

> † CYⲚ †ϢⲒⲚⲈ ⲀⲨⲰ †ⲀⲤⲠⲀⲍ[Ⲉ ⲈⲠⲞⲨⲬⲀⲒ]
> ⲚⲦⲈⲦⲚⲘⲈⲦⲘⲀⲒⲚⲞⲨⲦⲈ ⲈⲦⲦⲀⲒⲎ[Ⲩ ⲈⲢⲈ ⲠⲞⲤ]
> ⲤⲘⲞⲨ ⲈⲢⲞⲦⲚ ϨⲚ ⲤⲘⲞⲨ ⲚⲒⲘ ⲘⲠⲚ[ⲈⲨⲘⲀ]
> †Ⲕ.ⲞⲚ ⲈϤⲈϨⲀⲢⲈϨ ⲈⲢⲞⲦⲚ ⲈⲂⲞ[Ⲗ ϨⲀ ⲠⲈⲐⲞⲨ]
> 5.   ⲚⲒⲘ ⲈϤⲈⲤⲘⲞⲨ ⲈⲠⲈⲦⲚϪⲒ ⲘⲚ ⲠⲈ[ⲦⲚ† ⲈϤⲈ]
> ϨⲀⲢⲈϨ (*blotted*) ⲚⲚⲒⲒⲰⲦ ⲚⲀⲒ ⲈϤⲈ ?
> ⲚⲀⲦⲚ ⲚⲀϨⲢⲀ ⲚⲈⲈⲔϪⲞⲨⲤⲒ ⲈⲦϨⲒⲬ ?

The list (Nᵒ XLVII.) follows here without any interval.

" I greet and embrace &c. The Lord shall bless you with all spiritual blessings and shall keep you from all ill, and shall bless you in receiving (= your receiving) and in giving(?). He shall keep these Fathers for me(?), he shall ___? before the powers that be over (us? you?)

ll. 2-4. ⲈⲢⲈ ⲠⲞⲤ ⲤⲘⲞⲨ. The same formula in the Bishop's letter, *Ä.Z.* '92, 39, and a similar one *R.* V, 27.

ⲠⲚⲈⲨⲘⲀ†Ⲕ.ⲞⲚ. The gap contained, it seems, Ⲉ, probably from confusion with ⲆⲒⲔⲀⲒⲞⲚ.

l. 6. The blotted space contained, I think, nothing.

ⲚⲀⲒ. May be merely the Demonstrative; v. *Stern*, §. 244.

l. 7. Begins either with the Dat. 2 pl., for(?) ⲚⲞⲦⲈⲚ =) ⲚⲰⲦⲈⲚ, or with the Suff. 2 pl. of a causative, with final -Ⲁ for -Ⲟ.

ⲚⲀϨⲢⲀⲚ, "before, with us" is less probable than (ⲚⲀϨⲢⲀⲚ =)ⲚⲀϨⲢⲚ(Ⲛ)Ⲉ. What is still visible after Ⲁ is either Ⲙ or Ⲛ.

The Dialect is Sah., ⲘⲈⲦ = ⲘⲚⲦ being the only M.E. form.

XXII. Papyrus.   9¾ × 5⅞ in.

This letter is in a very mutilated condition. ll. 1-16 are connected merely by a band of fibre ¼ in. wide, with the lower part of the sheet, upon which illegible remnants of some 8 lines can be discerned. It is on the Verso of this lower portion — which was originally longer, — that the latter lines of the text are written, i.e. in the reverse direction to those upon the Recto; while the address is again in the same direct-ion as ll. 1-16. The space between the text on the Verso and the Ad-dress was occupied (vertically) by Arabic accounts. The material is thin; the colour, a light brown-yellow; the character, that of R. V, 51.

Recto:

    † ϩⲙ·ⲡⲗⲛ ⲙⲡⲛⲟⲩϯ ⲧⲉⲛϣⲓⲛⲓ ⲁⲩⲱ ⲧⲉⲛⲁⲥ

    ⲡⲁϫⲉ ⲛⲡⲟⲩⲭⲉⲓ ⲧⲉⲕⲙⲉⲧⲥⲁⲛ ⲉⲧⲛⲁⲛⲟⲩⲥ

    ⲁⲩⲱ ⲧⲓϣⲓⲛⲓ ⲁ̇ⲡⲁⲓⲱⲧ ⲡⲁⲡⲁ ⲫⲓⲗⲟ̅ ⲕⲁⲗⲱⲥ

    ⲁⲩⲱ ⲟ̅ⲏⲡϣⲓⲛⲓ ⲛⲡⲁⲡⲁ ⲡⲓⲙⲏⲛ ϩⲁⲗⲁⲓ ⲕⲁⲗⲟ̅ⲥ

5.   ⲁⲩⲱ ⲟ̅ⲏⲡϣⲓⲛⲓ ⲡⲇⲓⲁⲕ̅ ⲅⲉⲱ̅ⲣ ⲡⲁⲧⲁⲛϣⲉⲉⲓ

    ϩⲁⲗⲁⲓ ⲁⲩⲱ ⲛⲉⲓ ⲉϣⲁⲣⲉ ⲡⲑⲉⲕⲏ̅ ⲧⲙⲁϩ

    ⲥⲛⲟⲩϯ ⲕⲩⲣⲓⲁⲕⲏ ⲛ̅ⲧⲉⲓϩⲙⲏ ? ?

    ⲛ̅ⲧⲏⲓ ⲉⲩⲁⲡⲟⲕⲣⲓⲥⲓⲥ ⲁⲓⲧⲁϩ..ⲟ̇ ⲛ̅ⲡ̅ ⲡⲥⲁⲃⲁⲧⲟⲛ

    ⲁⲓⲭⲓ ⲧⲓⲱ̇ⲁ ϩⲓⲧⲉⲛ̇ ⲗⲉⲃⲗⲁⲓⲥ ⲧⲏ ⲟⲩⲛⲁⲓ ⲙⲉⲛⲏⲓ ⲉ̇

10.   ⲉⲡⲧⲟⲡⲟⲥ ⲁⲓϣⲓⲛⲓ ⲛⲥⲱⲕ ⲧⲁⲓⲥⲉⲓ ⲉⲧⲃⲏⲕ

    ϫⲉ ϣⲁϭⲏ ⲡⲉⲕϣⲓⲛⲓ ⲗⲟⲓⲡⲟⲛ ⲁ ⲡⲉⲓϩⲗⲁⲥⲁϩ

    ϭⲁⲩⲛⲓ ⲭⲛⲟⲩⲓ ϫⲉ ⲁⲕⲡⲟⲧ ⲉⲡⲁⲃⲩⲗⲱⲛ ⲗⲟⲓⲡⲟⲛ

    ⲁⲓϣⲟ̇ϣ..ⲁⲓⲡⲟⲧ ϩⲁⲑⲏ ⲫⲗ ⲁⲡⲁ̅ⲡⲁⲫⲓⲗⲟ̅

    ⲛ̅ⲟ̅ⲏⲡⲉⲃϣⲓⲛⲓ ⲗⲟⲓⲡⲟⲛ̅ ⲁⲃⲭⲛⲟⲩⲓ ϫⲉ ⲁⲕⲉⲓ ⲉⲛⲉⲓ

15.   ⲙⲉ ⲡⲁ...ⲩⲛ ?

    ⲡⲁⲥ ?

Verso:

    ? ⲉⲗⲧⲱⲃⲓ̇ ⲧⲏⲗⲉⲃ ⲉⲩⲧⲓⲧⲟⲛ ⲙⲉⲛⲏⲓ ϫⲉ

    ⲁⲩⲉϣⲃⲓⲧⲛ...ⲡⲉ̇ⲓⲉⲡⲓⲥⲕⲟⲡⲟⲥ ⲁⲃⲡⲓⲑⲓ

    ⲛⲡⲁⲛⲉ̅ ϣⲁⲛⲧⲉ ⲛⲉϣⲏⲛⲓⲱⲃ ϫⲉ ⲁⲛⲉⲟ̇ⲅⲉϣ

    ϣⲁⲗⲛ̇ ⲉⲛⲉⲥⲕⲏⲟⲩ ⲉⲓⲧⲉⲕⲗⲓⲥⲁ ⲁⲃⲧⲓⲧⲟⲛ

5.   ⲙⲉⲛⲏⲃ ⲡⲉⲃⲕⲉⲉⲃ ⲗⲟⲓⲡⲟⲛ ⲡⲁⲥⲁⲛ ⲁⲓ

    ϩⲱϫ ⲗⲁⲕ ϣⲟⲡⲓ ⲛⲉⲕϣⲗⲏⲗ ϩⲓϫⲱⲓ ϩⲉ ⲧⲉⲓ

    ϩⲁⲅⲓ[ⲁ ⲙⲡⲁⲣⲑⲉⲛⲟⲥ ⲧⲉⲥϭⲁⲙ ⲉⲧⲟⲩⲉⲃ ϣⲟⲡ

    ⲙⲉⲛⲏⲛ ⲁⲩⲱ ⲥⲧⲓⲧⲁⲁⲧⲥ·ⲙⲉⲛⲏⲛ ⲃⲗⲉϣ

Address:

    † ⲥ̅ⲩ̅ⲛ ⲧⲉⲉ̅ⲓⲧⲥ ⲡⲛⲙⲉⲗⲓⲥⲁⲛ   ⲕ̅ⲩ̅ⲣ ⲥⲁⲙⲟⲩⲏⲗ ⲡⲁⲡⲁϣⲉⲛ
    ⲉⲧ̅.ⲧ̅.   ⲡⲉⲃⲥⲁⲛ

Recto:

ll. 1–6. "In God's Name! I greet &c. thy good Brothership, and I greet my Father, Apa Philotheos fairly; and enquire thou for Apa Poimen and for the deacon Georgios, of Tansheei, fairly, on my behalf."

ⲁⲡⲁⲓⲱⲧ. ⲁ for ⲉ· is, in M.E., very unusual. v. ad Nᵒ XXIII¹³.

ⲟ̅ⲏⲡϣⲓⲛⲓ. v. ad Nᵒ XVI¹¹.

ⲧⲁⲛϣⲉⲉⲓ, mentioned in Nᵒ XLV, Rec.²⁹, and Append., P. Bodl., Rec.¹⁰·³⁵ Dr H. Petrie suggests ("Medum", p. 50,) that it is identical with ⲗⲩⲓⲃ, of which name the Arabic "Recencement" gives 5 examples in the district of Benisuef.

ll. 6. 7. "And I went to Sharé ──? the second Sunday in Lent."

ϣⲁⲣⲉ. This is perhaps but part of the name; cf. R. II, 66, ϣⲁⲣⲉⲡⲁⲛϭⲟⲗϯ.

I am not sure that №. XLV, Ver.² ,²³ ϣⲁⲣⲉ is a place-name ;(v. ad №.
XVI⁴.) Cf. №. XLV, Ver.⁷ and Append., P. Bodl., Rec.³⁵ ϣⲁⲣ?.

ⲛⲧⲉⲓⲟⲙⲏ is certain. ⲛⲧⲉ ⲡⲟⲙⲏ or ⲙⲡⲟⲙⲏ would be expected.

l. 9. Probably ϩⲓⲧⲉⲛ ⲛⲗⲉⲃⲗⲁⲓⲥ. The word = Sah. ⲡⲉϥⲣⲟⲉⲓⲥ (Peyr.), and is
found №. XXVI, ⲗⲉⲃⲗⲁⲉⲓⲥ, and №. XLV, Ver.¹⁴ ⲡⲉϥⲗⲁⲉⲓⲥ.

ll. 9, 10. Perhaps; "Take compassion on me and come to the Monastery"
(ⲧⲟⲡⲟⲥ), for Sah. ϯ ⲟⲩⲛⲁ ⲛ̅ⲙ̅ⲙⲁⲓ (v. ad №ˢ XII¹⁶, XIX⁷). Yet I know
no other instance of ϯⲛⲁ. The final ⲉ could also be read ⲉⲓ.

ll. 10, 11. "I have sought for thee, having written (ⲥⲉⲓ=ⲥϧⲁⲓ, R. V, 38.) of
thee that I intended to (or, that it is my habit to) enquire for
thee."

ll. 11–14. "For the rest, the old men, the sackcloth-weaver, told me that
thou wast gone to Babylon. Moreover, I have ―? and went to the
―? Apa Philotheos and enquired after him. And he further
told me that thou wast gone to the (pl.) ―?"

ϧⲗⲁ. I can but compare this with ϧⲉⲗⲗⲁ (Peyr.)

ⲥⲁϧⲃⲁⲩⲛⲓ probably = Zoega, 506, ⲥⲁϧⲧⲃⲟⲟⲩⲛⲉ, the ⲧ being lost before
(palatalised) ⲃ. ⲃⲟⲟⲩⲛⲉ, σάκκος, was dark-coloured hair-cloth;
v. Sirach, XXV, 19, ⲕⲁⲕⲉ ⲛ̅ⲑⲉ ⲛ̅ⲟⲩⲃⲟⲟⲩⲛⲉ, Ä.Z. '76, 117, ⲕⲙⲟⲙ ⲛ̅ⲑⲉ ⲛ̅ⲟⲩ-
ⲃⲟⲟⲩⲛⲉ, σακκοποιοι in Arsinoe, selling σχοινια τριχινα, occur in
Wien. Stud. '86, 114. The form ⲃⲁⲩⲛⲓ, Méms. de l'Inst. égypt. II, ii, and
Berl. P. 556? ; ⲃⲁⲩⲛⲉ, in №. XLVII.

ⲝⲛⲟⲩⲓ. I do not know whether, in the Djême texts, this could be rendered
"tell, inform" (Revill., A. et C. ⲛ̅ⲁ, ⲝ̅ⲑ̅.) Here "ask" seems improbable.

ⲡⲉⲓ-; v. ad №. XVII³.

Verso:

ll. 1, 2. "―? all the ―? contending with me that they were able to take us ―?
(? t̅ó) the Bishop".

ll. 2–5. I cannot divide the words here with certainty.

ⲡⲉⲃⲕⲉⲉⲃ ? for Sah. ⲙ̅ⲡⲉϥⲕⲁⲗⲁϥ (cf. №. XXVI, ⲡⲉⲗⲕⲁⲧⲉⲭⲓ = ⲙ̅ⲡⲉⲣ-) The form
ⲕⲉⲉ-, R. V, 47.

ll. 5–8. "Furthermore, my brother, I beseech thee (?) let thy prayers be for
me with the saintly Virgin, (that) her holy power be with us."

ϧⲱⲝ is, I suppose, the simpler form of ϧⲟⲭ ϧ̅ⲝ̅, "constrain"; its object
following with ⲉ-, like ϯϩⲟ, ⲕⲱⲣϣ. The present tense seems
obvious.

ⲧⲉⲥϭⲁⲙ for (ⲛ̅ⲧⲉ ⲧⲉⲥ-; or simply without prefix, ⲧⲉⲥϭⲁⲙ ϣⲟⲟⲡ.

Address: The writer, Samuel; the recipient, Shenoute. Note that the
letter was commenced with the 1 pers. pl. v. ad №. XXVII.

The Dialect is purely M.E.

XXIII. *Papyrus.* $9\frac{7}{8} \times 9$ in.

This fragt., and Nº XXIV, are remnants of the most extensive letters in the collection. The papyrus is strong and somewhat coarse-grained, but well prepared. The colour is light brown. From its character, which is large and without ligatures (cf. *Hyv., Alb.*, XII,3,) I should assign it to the latter years of the 10ᵗʰ cent. About ¼ of all the lines is lost (v. ad l.l.1,2) and l.l. 16–18 are much blurred.

Recto:
  ϯⲤⲨⲚ ⲦⲒⲰⲒⲚⲈ ⲀⲨⲰ ⲦⲒⲀⲤⲠⲀⲍⲈ ⲘⲀⲖⲖⲰⲚ ⲆⲈ ⲦⲒⲠⲢⲞⲤⲔⲨⲚⲈ ⲘⲐⲨⲠⲠ Ⲛ
  [Ⲉ]Ⲧ ⲘⲠⲚⲒⲔ ⲀⲨⲰ ⲈⲦⲬⲎⲔ ⲈⲂⲀⲖ ⲞⲚ ⲚⲀⲢⲈⲦⲎ ⲦⲎⲢ ⲘⲠⲚⲀ ⲈⲦⲞⲨⲀⲀⲂ
  ⲈⲢⲞⲨⲚ ⲚⲚⲀⲞⲤ ⲚⲒⲰ ⲦⲎⲢⲞⲨ ⲈⲦⲚⲈⲘⲀⲔ ⲚⲞⲞⲨⲀⲦⲈ ⲠⲀⲞⲤ ⲚⲒⲰ
  ⲔⲒⲠⲢⲒⲀⲚ ⲘⲚ ⲚⲈϤⲤⲚⲎⲨ ⲦⲎⲢⲞⲨ ⲘⲚ ⲞⲨⲀⲚ ⲚⲒⲘ ⲈⲦⲚⲈⲘ
5. ⲒⲎⲤ ⲠⲈⲬⲤ ⲈⲠⲒⲦⲀ ⲆⲈ ϯⲦⲀⲘ ⲘⲠⲀⲞⲤ ⲚⲒⲰ ⲜⲈ ⲀⲒⲤϦⲀⲒ ⲠⲒⲤⲚⲀ[Ⲩ]
  ⲈⲚⲚⲀϦⲘ ⲈⲠⲈⲐⲞⲞⲨ ϦⲒⲦⲚ ⲦⲂⲰⲒⲐⲒⲀ ⲚⲈⲔⲰⲖⲎⲖ ⲈⲦⲞⲨⲀⲀⲂ
  ⲚⲒⲰ ⲜⲈ ⲀⲒⲞⲨⲀⲀⲦⲈ Ⲉ ⲈⲦⲠⲰⲖⲒⲤ ⲘⲚ ⲠⲀⲒ ⲔⲈⲖⲈⲤ ⲔⲀⲦⲀ ⲐⲎ
  ⲠⲒⲤⲔ ϦⲀⲐⲎ ⲠⲀⲤ ⲠⲈⲦⲢ ⲘⲚ ⲠⲀⲤ ⲔⲞⲤⲘ[Ⲁ] ⲜⲈ ⲰϢⲠⲈ ϦⲘ
  ⲀⲘⲠⲰ ⲈϦⲚⲦ ⲦⲞⲨⲔⲈⲈⲨ ϦⲀ ⲐⲎⲨⲠⲀⲚ ⲦⲈ ⲠⲚⲞⲨ ⲞⲨⲀⲢⲠⲞⲨ
10. ⲠⲰⲦ ⲈⲠⲈⲠⲒⲤⲔ ⲦⲈ ⲆⲈⲖⲈⲘⲎ ⲠⲰⲦ ϦⲀⲐⲎ ⲘⲞⲨⲤⲎ ⲚϤⲦⲀⲘ
  ⲀϤⲞⲨⲰϯ ⲘⲈ ⲦⲈⲖⲈⲘⲎ ⲈⲠⲒⲤⲔ ⲀⲂⲂⲒ ⲠⲀⲤ ⲔⲞⲤⲘⲀ ⲀϤ
  Ⲁ ⲠⲒⲀⲖⲔⲈⲚⲰ ⲠⲀⲒ ⲈⲒ ⲔⲀⲚ ⲔⲈⲞⲨⲈ ⲀⲂⲒ ⲀⲚⲀⲔ ⲈⲦⲰⲦⲰⲢⲒ ⲚⲀ
  ϦⲈⲒ ⲠⲤⲀⲚⲈⲠⲢⲰⲘⲈ ϦⲘⲀⲀⲤ ⲈⲚⲦⲈϤ Ⲁ ⲠⲀⲤⲀⲚ ⲔⲞⲤⲘⲀ ⲦⲒ ⲚⲈⲚ
  ⲈⲢⲀϤ ⲀⲨⲰ ⲠⲀⲞⲤ ⲚⲒⲰ ⲔⲀⲦⲀ ⲚⲈⲰϢⲒⲚⲈ ⲚⲦⲀⲨⲠⲰϦ ⲈⲢⲀⲚ ϦⲈⲒ Ⲧ
15. ⲈϦⲞⲨⲚ ⲘⲠⲞⲨⲔⲈ ⲞⲨⲀⲖⲖⲀⲘⲎⲢ ϦⲈ ⲠⲘⲀⲢⲎⲤ ⲚⲔⲎⲘⲈ ⲞⲨⲀⲖⲖⲀ Ϧ
  ⲘⲈ ⲚⲈⲨⲔⲀ ⲘⲚⲈⲨⲬⲰ ⲘⲀⲤ ⲜⲈ Ⲁ ⲠⲢⲰⲘⲈ ϦⲰⲚ ⲈϦⲞⲨⲚ ⲀⲨⲰ ⲠⲢⲞ
  ⲠⲈ ⲀⲤⲤⲰⲂⲰⲢ ⲚⲈⲢⲈⲘⲠⲞⲨⲤⲒⲢⲈ ⲘⲠⲦⲀⲰ ⲈⲨⲚⲎⲨ ⲚⲀⲚ ⲀⲨⲦⲀⲘ
  ⲦⲀⲘⲀ ⲚⲈⲨ ⲠⲈⲦⲚⲀ? ϪⲒ ⲠⲚⲞⲨ Ⲛ? ⲀⲞⲤ ⲘⲠⲀⲢ ⲚⲦⲀⲔ ⲠⲈⲔϦⲎⲦ
  ϪⲒⲘⲞⲒⲈⲒⲦ ⲚⲀⲔ ⲚϤⲤⲔⲈⲠⲀⲌⲈ ⲘⲀⲔ ⲚⲘⲀⲔ ⲚϤⲦⲀⲔ ϦⲒϪⲰ
20. ⲈⲖⲀⲞⲨ ⲘⲠⲈⲐⲞⲞⲨ ⲈⲔⲞⲨⲀⲬ ⲚⲤⲰⲘⲀ ⲠⲨⲬ ⲠⲚⲀ ⲚⲀⲒ ⲀⲒⲤϦⲎⲦⲞ[Ⲩ]
       (space) ⲚⲈⲔⲈⲨ ⲈⲦⲞⲨⲀⲀⲂ ✝

Verso: ⳰ⲢⲈⲈⲘ (space) ⲔⲨⲢ ⲀⲂⲂⲒ ⲈⲀⲢ Ⳝ ϥⲞⲤⲚⲒⲔ ⲘⲈ ⲚⲒⲔ ϯⲈⲖⲀⲨⲤ

For the cross above l.1, v. Nº XIII.

l.l.1,2. Might be completed thus; 1,[ⲚⲞⲨⲈⲢⲎⲦⲈ ⲘⲠⲀⲞⲤ ⲚⲒⲰ], 2,[ⲀⲨⲰ ⲦⲒⲰⲒⲚⲈ ⲈⲠⲤⲞⲞⲨϦ]

ⲘϦⲨⲠⲠ for ⲘⲠϦⲨⲠⲞⲘⲞⲆⲒⲞⲚ (ὑποπόδιον). The preceding Preposition varies; R.V,27,29, ⲈⲬⲚ; *Berl.,* P.3260, M (= *Göttingen,* Cod. M.S. Or.,25⁸, N ; R.V,36, Ⲉ.) Cf. the formula in Nº XXV.

ⲈⲦ and ⲠⲚⲒⲔ, v. ad Nº XIIˢ.

ⲈⲦⲬⲎⲔ ⲈⲂⲀⲖ. This epithet Ä.Z. '85, 73.

ⲀⲢⲈⲦⲎ. Cf. R.V, 25, ⲔⲀⲦⲀ ⲚⲈⲀⲢⲈⲦⲎⲞⲨ ⲦⲎⲢⲞⲨ ⲘⲠⲚⲞⲨⲦ ⲘⲈ ⲚⲈⲖⲞⲘⲒ.

ⲘⲠⲚⲀ = ⲘⲠⲚⲚⲀ.

l.3. ⲒⲰ. This ⲧ has the form ⳑ throughout.

ⲚϨⲞⲨⲀⲦⲈ. v. ad Nᵒˢ XII⁵ and XX⁵. "The Congregation of all my Lords Fathers that are with thee, the foremost (of them, namely,) my Lord Father [N.N.]."

l.5. ⲈⲠⲒⲦⲀ ⲆⲈ ⲦⲦⲀⳘ. This formula in Nᵒ XXVII.

l.6. [Ⲧ]ⲈⲚⲚⲀϨⳘ, intransitive, as R. V, 29, 46, 47.

ⲚⲈⲔⲰⲖⲎⲖ = ⲚⲚⲈⲔ‧.

l.7. ⲞⲨⲀⲀⲦⲈ. v. ad Nᵒ XII¹² and here, l. 11, ⲞⲨⲰⲦ.

‧ⲉ, "5 solidi(?)." Dots precede the sums thus throughout App., P. Bodl., also A.Z. '85, 41 (Nᵒ X), ib., 38 (= Berl. P. 3227) and Nᵒ XVIII⁸, XXIV²⁹,³², XXXVI.

ⲠⲰⲖⲒⲤ, as R. II, 58, 62; V, 47, 48, A.Z. '85, 33, 34; Nᵒ XXIV³. Probably Arsinoe, though it might be the metropolis of another Nome (v. Wilcken, Observationes.)

ⲔⲈⲖⲈⲤⲦ ? = Colestius (Pape, 643.)

l.8. ϨⲀⲐⲎ[Ⲛ]. v. l. 10 and Nᵒ XII¹⁶, R. V, 57.

ⲉ̅, also A.Z. 78, 25; here = ⲤⲀⲚ, not ⲤⲞⲚ; v. ad l. 13. Cf. likewise l. 5, ⲦⲀⳘ and l. 18, ⲦⲀⲘⲀ.

Ⲭ[Ⲉ] ⲈⲰϢⲠⲈ ⲠⲢⲰⲘⲈ ϨⳘ[ⲀⲀⲤ?], or, Ⲭⲉ ⲠⲢⲰⲘⲈ ⲰϢⲰⲠⲈ ϨⳘ. Ⲭ for Ⲭⲉ is frequent; e.g. R. V, 29, 42, 44; Berl. P. 3251, 5553.

l.9. ⲈϨⲢⲦ, "(he went) down" (? = northwards; v. Stern, §. 576), rather than "before them", ⲈϨⲢⲦ[Ⲧ]ⲞⲨ; for an Imperative, ⲔⲈⲈⲨ, seems, in this narrative, improbable.

ⲔⲈⲈⲨ, = Sah. ⲔⲀⲀⲨ, is found R. V, 47. For ⲦⲞⲨ- (= Ⲛ̅ⲦⲞⲨ-), v. ad Nᵒ XII²¹.

ⲐⲎⲨⲠⲀⲚⲦ. Cf. Pape, 495, Θεόφαντος, and ib., 502, ff., initial Θευ- for Θεο-.

ll. 10, 11. ⲆⲈⲖⲈⲘⲎ, ⲦⲈⲖⲈⲘⲎ; probably the same. Cf. the name ﺩﻟﻤﻰ = δελεμη, R. V, 62.

ⲘⲞⲨⲤⲎ ? = ﻣﻮﺳﻰ.

ⲈⲠⲒⲤⲔ̇ ? for ⲈⲠⲈⲠⲒⲤⲔⲞ[ⲠⲞⲤ].

ⲀⲂⲂⲒ ? The Bishop's name. It recurs in the address, apparently as the name of the recipient, thus making the explanation, ⲀⲂⲂⲒ = ⲀϥϥⲒ unlikely.

l.12. ⲠⲒⲀⲖⲔⲈⲚⲰ. Cf. Nᵒ XVIII, ⲠⲀⲖⲔⲈⲚⲰ, ⲠⲀⲖⲔⲎⲚⲰ; XXVI, ⲠⲀⲖⲔⲈⲈⲰ; XLV, (ⲚⲈⲢⲰⲘⲈ) ⲠⲀⲖⲔⲈⲈⲒⲰ. If these are forms of but one Arab. word (with doubled Article,) I suppose them to transcribe ﺍﻟﺸﻚ, (yet ⲕ persistently for ﺵ is strange,) and to mean rather "Military Official" than "Soldier", collecting the imposed contributions, (v. Nᵒ XLV,) illustrated by Arabic M.S.S. from Mid. Egypt (v. "Führer"-Rainer, 1. Th., Nᵒˢ 583, 504, 504a, 507, 508, 510, 544. Nᵒ 634 shows an Arab garrison in Arsinoe.) No Coptic word for "Soldier" in these texts. The Djêmê papyri show ⲢⲘⲠⲘⲒⲖⲎⲤ (Brit. Mᵐ Nᵒ XL*), the Memphitic

---

* Sic, twice; not ⲠⲘⲒⲚⲎⲤ as Goodwin, A.Z. '69, 74. Still, it might be a place-name; cf. Revill, A. et C., ⲠⲦ̅, ⲠⲦⲞⲞⲨ ⲘⲠⲘⲒⲖⲈ (so Ciasca.)

Passports, ⲙⲁⲧⲟⲓ, (*Revill., A. et C., p̄ā.*)

ⲉⲓ ⲕⲁⲛ ⲕⲉⲟⲩⲉ ⲁⲃⲓ, for Sah. ⲏ ⲕⲁⲛ (ⲕⲁ̈ⲛ) ⲕⲉⲟⲩⲁ ⲁ̣ϥⲉⲓ (v. *A.Z.* '84, 150.) "Even
though another have gone, I (it is that) will go surety for(? him
ⲛⲁϥ).

ⲱⲧⲱⲣⲓ; also in the Memph. Passports; v. *A.Z.* '85, 148, 150.

l. 73. ϩⲉⲓ; v. ad N⁰ XII¹².

ⲥⲁⲛⲉⲡⲣⲱⲙⲉ. Perhaps ⲉⲡ· for a Sah. *ⲁⲡ· (from ⲱⲡ; v. *Stern*, §. 173.)
For the census in the Arabic period v. "*Führer*"-*Rainer*, I. Th.,
N⁰ 539. If ⲥⲁⲛ were Vocative, the Art. possess. would be required.

ⲉⲛⲧⲉϥ ends the sentence; or, ⲁⲡⲁⲥⲁⲛ ⲕ·, for ⲉⲡⲁⲥⲁⲛ ⲕ·.

l. 14. ⲕⲁⲧⲁ ⲧⲉ., "According to the news that have reached us, lo, —".

l. 15. ⲙⲡⲟⲩⲕⲉ, "They have not left—? in the South of Egypt." Krall's ⲕⲏⲙⲉ
= Fostat (*R.* II, 50,) is here, at least, impossible.

l. 17. ⲁⲥⲥⲱⲃⲱⲣ seems to be Arabic; ? اصوار.

ⲡⲟⲩⲥⲓⲣⲉ ⲙⲡⲧⲁⲱ. A Busiris ϩⲙ ⲡⲧⲟⲱ ⲛⲱⲙⲟⲩⲛ is mentioned *R.* II, 64.
ⲧⲁⲱ, like ⲡⲟⲗⲓⲥ, would have a special meaning for our correspondents, which they had no need farther to define.

l. 19. "[The Lord] lead thee and shield thee, and set thee in [a place of rest,
apart from] all evil."

ⲭⲓⲙⲟⲓⲉⲓⲧ ⲛⲁⲕ, according to Boh. usage; v. *Stern*, §. 565. The phrase is
found *Berl., P.* 3285; *R.* II, 58; V, 45, 46.

ⲥⲕⲉⲡⲁⲍⲉ; v. *R.* II, 57; *Berl., P.* 5559, both with ⲙⲙⲟⲕ. Possibly ⲛⲙⲁⲕ = ⲛⲙⲁϥ,
but probably it is an error.

ϩⲓⲭⲱ; v. ad N⁰ XVIII.

l. 20. ⲉⲕⲟⲩⲁⲭ ⲧⲉ.; v. ad N⁰ XI⁷.
The line might be continued; [✝ϩⲟ ⲁⲣⲓⲡⲁⲙⲉⲉⲩⲉ ϩⲛ].

l. 21. ⲉⲩⲭ = εὐχή. The Greek word (instead of ⲱⲗⲏⲗ) is unusual.

Verso: I can make very little of the Address. The recipient's name is
apparently ⲁⲃⲃⲓ (v. ad *l.* 11,) and 2 titles, joined by ⲥ, follow it.
After the Chrysmon one looks for the name of the writer.

M.E. forms are in the majority, though the text has Sah. ⲱⲓⲛⲉ, ⲥϩⲁⲓ,
ⲥⲛⲏⲩ, ⲟⲩⲁⲁⲃ, ⲛⲓⲙ, ⲧⲉ., Boh. ⲟⲩⲁⲣⲡ· (ⲟⲩⲟⲣⲡ·), ⲱⲧⲱⲣⲓ and, *l.* 19, ⲛⲁⲕ;
nor is ⲗ substituted for ⲣ.

XXIV Papyrus (v. N⁰ XII.)   17 × 5⅜ in.
This was the original letter upon the sheet. (v. ad N⁰ XII²⁶⁻²⁸,) and far

the longest in the collection. About one half of the papyrus has disappeared (v. ad l.1). The character much resembles that of N° XIV (pl. 3), although twice as large. The text runs in the reverse direction with that of N° XII. A colon frequently, a double-colon rarely, divides the words.

✝ ⲤⲨⲚ ⲦⲓⲰⲓⲚⲓ ⲈⲦⲈⲔⲘⲈⲦⲘⲀⲓⲚⲞⲨ̅
ⲈⲂⲀⲖⲢⲓⲦⲈⲚ ⲠⲚⲞⲨ̅ ⲘⲚ̅Ⲛ̅ⲤⲀ ⲚⲀ[ⲓ]
ⲦⲀⲚⲒ ⲈⲦⲠⲰⲖⲒⲤ ⲢⲒⲰⲰⲤ : ⲀⲢⲀ
ⲘⲈ ⲚⲢⲢⲀⲰ ⲢⲒⲬⲰⲔ · ⲈⲖⲦⲀⲄⲀⲠ[Ⲏ]
5. ⲚⲤⲈⲘⲈⲰⲚ · ⲀⲢⲀⲠⲰ : ⲈⲨⲠⲀ
ⲀⲢⲀ ⲚⲠⲈⲢⲦⲒⲞⲨⲎⲦⲈⲤ ⲚⲀⲒ Ⲛ
ⲖⲀⲨ ⲚⲤⲀⲒⲎ ⲔⲀⲦⲀⲖⲀⲔ ⲀⲢⲀ ⲦⲒ
ⲈⲖⲦⲘⲈⲦⲤⲀⲚ ⲦⲒⲞⲨⲎⲦⲈⲤ ⲚⲀ
ⲦⲀⲀⲠⲞⲔⲢ ⲢⲀⲦⲎⲔ ⲈⲔⲦⲈⲨ Ⲛ
10. ⲦⲈⲒⲦⲞⲨ ⲚⲤⲈⲘⲈⲰⲚ · ⲀⲨⲒ ⲦⲀⲀ
ⲖⲀⲔ ⲬⲈⲚⲦⲞⲨ ⲘⲀⲚ ⲔⲈⲚ ⲀⲢⲀ
ⲘⲈ ⲠⲈⲨⲤⲀⲚ · ⲔⲀⲦⲀ ⲐⲎ ⲚⲦⲀⲨⲀⲢ
? ⲈⲬⲒ ⲚⲦⲈ ⲢⲰⲘⲒ ⲢⲒⲬⲰⲔ
ⲤⲈⲨⲎⲢ ⲦⲀⲘⲀⲒ ⲘⲈ ⲤⲈⲘⲈⲰⲚ
15. ⲚⲈⲚⲞⲨⲒ̈ · ⲚⲚⲈⲔⲰ[Ⲉ]ⲘⲒⲔⲰⲚ
ⲖⲈ ⲚⲈⲔⲰⲎⲢⲈ ⲦⲒ ⲚⲈⲚⲞⲨⲒ̈ Ⲣ
ⲖⲀⲔ ⲘⲈⲔⲤⲦⲀ ⲚⲈⲨⲚⲞⲨⲒ̈?
ⲚⲈⲨⲀⲢ ⲢⲈⲔ ⲈⲢⲀⲨ ⲠⲀⲖ ⲬⲞⲨⲂ
ⲬⲰⲚ · ⲚⲠⲈⲔⲈⲒⲦⲞⲨ ⲚⲦⲢⲎ
20. ⲚⲦⲀⲨⲢⲒⲤⲒ ⲚⲠⲈⲔⲦⲒⲞⲨⲖⲀⲢ

ⲀⲨⲰ ⲚⲠⲈⲢⲔⲈⲦⲈ ⲠⲘⲒⲤⲦⲒⲚ
ⲘⲀⲚ ⲞⲨⲢⲰⲒ̈ⲈⲚⲦⲈ ⲠⲈⲒ : ⲚⲀ
ⲢⲒⲬⲰⲔ ⲚⲠⲀⲢⲀ ⲠⲰⲈⲘⲀ · Ⲗ
ⲤⲀⲠ · ⲀⲨⲰ ⲢⲈ Ⲡ̅Ⲁ̅Ⲓ̅ ⲄⲀⲂⲢⲒ ⲂⲈ
25. ⲚⲠⲈⲔⲦⲒ ⲢⲀⲨ ⲚⲈⲔⲠⲀⲖ Ⲛ̅
? ⲈⲚⲦⲈ ⲦⲈⲒ · ⲰⲀⲔⲦⲒ Ⲛ
ⲚⲀⲬⲰⲤ ⲂⲀⲖ · ⲖⲒⲠⲞⲚ ⲰⲒⲚⲒ
ⲘⲈⲬⲈⲨ ⲬⲈ ⲘⲀⲢⲈⲨ ⲦⲀⲘⲦ Ⲓ
ⲉ̇ⲩ̇Ϯ ⲔⲈ : Ⲉ ⲚⲚⲞⲨⲒ̈ ⲚⲀⲒ · Ⲱ
30. Ⲓ̈Ⲉ ⲘⲀⲖⲈⲨⲠⲰⲦ ⲚⲀⲨ · ⲖⲒⲠ Ⲑ
ⲦⲀⲦ ⲠⲈⲨⲢⲎⲦ ⲢⲰⲞⲨ Ⲁ ⲠⲀⲤⲀ
: ⲔⲂ̇ Ⲛ̅Ⲛ̅Ⲱ̇ⲔⲀⲨ ⲂⲀⲖ ⲈⲚⲈⲢ
ⲈⲢⲞⲨⲚ ⲈⲠⲈⲨⲢⲒⲤⲒ ⲘⲈ ⲠⲈⲨⲤⲀⲚ̇
ⲚⲎⲢⲠ · ⲚⲠⲈⲖⲦⲀⲔⲀⲨ ⲚⲦⲀⲀⲦ
35. ⲂⲀⲖ · Ⲁ̇·ⲀⲚⲈⲨ ⲚⲈⲰⲦⲈⲔⲦⲈⲒⲖ
ⲚⲈⲰ ⲦⲀⲖⲰⲰⲢⲒⲌⲈ ⲘⲘⲀⲔ·Ⲣ
Ⲛ̇ⲰⲀ̇ⲔⲦⲈ? ⲚⲀⲒ ⲚⲞⲀ̇ⲒⲎ ⲦⲀ
Ⲩ̈Ⲓ ⲚⲎⲢⲠ̅ ·̇·̇ ⲔⲈ̣ⲞⲨ ⲂⲀⲖ ⲚⲈⲔ·
? Ⲛ·̇·̇ ⲔⲞⲨⲢ ⲔⲀ ⲚⲈⲒ ⲢⲰ
40. ? ⲠⲔⲈⲢⲒ · ⲦⲒⲰⲓⲚⲓ ⲢⲀ

Below l. 40 is a wide margin.

l.1. may be completed thus; [ⲚⲤⲀⲚ(?) ⲈⲦⲦⲀⲒⲎⲨ(?) ⲦⲎⲢⲎⲚⲒ ⲚⲀⲔ]. v. ad N° XII.

l.3. ⲦⲠⲰⲖⲒⲤ ; v. ad N° XXIII.

l.4. ⲈⲖⲦⲀⲄⲀⲠⲎ; v. Ä.Z.'85, 29; Berl., P. 5642, and often upon tomb-stones.

l.5. ⲀⲢⲀⲠⲰ; cf. Zoega, 136, ⲀⲢⲀⲠⲞⲖⲰⲚ, Ὡραπόλλων.

ll. 6, 8. ⲎⲦⲈⲤ. ? = εἶδος. Cf. Ä.Z.'92, 39, ⲈⲒⲦⲎⲤ, ⲒⲦⲎⲤ, ⲈⲒⲦⲞⲤ, where it stands alone; likewise in Revill., A. et C., θ; while ib., ⲒⲀ, ⲈⲒⲆⲞⲤ ⲘⲠⲈⲚⲒⲠⲈ, Lagarde, Aegypt., 230, ⲈⲒⲆⲞⲤ Ⲛ̅ⲈⲒⲖⲀⲨ (= "Can. Apostol." σκεῦος ὀδόνης,) it has closer definition.

l.7. This recalls N° XV.

l.11. ? = Sah. ⲬⲈ Ⲛ̅ⲦⲞⲨ Ⲙ̅ⲘⲞⲚ ⲔⲎⲚ, "bring them to us (and) it suffices."

ll. 15, 16. ⲚⲈⲚⲞⲨⲒ̈ = Sah. Ⲛ̅ⲚⲞⲨⲂ, rather than ⲚⲀⲚⲞⲨⲒ̈ (cf. l. 29.)

l.17. ⲤⲦⲀ, M.E. Stat. constr. for ⲤⲦⲞ ; v. Stern, §.337.

l.18. ⲀⲢ ⲢⲈⲔ, perhaps for Sah. ⲀⲢⲈ ⲢⲀⲦⲔ̅; cf. R. II, 44, ⲈⲂⲈⲀⲢⲒ ⲢⲈⲂ, N° VI, Rec.', ⲀⲢⲒ ⲢⲀⲨ.

l.19. ⲈⲒⲦⲞⲨ, as Boh. ⲀⲒⲦⲞⲨ (v. Stern, §. 342); cf. Recueil, XI, 116, ⲈⲒⲤ = Sah. ⲀⲀⲤ.

l.24. ϩε for ϩει; *v. ad* N.° XII¹².

ΓΑΒΡΙ[ΗΛ]; *cf. the abbreviation l.5 above. Note that the writer of* N.° XII *is also named Gabriel.*

l.l. 29, 32. :ε̅, :κβ̅. *For this double dot, v., e.g.,* R.V, 46. *The letter following* κβ̅ *has been altered and may be* ⲁ.

The Address; v. ad N.° XII²⁹. "(From) the Archdeacon Philotheos, the Arch-Presbyter, (to?) Georgios, in the Lord,"— *so the position of the Chrysmon seems to require. But can these two offices be combined in one person? For* ⲉⲛ ⲕ̅ⲱ̅, *v.* N.° XVII.

The Dialect is M.E.

XXV. *Papyrus.*   2½ × 8½ *in.*

The papyrus is very dilapidated; a mere net-work of fibres in several places. It is of a faint gray-yellow colour, and bears a peculiar character, quite without ligatures. The ⲁ *has an angular form, similar to that in* N.° 1. *I think the final phrases indicate that not many words are lost. Missing letters are represented by dots.*

Recto: ϯ ϩⲁⲧϩⲏ ⲙⲛ ϩⲱϥ ⲛⲓⲃ[ⲓⲓ] ϯ ϯ ⲩ ⲓ ⲛ [ⲓ] ⲁ̄ⲩⲱ ϯ[ⲁ]ⲥⲡⲁⲍⲉ [ⲙ]ⲡϣⲁ[ⲓ]ⲱ ⲛⲛⲉ
ⲟ[ⲁⲗ]ⲗⲁⲩⲭ ⲙⲡⲁⲡⲣⲟⲥⲧⲁⲧⲏ[ⲥ] ⲛⲟ̄ⲥ ⲛ[ⲓ]ⲱⲧ ⲁⲩⲱ ⲡⲗⲁⲟⲥ ⲧⲏⲗϥ [ⲛ̄]ⲛⲟⲣⲑⲟ
ⲇ[ⲟ]ⲝⲟⲥ ⲕⲁⲧⲁ ⲧϩⲛ ⲛⲧⲁⲁⲕⲭⲁⲁⲥ ⲉⲗⲗⲓ ϩ..ⲓⲁⲙ ⲉⲧⲃⲉ ⲡ[ⲕ]ⲁⲙⲁⲥⲓ
ⲭⲉ ⲛⲁⲛⲟⲩϥ ⲁⲩⲱ ϣⲁϥⲉⲗϣⲉⲩ ⲛⲏⲕ ϩⲉⲓⲧⲉⲥ...ⲁⲓⲧⲛⲁⲩ ⲧϩⲟⲗⲟ
5.   ⲕⲱⲧⲥⲓ ⲛⲏⲕ ⲙⲛ ⲡⲁⲗⲱⲙⲓ ⲉⲧⲉ ⲡⲣⲁⲩ ⲡⲉ ϩⲁⲛⲭⲕ ⲭⲓⲧⲥ ⲛⲧⲁ.ⲩ
ⲧ̄ⲛⲁⲩϥ ⲛⲏⲓ ⲁⲩⲱ ϯ.ϥ̇. ⲛⲉⲥⲙⲓⲁ ⲛⲏⲓ ⲛϩⲗⲟⲩ ⲥ̄ⲛⲉϥ : ⲗⲟⲓⲡⲟⲛ̄ ⲗⲗⲁⲩ
ⲛⲛⲁⲡⲟⲕⲣⲓⲥⲓⲥ ⲉⲗⲉ ⲧⲉⲕⲙⲉⲧⲓⲱⲧ ⲕⲉⲗⲉⲅⲉ ⲙ̇[ⲙ̄]ⲁϥ ⲕⲉⲗⲉⲅ[ⲉ] ⲙ̇ ?
ⲙ̇.ϥ ⲙ̇ⲡⲉⲕⲱϩⲗⲓ ⲁⲩⲱ ⲡⲉⲕϩⲉⲗ ϯⲥⲉϥⲧⲱⲧ...ⲉⲛ̄ⲟⲩϩⲉⲓ ?

Verso: ϯ ⲧⲉⲓⲥ ⲙⲡⲁⲡ[ⲣⲟⲥⲧⲁ]ⲧ[ⲏⲥ] ⲛⲓⲱⲧ ⲁ̄ⲡⲁ ⲅ̄ⲉⲟ̄ⲝ [ⲡⲁⲣⲭ]ⲏⲙⲁⲛⲧⲣⲓⲧⲏⲥ +
[ⲕ]ⲟⲥⲙⲁ +++

"Before all things, I greet and kiss the dust of the feet of my Patron, Lord and Father and all the people that are orthodox. According as thou saidest to me in Fayyum(?) concerning the cloak, that it is good and is (? could be) of use to thee; lo, ___? I sent the solidus to thee with my servant, namely Prau(?) Take it ___? Send it to me and give ___? to me for two days. For the rest, if thy Fathership command any answer, so command it of thy son and slave. I am ready ___? welfare ___?"

Address; "For my Patron (and) Father, Apa Georgios, the Archimandrite;

(from) Kosma."

For the cross above l.1, v. Nº XIII.

l.1. �②ⲁⲧ②ⲏ ⲧⲉ.; variants R.V,24. The genitive ⲛ(②ⲱ④) coincides regularly with the final ⲛ of ⲙⲉⲛ.

ⲡⲉⲩⲁⲓⲱ ⲧⲉ. Cf. R.V,36; A.Z.'85,29; Quatrem., Rech⁵, 248; and, for a similar expression, Ostr. Prof. Sayce, †ⲟⲩⲱϣⲧ ⲙ̄ⲡⲓⲭⲛⲟⲥ (ἴχνος) ⲛ̄ⲛⲟⲩⲉⲣⲏⲧⲉ ⲉⲧⲧ ⲛ̄ⲧⲉ[ⲕ]ⲑⲉⲟⲥⲉⲃⲉⲓⲁ ⲛ̄ⲓⲱⲧ, Berl. P.3246, ⲉⲝⲛ ⲡ̄ⲡⲓⲭⲛⲟⲥ ⲛ̄ⲛⲟⲩⲉⲣ-ⲏⲧⲉ ⲙⲡⲁⲭⲟⲉⲓⲥ, Ostr. Goodwin, Brit. Mᵐ M.S. Ad.31291, †ⲡⲣⲟⲥⲕⲩⲛⲉ ⲙⲡⲉⲓⲭⲛⲟⲥ ⲛ̄[ⲛ̄]ⲟⲩⲉⲣⲏ[ⲧⲉ] ⲛⲧⲉⲕⲉⲩⲗⲁⲃⲓⲁ ⲉⲧⲧ.

l.2. ⲡⲣⲟⲥⲧⲁⲧⲏⲥ; also R.V, 26,31,32 and (perhaps) A.Z.'85,37.

ⲟⲣⲑⲟⲇⲟⲝⲟⲥ; merely opposed to heresy in general, or perhaps refers here to the divisions in the Egyptian Church. In 512, a Fayy. M.S. speaks of a monk as ⲡⲟⲧⲉ ⲙⲉⲛ Μελιτιανος ⲛⲩⲛ δε ορτοδοξος (Rev. des Ét⁵ gr⁵, '90,134), and about 740, the Jacobite Patriarch, Chael, is made to speak of the "fides orthodoxa" of Dioscorus, and of his followers as "orthodoxi" (Renaud., Hist. Patr. Alex., 214.)

l.3. ⲛⲧⲁⲗ-; v. Stern, §.374, and A.Z.'85,37.

②..ⲓⲁⲙ; possibly ②ⲓ(or ②)ⲡⲓⲁⲙ, for ②ⲉ ⲡ·. Cf. ②ⲓ = ②̄ⲙ R.II,61, Nº XXVI". ②ⲉ or ②ⲏ cannot be read here.

[ⲕ]ⲁⲙⲁⲥⲓ; probably, because of καμάσιον, Du Fresne.

l.4. ②ⲉⲓⲧⲉⲥ; cf. with this the form ②ⲉⲓⲧ, R.V,51 and? A.Z.'85,35.

ⲧⲛⲁⲩ; cf. R.V,48, ⲛⲕⲧⲛⲁⲩⲧ④.

l.5. ⲡⲣⲁⲩ; if indeed a name, cf. Zoega, 53 (Boh.) ⲡⲓⲣⲱⲟⲩ.

l.6. A possible reading is † ⲏⲡ; but what follows it?

l.7. ⲕⲉⲗⲉⲩⲉ; cf. R.I,24.

ⲙⲙⲁ④ marc.; i.e. ⲗⲁⲗ④.

l.8. ②ⲉⲗ; cf. Mém. de l'Inst. ég.II,ii, ②ⲉⲗ, δοῦλος, and? Recueil XI,147,②ⲉⲗ

Address: ⲅⲉⲟ② or ⲅⲉⲟ†. The latter would imply that Kosma was Archi-mandrite. But the servile tone of his letter makes this less probable. For the triple Chrysmon, v. R.V,26, and cf. ib., 40.

The text displays the most marked M.E. characteristics; e.g., ⲗ for ⲣ, -ⲓ for -ⲉ, Perf.-ⲁⲗ- for -ⲁ-, ⲛⲛ-(l.8) for ⲛ·.

————————

XXVI Papyrus (from Hawara.) $5\frac{3}{4}$ × 6 in.

A leaf of thin but coarsely-ribbed material, of yellow-brown colour. Its character is distinguished by (traced); ⳬ =ⲃ, ⲩ,ⲭ =ⲗⲉ, ·⳿ =ⲟⲩ, ⲧ =ⲧ, superscript. It may be placed beside that of Nᵒ XX. Below and to the left of the text, the margin remains. There is no address (cf. Nᵒ XVIII.)

[Ϯ]ϩ[ε ⲡ]ⲗⲉ[ⲛ] ⲉⲡⲛⲟⲩⲧⲓ ⲛⲱ[ϣ]ⲁⲣⲉⲡ…?

ⲭⲁⲉⲓⲥ ⲓ̈ⲱ ⲉⲧ̈ⲧ̈ ⲁⲩⲱ ⲡⲓϣⲓⲛⲓ ⲉⲟⲩⲁⲛ ⲛⲓⲃⲓ ⲉⲧⲧⲓ

ⲛ ⲟⲩⲛⲁϭ ⲱⲁ[ⲟ]ⲩⲕⲟⲩⲓ ⲧⲏⲣⲏⲛⲓ̈ ⲡⲛⲟⲩⲧⲓ ⲛⲉⲕ ⲙⲉⲛⲉ[ⲥⲁ ⲛⲉⲓ…?

ⲁ ⲡⲁⲗⲕⲉⲉⲱ ⲥϩⲉⲓ ⲛⲉⲕ ⲍⲉ ⲟⲩⲁⲧⲉ ϩⲉⲛⲡⲁⲣⲉⲥ ⲛ[ⲉ̇ⲓ…?

5. ⲁϩⲁ ⲥⲛⲉⲩ ⲛⲁⲛⲟⲩϩ ⲙⲁⲛ ϩⲉⲓ ⲡⲗⲱϣⲓ ⲥϩⲉⲓ

ⲡⲓⲁⲥⲁⲧⲉⲣ ⲁϩⲁ ⲡⲓⲥⲛⲉⲩ ⲛⲁⲛⲛⲟⲩϩ ⲁϩⲁ ⲡ

ϩⲉⲛⲡⲁⲣⲉⲥ ⲛⲉⲓ ⲁϩⲁ ⲡⲁⲥⲁⲧⲉⲣ ⲁϩⲁ ⲡⲥⲛⲉ[ⲩ̇…?

ⲁϩⲁ ⲡⲉⲗⲕⲁⲧⲉⲭⲓ ⲡⲁⲗⲉⲃⲗⲁⲉⲓⲥ ϩⲓ ⲡⲟⲩ

ϩⲉⲓ ⲡⲉⲧⲁⲃⲥϩⲉⲧⲃ ⲁⲓⲧⲁⲙⲁⲕ ⲉⲗⲁⲃ ⲉⲗⲉ ⲡⲭⲁ[ⲉ̇ⲓⲥ…?

10. ⲡⲁⲭⲁⲉⲓⲥ ⲓ̈ⲱ ⲕⲉⲗⲉⲩ ⲛⲧⲉⲃⲥϩⲉ ⲡⲉⲃϣⲓ[ⲛⲓ…?

ⲧⲉⲛⲭⲁⲓ[ⲥ ⲉ]ⲃⲁⲗ ϩⲓ ⲡⲟⲩⲱ ⲱ ⲉⲡⲛⲟⲩⲧⲓ ⲟ[ⲩ]ⲭⲉⲓ ϩⲓ ⲡⲟ̄ⲥ +

l.1 cannot be completed with certainty, so the amount lost remains doubtful.

l.2. Note the elision of liquids here and in l.10, ⲭⲁⲉⲓⲥ[ⲛ]ⲓⲱⲧ, l.3, ⲧⲏⲣⲏⲛⲓ [ⲙ]ⲡⲛⲟⲩⲧⲓ, l.8,[ⲙ]ⲡⲉⲗⲕⲁⲧⲉⲭⲓ.
ⲉⲧⲧⲓ. What formula is this? ⲓ is certain.
l.3. ⲛⲁϭ–ⲕⲟⲩⲓ; v. ad Nᵒ XIII⁵.
ⲧⲏⲣⲏⲛⲓ ⲝ.; v. ad Nᵒ XII".
l.4. ⲡⲁⲗⲕⲉⲉⲱ; v. ad Nᵒ XXIII¹².
ⲛⲉⲕ. The middle letter has been altered.
ϩⲉⲛⲡⲁⲣⲉⲥⲛ?; seems to recur in l.7. Cf. perhaps Nᵒ XVI.
ll.5.6. ⲁⲛⲛⲟⲩϩ; "Rope maker" (for Sah.*ϩⲁⲛⲛ', like ϩⲁⲛⲛⲟⲩⲃ). But this is a mere guess.
l.5. ⲡⲗⲱϣⲓ; cf. Zoega, 561, ⲡⲉⲧⲣⲱϣⲉ, "The Overseer"(of a bakery.)
ll.6,7. ⲁⲥⲁⲧⲉⲣ; ? Arabic, with the Article. Yet one would expect ⲁⲥⲥ'.
l.8. ⲕⲁⲧⲉⲭⲓ; v. ad Nᵒ XIV⁶.
ⲗⲉⲃⲗⲁⲉⲓⲥ; =Peyr, Sah. ⲣⲉϥⲣⲟⲉⲓⲥ; M.E., Nᵒ XLV, Ver.¹⁵, ⲣⲉϥⲗⲁⲉⲓⲥ.
l.9. "Lo, what he has written, I have told it thee."
ⲁⲓⲧⲁⲙⲁⲕ ⲉⲗⲁⲃ; v. Stern, §.510 (p. 334).
l.10. ⲕⲉⲗⲉⲩ. The final -ⲉ has lapsed, owing to the following ⲛ. Cf. Nᵒ XXVIII, ⲕⲉⲗⲉⲩ ⲉⲥϩⲁⲓ.
l.11. ϩⲓ = ϩⲉ = ϩⲙ̄. v. ad Nᵒ XXV³.

The Dialect is purely M.E.

XXVII Papyrus. $6\frac{1}{2} \times 10\frac{5}{8}$ in.

A yellow-brown papyrus, bearing also Nº XXVIII. This face has been cleared of a former to receive the present text, — the blank margins retain their darker tint. The sheet was afterwords folded (in both directions), so as to bring the address line to the outside. The character is a poor example of the class of *Hyv.*, *Alb.*, XX.

ϯCΥΝ ΤΕΝϢΙΝΙ ΕΕΠΕΚΟΥΧΑΙ ΝΕΜ ΝΗ ΕΤΝΕΜΑΚ

ΕΠΙΤΑ ΔΕ ϯΤΑΜⲰ ΝΤΕΚΑΓΑΠΗ ΧΕ ΑΙΕΡΔΕΚ[ⲓ̈]ΝΠΕΙΚ̄C̄

ϨΑΙ ΑΙΕΡΝⲰΕΙΝ ΝΝΗ ΕΤΑΚΕΡC[Ⲏ̄]ΜΑΝΕ Μ̄ΜⲰ[ΟΥ ?

ΑΝΑΓΓΕ ΚⲰ ϯϨΑΤΙΚΑϢ Ϩ ϯΠ..CϨΑΙ ΝϨΑΘ̇Ρ̇Ε ?

ΠⲰΑΧΙ CϨΑΙ ΝΑΙ ΝΑΙ ϢΑ ⲫϯ ΟΥⲰϢ ΟΥΧΑΙ ϨΝ[Π̄C̄ ϯ

Address (on same face, but in reverse direction);

[ϯ ΟΥΕΝΑ̇]ΒΡΙ Π̅Ρ̅ CΕΝⲞ̊ Ⲇ̈Ⲓ (space) ϯ CΫ́ΜΕⲰΝ ΕΝΚⲰ̄ ϯ

"We enquire after thy welfare and those that are with thee. Thereafter, I inform thy Benevolence that I have received thy letter (and) have taken knowledge of the matters which thou hast indicated. It is needful to leave the —? and the —? Write to Hathré the news. Write to me so long as God will! Farewell in the Lord!"

Address; "Onnophrios, presbyter, and Senuthios, deacon; Simeon, in the Lord."

l. 1. ΕΕΠΕΚΟΥΧΑΙ. Cf. *R.* II, 58, 61, ΕΕCϨΕΙ.
The line may have had another word; perhaps ΤΗΡΟΥ.

l. 2. ΕΠΙΤΑ ΔΕ; v. ad Nº XXIII⁵.

ΑΓΑΠΗ; v. *R. V,* 29, ΝΕΤΝΕΑΓΑΠΗ.

ΕΡΔΕΚΊ for δέχεσθαι. Cf. *R.* II, 56, ασισρδεχι νεκοχασι. Κ for Χ is remarkable; v. *Stern*, § 16.

l. 3. ΕΡΝⲰΕΙΝ, for νοεῖν.

ΕΡCΗΜΑΝΕ for σημαίνειν. With Μ̄ as guide to the word-division, no other reading suggests itself.

l. 4. ΑΝΑΓΓΕ, for ἀνάγκη. These words could be variously divided; e.g, ΑΝΑΓΓΕ[Ε]ΚⲰϯ ϨΑ ΤΙΚΑϢ, when ΚΑϢ (fem.) would be a new word. As it stands, I take the first ϯ (for Ν̄ϯ,) as the Art. fem., — the second may be the imperative, "give," — and ϨΑΤ˙ for the Nomen agentis of ϨΙΤΕ. But the explanation is unlikely and unsatisfactory.

ϨΑΘΡΕ; uncertain, owing to the blank space between Θ and Ρ.

l. 5. The first ΝΑΙ is conjectural. ΝΕΙ (but not ΝΗΙ,) were possible; but the word-sequence is against this.

Ⲫϯ. The Φ is very angular.

Address: One expects this to begin with the recipients and end with the writer's name. The use of sing. and plur. in this letter would imply the reverse. Yet other letters are equally inconsequent; v. N.ᵒˢ XI, XXII, XXIV. For ⲈⲚⲔ[ⲨⲢⲒ]ⲱ, v. ad N.ᵒ XVII, Ver.

The text has a notable Boh. tendency, conspicuous in Ⲫϯ, ⲘⲘⲰⲞⲨ, ⲚⲎ ⲈⲦ·, ⲈⲦⲀⲔ·, and in the Greek verbs with ⲈⲢ·.

XXVIII *Papyrus.* (v. pl. 1.) $6\frac{1}{2} \times 10\frac{1}{8}$ in.

Upon the same leaf as N.ᵒ XXVII, but in a very different character. The text is so little intelligible, that,—taking N.ᵒ XXVII to be a more recent ad-dition,—one might suspect the loss of a considerable part of the leaf upon the right side.

```
   ᶦⁿϯ ⲦⲓⲦⲀⲘⲀ ⲘⲠⲀⳂⲀⲈⲓⲤ ⳉⲈ ⲀⲨⲤⲀⲚ ⲔⲀⲦ ⳋⲀⳋⲦⲎⲚ?
       ⲀⲂⲦⲀⲘⲀⲚ̀ ⳨ⲈⲢⲉ̣̂ ⳡⲉⳡⲃ ⲈⲚⲀⲈⲘⲦⲞⳅⲈ ⳋⲀⳋⲦⲚ ⲞⲨ?
       ⳡⲱⲤ ⲈⲠⲀⳋⲦⲢⲈ ⲠⲈ ⳨ⲓⲦⲞⲨ Ⲁ ⲦⲈⲔⲀⲎⲤⲓⲀ
       ⲔⲈⲀⲈⲨ ⲈⳅⳋⲀⲓ ⲞⲨⳅⳋⲀⲓ ⲚⳋⲀⲦⲢⲈ ⲂⲱⲓⲚⲈ ⲘⲘⲀⲂ
   5.  ⲂⲱⳡⲀⲚⲤⲦⲨ⳨Ⲉ ⲞⲨⲀⳋⲀⲐⲞⲚ ⲈⳡⲱⲠⲈ ⲤⳋⲀⲓ ⲚⳋⲚ̀
       ⲈⲔⲞⲨⳡⳋ ⲚⲦⲈⲚⲦⲞⲀⲘⲀ ⲠⳡⲱⲤ ⲘⲀⲚ ⲞⲨⲢⲰⲘ
       ⲚⲦⲀⲂⲘⲞⲨ ⲀⲨⲱ Ⲁϥ⳨ⲀⲀⲤ ⲈⲢⲈ ⲤⲀⲨ ⲚⲢⲰⲘⲈ Ⲙ
       ⲎⲢⲈ ⲘⲠⲀⲦⲈⲂⲘⲞⲨ ⳨ⲞⲈⲓⲤ ⲦⲈⲨ ⳋⲀⳋⲦⲎⲂ
       ⲚⲦⲈⲚⲦⲂ ⲘⲠⳡⲱⲤ (finis.)
```

ll.1–3. Perhaps, "I inform my Lord that a brother has slept with us(?) and has told us(?) that there are seven "planters"—by a (?) shepherd —?

ⲀⲨⲤⲀⲚ[Ⲛ̀]ⲔⲀⲦ rather than Ⲁ ⲞⲨⲤⲀⲚⲒⲔⲀⲦ, "mason", for the needful verb is wanting.

ⲀⲈⲘⲦⲞⳅⲈ; cf. Peyr., Sah. ⲢⲈ⳨ⲦⲰⳅⲈ.

ⳡⲱⲤ must have the Art. indef. if the following Ⲉ· is correct. v. *Stern*, §.407.

ⲠⲀⳋⲦⲢⲈ may = "who is my twin-brother", or, more probably, be the name; "my (son, brother, ?) Hatre" (v. l. 4) However I do not know if the Pron. poss. can be thus used.

The division of the next words is unclear. That given seems at variance with the Pron. Ⲃ = ⳨, in l. 4.

l.4 ⲔⲈⲀⲈⲨ[Ⲉ̀] ⲈⳅⳋⲀⲓ, as in N.ᵒ XXVI.

l.5 ⲤⲦⲨ⳨Ⲉ for στοιχεῖν. Its object with Ⲉ·,(ⲈⲞⲨⲀⳋⲀⲐⲞⲚ), as in the Djême texts.

l.7. ⲟⲁⲩ = Sah. ⲥⲟⲟⲩ.

l.8. Perhaps ⲭⲉ ⲉⲓⲥ ⲧⲉⲩ, for Sah. ⲧⲁⲁⲩ; though ϯ in M.E. usually accords with the Boh.; ⲧⲉⲓⲧⲛ.

The Dialect is purely M.E., with the exception of ⲣⲱⲙⲉ, ⲥϩⲁⲓ, ⲉϣⲱⲡⲉ.

XXIX Papyrus.

$11\frac{3}{4} \times 3\frac{3}{4}$ in.

A strip of (now) extremely thin papyrus, the transverse layer having entirely disappeared. The colour is of the lightest; the characters of medium size, slender and comparable both with *Ä.Z.* '85, Taf. I, vi, and *R.V.*, 51.

[?ⲅⲁⲑⲏ ⲙⲉⲛ ϩⲱϥ ⲛⲓⲙ ⲧⲓ[ϣ]ⲓⲛⲓ ⲧⲉ.	ⲛⲡⲁⲟⲥ ⲛⲓⲱⲧ ⲛⲓϭ ⲡϣ
ⲓⲱ[ⲧ ⲉⲧⲧⲁ[ⲓ]ⲏⲟⲩⲧ	15. ⲱϫⲉ̇ⲭⲓ ⲉⲡⲉⲓ . . ⲁⲕⲥⲁ̇ⲧ
ⲉⲓ ⲁⲃ	ⲡⲉⲧⲉⲙⲉⲩⲉ̇ⲡⲩⲝ̄ⲡ̄ⲉ
ⲙⲉ ϩⲉⲛⲥ	ⲡⲣⲟⲥⲕⲩⲛⲓ ⲛⲧⲉⲕⲙ
5. ⲛⲡⲉⲛⲟ̄ⲥ ⲛⲓⲱ[ⲧ	ⲁⲡⲁ ⲙⲉⲗⲁ ⲙⲉ̇ ⲡⲥ̇ⲏ̣ⲏⲡⲉ
ⲣ ⲁⲃⲣⲁⲙ ⲉ̇ⲛⲁⲓ	ⲉⲃⲁⲗ ϩⲓⲧⲛ
ⲧ̣ⲓ ⲧⲁⲙⲁ ⲛⲡⲁⲟ̄ⲥ ⲛⲓⲱⲧ	20. ⲡⲛⲉⲩⲙⲁ
ⲧⲉⲡ ⲙⲉⲛ ⲧⲁⲥⲱⲛⲓ ⲁ	ⲛ̣ⲑⲁⲛⲁⲥⲓⲟⲥ
ⲧⲉⲥⲕⲟⲩⲛϣⲏⲏⲗⲓ ⲛⲉⲓ ⲥ	ⲛⲉⲥⲛⲏⲟ̣ⲩ̣
10. ⲕⲥⲁⲟⲩⲛ ⲁⲛⲧⲱⲓϭ ⲣⲁϩⲩ	ⲭ
ⲉⲧⲃⲏⲧⲥ ⲛⲕⲉⲥⲁⲡ ⲭⲉ ⲧⲉ	ⲕ. ⲉⲃⲁ[ⲗ]ϩ
ⲉⲗⲡⲁⲅⲁⲑⲟⲛ ⲥϩⲉⲓ ⲛⲡⲗⲛ[ⲁ̣	25. ⲩⲛ
ⲛⲃⲥⲩⲛⲁⲅⲉ ⲛⲙⲁⲩ ϣⲁ	ⲁⲅⲓ.ⲡ

The margin remains above l.1 and to the left of ll. 17-19.

It can be gathered that the writer addresses a superior (ll. 2, 7) whose sister and her daughter he also greets (ll. 8, 9) and whom he begs to write to "Apa —?" (l. 12.) Greetings are sent to "Apa Mela and the rest (of the brethren)" (ll. 17, 18,) and "(peace or a blessing) from (God to thee)" (l. 19; cf. ad Nº XII".) ll. 21-26 may be a post-script.

l.9. ⲕⲟⲩⲛϣⲏⲏⲗⲓ; v. ad Nº XVI⁴.

ll.10.14. ⲕ̣ may be ⲕⲓ; both equally unintelligible to me.

l.18. ⲙⲉⲗⲁ? = Mélas.

The Dialect is M.E.

XXX Papyrus. 5½ × 5 in.

Thin material and very light colour. The character shows frequent ligatures, very similar to those of R.V,51. The margins remain at top, bottom and upon the left side.

sic + ϩϵM ΠΛϵN ΠΝΟΫ Νϲῳ[ΑΡϵΠ ϫ.

ϫϵΙ ΤϵΚΜϵΤϪΛϵΙϹ ΝϹΑΝ ϵΤΤΑΙΗΟΫ

ϵΠΑΡΘϵΝⲰϹ ΤϵΛϵΒ ϵϪΙΝ ΟΥΚΟΥ[Ι ϲῳΑ ΟΥΝΑϭ ΜϵΝϵ]

ϹΑ Νϵ̣Ι ̣ΤΙΤΑΜΑ ΜΑΚ ϫϵ Λ ΝΑϹ̇

5. ΡΙΑ ΚϵϵΥ ϩΟΥΝ ΤϵΚΛϵϹΙΑ Λῖ ϩϵ

ΤΙΟΥ ΜϵΝΗΥ ΤΟΥΚϪϩΙ ΛϵΒ Μϵ ϩϵ

ϪΥⲰ ϩϵΙ ⲇ̣ⲓ̅ ⲇ̅ ϩϵΝϵΟΥ ΝϵΡΠ ΛΟΥϵΙΝ

ΤϵΚΛϵϹΙΑ ϭϵΠῳΙΝΙ ΤϵΚ̇

ΑΠⲰΚΡΗϹ ΤΑΙΤΟΥ Τ̇ΙΡΗ[Ν]Η Νϵ̣Κ ϫ.

l.2. [ΟΥ]ϫϵΙ, with the ligature (traced) 𝔛𝔶 (also l.l. 4,7.)

l.l.2,3. Perhaps [Μϵ ΠϹῳΟΥΛϩ ϵϩΟΥΝ ΝΝ]ϵΠΑΡΘϵΝⲰϹ, o͞r, ΠϵΚϹῳΟΥΛϩ....ϵ[Μ̅] ΠΑΡΘϵΝⲰϹ. Some such masc. word is required by ΤϵΛϵΒ. Whether the reference is to a congregation of Nuns can not be decided.

ϵϪΙΝ; v. ad. N° XIII⁵.

ΚϵϵΥ; v. ad. N° XXII, Ver.⁵.

ϵΚΛϵϹΙΑ; presumably for ἐκκλησία, as in Berl., P. 3267, Ν̅ϩΟΥΝ ΤϵΚΛΗϹΙΑ, and N° XXVIII.

l.6. ΜϵΝΗΥ; v. ad. N° XIX⁷.

ΤΟΥΚΑ ΤϩΙ ΛϵΒ ?= Sah. Ν̅ΤΟΥΚΑ ΤϩΗ ϵΡΟϤ. But this does not assist trans-lation.

l.7. "And here are 4 double-kerameion (v. Wilcken in N° XLV, Rec!.) jars of wine." For ⲇⲓⲓ̅, v. A.Z. '78, 70, ΤΙΠΛΗ =? διπλῆ, a wine measure (Stern) also ib., 75, ΔΙΔΙΠΛΑ.

ϩϵΝϵΟΥ ? for Sah. ϩΝΑΑΥ. Cf. R.V, 32, ϩΝϵΥ.

ΛΟΥϵΙΝ, φορτίον. If so, something must be supplied before it; perhaps a second Π.

l.8. ϭϵΠῳΙΝΙ; v. ad. N° XVI".

l.9. ΑΠⲰΚΡΗϹ could be read ΑΠⲰΚΡΙϹ. Cf. R.I, 24, V, 55, ΑΠΟΚΡΙϹ = ἀπόκρισις.

ΤΑΙΤΟΥ; usually ΤϵΙΤΟΥ = Sah. ΤΑΑΥ.

Verso; † ϹΥΝ̄---?, in a different hand and in the reverse direction.

The Dialect is M.E.

_____

XXXI Papyrus. 5 × 4½ in.

The bottom corner of a letter, written upon thin, light-coloured papyrus, in a

clear character, free from ligatures. κ is (traced) Ⲕ and ⲍ, Ⲍ . ⲙ and ⲛ
are very ambiguous. For ⳉ, v. p. 27. There are traces of lines above l. 1.

ⲧⲁⲙⲟⲓ ⲭⲉⲃⲏⲣ ⲡⲉ ⲡⲉⲥⲇⲟⲙ

ⲕⲟⲥⲧⲁⲛⲧⲛⲟⲥ ⲧⲉϥⲛⲁⲇⲥ

ⲕⲉⲗⲉⲃⲓ ⲥⳉⲏ ⲡⲉⲕ

ⲧⲁⲃⲟⲣϥ ⲙⲁⲥ ⳉⲁ

5.   ⲛ̄ⲥⲁ ⲟⲩⲟⲛ ⲛⲓⲃ

ⲭⲁⲓ ⳉⲉⲙ ⲡⲟ̄ⲥ

+

l. 1. ⲭⲉⲃⲏⲣ = ? ﻞﺒﺣ . Cf. R. V, 38, ⲭⲉⲡⲓⲣ.
From ⲡⲉⲥ- it would seem that a woman's property is in question.
l. 2. The last letter is not ⲉ.
l. 3. ⲕⲉⲗⲉⲃⲓ; for κελεύειν.
ⲥⳉⲏⲧ; ? for the Qualit. ⲥⳉⲏⲟⲩⲧ. The ⲧ has the form ⲧ.
l. 4. ⲃⲟⲣϥ; possibly for ⲟⲩⲟⲣⲡ. Cf. R. V, 41, 42, ⲃⲟⲣⲡ.

The interest of this fragt. lies in its use of ⳉ. There are no M.E. forms;
ⳉⲟⲙⲧ might be held Boheiric.

———————

XXXII Parchment. (v. Nº XXXIII.) $2\frac{1}{2} \times 2\frac{3}{4}$ in.
Very mutilated and brittle. The disconnected letters above the text
and the nature of the text itself give the impression of a mere writing
-exercise. The other face bears Nº XXXIII. The character is uncial and
similar to that of Ciasca, Sacr. Bibl. Frag. I, pll. X, XI, XVII; Hyv., Alb. IX (Br. M.), XI.*

ⲟ̇ⲙ ⳋ ⲭⲯⲓⲕⲍ

ⲭⲫ ⲫ ⲟⲙ ⲡⲣⲁⲛ ⲫ

ⲌⲌ ⲌⲌ ⲭ ⲯ ⲍ ⲯ ⲟ ⲫ

ⳉ

ⳋ ⲥⲩ̇ⲛ ⲟⲙ ⲡⲣⲁⲛ ⲙⲟ̄ⲥ [ⲓⲥ] ⲡ

ⲭⲥ ⲡⲉⲛⲛⲟⲩⲧⲉ ⲟ̇ⲓⲟⲩⲥⲟⲡ

ⲟ̇ⲛ ⲟⲩⲛⲟϭ ⲛⲡⲁⲣⲟⲩ

ⲉⲟⲩ ? ⲛⲟⲩⲧ̇ⲓ

l. 1. ⲥⲩ̇ⲛ ⲟⲙ ⲡⲣⲁⲛ ; v. ad Nº XV'. A rare formula in these letters. It occurs
      (without ⲥⲩ̇ⲛ) in Boh. texts, e.g. Nº XXXIX, Hyv., Alb. XXI.

———————————————————

* Two of these are dated; Hyv., Alb. IX, where the colophon (only!) gives A.D. 1006, and
ib. X = Ciasc. XI, where C. reads A.D. 803, Hyv. (whose facsimile justifies him) A.D. 1003.

l.3. ΠΑΡΟΥ[ϹΙΑ] *hardly seems appropriate; but I see no alternative.*

The presence of ϩ, *even among the letters of less common use, is remark-able where the text is clearly Sah. Its form (v. p. 27,) may be classed with that in Hyv., Alb. XIX (1st script,) A.D. 962.*

XXXIII *Parchment.* $2\frac{1}{2} \times 2\frac{3}{4}$ *in.*

The same leaf as N° XXII. The character is almost identical.

ϯ ϹΥⲚ̄ Ⲛ̄ϢⲞⲢⲠ̄ ⲚϨⲰⲂ

ⲚⲒⲘ ⲦⲒϹϨⲀⲒ ⲀⲨⲰ ϯ

ϢⲒⲚⲈⲒ ⲈⲠⲞⲨⲬⲀⲒ Ⲛ̄ⲠⲀ

ⲘⲈⲢⲒⲦ ⲚⲈⲒⲰⲦ?ⲀⲒ

5.   ⲞⲨⲬⲀⲒ Ⲛ̄ⲞⲨⲞⲚ ⲚⲒⲘ

?ϯⲘ̄ⲦⲞⲚ Ⲙ̄ⲠⲈⲔⲀ̄

[Ⲣ]ⲒⲞⲚ Ⲙ̄ⲠⲚ̄Ⲁ̄?ⲈⲪⲎ

ⲦⲈⲔⲘⲚ̄ϯϯ

l.4. The missing letter seems to have been Ⲛ *or* Υ. Ⲕ *could scarcely be read and is improbable.*

l.6. Perhaps there was nothing before ϯ. *For this phrase, v. ad N° XII?.*

The Dialect is Sahidic.

XXXIV *Papyrus.* $3\frac{1}{2} \times 7\frac{1}{2}$ *in.*

Coarse papyrus of grey-brown colour. The character is regular and much like that of N° XIV (pl. 3). There are margins at the top and on the right.

Recto: ϨⲀⲘϢ[Ⲉ̇]...ⲢⲰⲘⲈ ⲠⲈ Ⲛ̄ⲀϹΥϹⲦⲢⲞⲫⲞϹ Ⲛ̄ϥ̇ⲚⲞⲒ Ⲛ̄

ⲤⲢ̄ⲂⲈ Ⲉ..ⲰⲰⲖⲈ ϨⲀⲦⲎⲔ ϯϨ̇ⲒϹⲈ ⲚⲀⲔ ⲀⲘⲞⲨ ⲈⲠⲘⲞ

ⲤⲞⲔ ⲘⲚ [ⲖⲈ]ϨⲰⲚⲈ ⲘⲚ̄ ⲦⲀⲚⲰϢⲎ ⲐⲈ ⲞⲨⲚ Ⲛ̄ⲦⲀⲒ

Ⲛ̄ⲤⲀⲖⲒⲖ ϪⲈ̄ Ⲛ̄ⲅ̄ϹⲞⲞⲨⲚ ⲀⲚ ϪⲈ ϥⲢⲞⲨ Ⲕ̄ⲤⲞⲞⲨⲚ ⲄⲀⲢ

5.   ⲰⲘⲚ̄ ⲘⲘⲀⲨ [Ⲛ̄Ⲥ]ⲀⲂⲖⲖⲀϥ̈ ⲀⲨⲰ ⲀⲚⲒ ⲠⲔⲀⲆⲞⲨϹ Ⲛ̄ϨⲞ

Verso: ϯ ⲦⲀⲀϹ ⲚⲠⲈⲚⲤⲞⲚ [Ⲙ̄]Ⲙ[ⲀⲒⲚ]ⲞⲨ[ⲦⲈ] ϥⲉ.

l.1. Before ⲢⲰⲘⲈ *one could read a* Υ; "*he is a careless man, he knows* not how to ___?" This seems to refer to a Carpenter.

l.2. †ⲦⳒⲤⲈ ꝛc. "Give thyself the trouble to come to the monastery(?)"; lit., "trouble thyself, come."

l.3. Possibly [ⲡⲉⲗⲟⲓ]ⲥⲟⲕ, for which v. ad Nº XLV, Ver.²⁵. In that text the two fol-
-lowing places likewise occur.

ⲗⲉⳡⲱⲛⲉ, Illahun; cf. R. II,58, ⲗⲓⳡⲱⲛⲉ; A.Z. '85, 30, ⲗⲉⳡⲱⲛⲏ (Nº III⁵, sic original)
Nº XLV, Rec.⁷, Ver.¹⁵; Append., P. Bodl., Rec.¹³,¹⁴, ⲗⲉⳡⲱⲛⲓ.

ⲦⲀⲛⲱϣⲏ is found Nº XLV, Rec.¹, Nº XLVI (perhaps), also Greek in Denkschr.
(Wien) XXXVII, 103, ⲇⲣⲱϫⲏ. I have no identification to suggest.

ⲑⲉ; for Ⲛⲑⲉ, "Like, therefore, as I have ___?"

l.4. ⲟⲁⲗⲓⲗ; Peyr., "Water-wheel."
"He knows not what he is doing. For thou knowest ___?

l.5. " ___? there except him. And bring the jar (κάδος) of ___?"

The Dialect is Sah.,— a fact to be noted when considering the localities
mentioned.

———————————

XXXV *Papyrus.* 3½ × 4½ in.

A very fine, light-coloured fragt. The character has few ligatures,
except in l.5. ⲙ inclines to the Greek form. There are margins at the
top and on the right side. Some fibres remaining below, show traces
of writing. There has been also a line (? address) on the back.

ⲉⲓϣⲟⲟⲡ ⳓⲚ ⲡⲥⲀⲂⲈⲦ ⲟⲚ ⲡⲧⲟϣ ⲙ̄

[ⳓⲏ]ⲅⲟⲩⲙⲉⲛ[ⲟⲥ] ⲙ̄ⲡⲙⲟⲚⲀⲤⲦⲏⲣⲓⲟⲛ

ⳇ ⲚⳡⲟⲗⲟⲕⲟⲦⲦⲓⲛⲟⲥ ⲉⳡⲟⲩⲛ

ⲉⲓⲟⲩ . . ⲚⲅⲉⲦⲚⳡⲀⲦⲓⲱⲤⲩⲛⲏ

5.   ⲕⲀⲓⲇⲉⳡ ⲓⲛⲀ⫽ †

l.1. "(I, N.N.,) dwelling at Psabet, in the Nome of ___?"

ⲡⲥⲀⲂⲈⲦ; "The Wall" (So Isaiah XXXVI, 11; Méms. de l'Inst. égypt. II, ii.) It recurs
Nᵒˢ XLV, Ver., XLVI. I take it to be the "Safet," so frequent in Mid. Egypt.
Write "Nehia Safet" (Ibn Rudwan in Quatrem., Méms., I, 393,) cf.
نهيا صفط (Abdellatif, ed. de Sacy, 675.) "El Safet" (Descript. de l'Ég.) is
8 kil. S.W. of Feshn. Perhaps the varying orthography points to an
Egyptian word; cf. Abdellat., صفط; Descript., سفط; Recencemt., سفس.

ⲡⲧⲟϣ ⲙ̄. Among the Mid. Egyptian Nomes our alternatives — owing to the
ⲙ̄ (for Ⲛ·),— are ⲡⲉⲙϫⲉ, ⲡⲓⲀⲙ and ⲙⲉϭⲓ (v. the list in Champol., l'Ég.
sous les Phar. I, 372.)

l.3. The sum ended probably with ϩ̄.

ϩΟⲗΟΚΟΤΤΙΝΟⲥ is a Sah. (or Greek) form.

The payment is to be made "into," ⲉϩΟⲨⲚ, some place (as, e.g., *A.Z. '91, 21*). For the person paid has rather Ⲛ̄; e.g., *A.Z. '91, 14*, ⲦΙ--ⲚⲠⲀⲢⲬⲰⲚ; *Br. m̄.* *Pap. XL*, ⲀⲔϯⲞⲨϩⲀⲗⲀΚΟΤΙⲚΟⲥ ⲚⲀⲓ; *Revill., A. et C. ϥ̄ⲑ*, ⲦΙ--ⲚⲦⲈⳅⲞⲨⲥΙⲀ.

l.4. Ends with a Greek word which I cannot identify. It seems like *ἀϲτιοσύνη (?? "debt")*. Its Prefix may be Ⲛ̄ⲦⲈ ⲦⲚ̄ or Ⲛ̄ ⲦⲈⲦⲚ̄.

l.5. This and N° XLIII are the only dated frags. in the collection. Here it can be gathered merely that the year was the 13th, 14th or 15th of an Indiction.

The Dialect is purely Sahidic.

XXXVI Papyrus. $3 \times 5\frac{3}{4}$ in.

Very fine, brown material. The character is not unlike that of N° XIV *(pl. 3)*. All lines, except *l.4*, are incomplete. *l.5* was not the last.

Recto: [ϯ ϩⲉ ⲠⲗⲈⲚ ⲈⲠⲚΟⲨⲦΙ Ⲛ]ϭⲨⲀⲢⲈⲠ ⲀⲚⲀⲔ ⲦⲈ ⲠΙⲗⲰⲦΙ ⳙ ⲤΙⲤΙⲚⲚ[Ⲁ]
          ⲄⲈ]ΟⲢⲄΙ ΚⲀⲦⲀ ·ⲉ, ⲈⲦⲤΙⲦΙⲰϩΙ ⲠⲈ ⲂΙⲦⲀⲀ
          Ⲛ̄ ⳙ ⳯ⲀΙⳙΟⲨⲚ ⲦⲀΙⲦⲰⲦ ⳙⲈ
              (space)   ϧ ψⲀⲦΙ (space)
          5.   ⲚⲚ·ϭ̄ ⲚⲦⲈⲚⲦⲰⲦ

Verso: (in the reverse direction; very faint;)
              ϯ ⲦⲀⲀⲥ ⲀⲢ?⫽

l.1. ⲠΙⲗⲰⲦΙ. The preceding ⲦⲈ is quite certain and is either an error, for ⲠⲈ, which the formula requires, or ⲠΙⲗⲰⲦΙ is fem. Cf. *Parthey*, Φιλῶτος *(genit.) fem.*; but *Zoega, 64*, ⲠΙⲗΟⲦΟⲥ m., and (perhaps) *Berl., P. 3248*, ⲠⲈⲗΟⲐⲈ m. Besides, I do not know that ⲩⲓος can, in such cases, = "daughter".

ⲤΙⲤΙⲚⲚ[Ⲁ]; Cf. *Pape, 1400*, Σισιννᾶς, Σισίνης ⲧⲉ., *Wien. Stud. '86, 216*, Σισίννιῳ. The ending is uncertain.

l.2. ΚⲀⲦⲀ ⲧⲉ.; "to the amount of (?) 5½ solidi (?) for the sown field. They have been paid to (me?)." For the sum, v. ad N° XXIII[7].

ⲂΙⲦⲀⲀⲦ = Sah. ⲈϥⲈΙ ⲈⲦΟΟⲦ·, "come to hand"; v. *A.Z. '84, 157*; *ib. '85, 37*; *Berl., P. 5561*. The Prefix is masc. sing. presumably on account of νομισμάτ-ιον or of ϩΟⲗΟΚΟⲦⲦΙⲚΟⲥ.

l.3. ⳙⲀΙⳙΟⲨⲚ = ⲟⲗⲟⲁⲟⲗⲟ. It occurs *R. 1, 16, 65; V, 53*.

ⲦⲀΙⲦⲰⲦ ⳙⲈ; also in N° XXXVII and *A.Z. '91, 4*. It seems to be Perf. II, 1 sing.

and to mean, "I have agreed with him," or it may be the Relat. Perf II. In l.5, "we are agreed."

l.4. ⲯⲁⲧⲓ; Cf. Revill., A. et C., ⲡ̄ⲏ, Ä.Z. '84, 155, ⲯⲁⲧⲏ m., ib., 157, ⲡⲉⲥⲁⲧⲉ m.

l.5. (traced);   ↗ ⲥⲯ̄ ⲫⲫ

The Dialect is M.E.

XXXVII. Papyrus.   10 × 4½ in.

The material is thin and light coloured; the character, irregular and resembling both № XXVIII (pl. 1) and Ä.Z. '35, Taf. I, 1. On the back are remnants of an Arabic text. Above l. 1 is a margin, 4 in. wide. There are traces of lines below l. 9.

Recto:

    [Ϯ ϩⲉ ⲡⲗⲉⲛ ⲉ̄ⲡⲛⲟⲩⲧⲓ ⲛⲱⲁⲣⲉⲡ ⲛϩⲱⲃ
    [ⲛⲓⲙ ⲁⲛ]ⲁⲕ ⲡⲉ ⲧⲁⲛⲓⲉⲗ ⲧⲁⲓⲥϭⲉⲓ
      ⲅⲉⲱⲣⲅⲓ ⲧⲁⲓⲧⲱⲧ ⲙⲉ
      ϩⲗⲩ ⲛⲓⲙ ϩⲟⲩⲛ ⲡⲥⲁⲃ
  5.   ⲉⲗ ⲥⲁⲃⲁⲗ ⲡ.ϩ̇ⲙⲗⲉ
      ⲁⲡⲁ ⲓⲥⲁⲕ ϩⲗⲑⲏⲓ ⲧⲁ̇ⲩ
      ϩⲉⲛ ⲛⲏⲃ ⲕⲁⲧⲁ ⲑⲏ ⲛ
      ⲟ̇ⲁⲛ ⲡⲉⲃ ϣⲉⲣⲉ ⲃⲁⲗ
      ⲙ̇ⲉⲩⲥ ⲁϩⲗ ⲱ ⲕⲁⲧⲟ̇ⲩ

Verso: ⲡⲓⲧⲁⲅⲓ ⲡⲟ̇ⲁⲣⲁ̇

Recto: l. 3 may have begun with ⲧⲁⲓ ϣⲓⲛⲓ.
ⲧⲁⲓⲧⲱⲧ ⲙⲉ; v. № XXXVI.
l. 5. The missing letter was a narrow one; perhaps ⲓ. What follows it is not ⲁ.

Verso: ⲡⲓⲧⲁⲅⲓ ? = Πιττακός or Πιττάκιον, rather than πιττάκιον, "note." Yet cf. Recueil VI, 66, where the Verso of a Contract bears ⲡⲉⲭⲁⲣⲧ ⲓⲥⲁⲗⲕ (i.e., the writer).
ⲡⲟ̇ⲁⲣⲁ[ⲙⲉⲩⲥ], κεραμεύς perhaps. Cf. № LIII, ⲟⲁⲣⲁⲙ[ⲉ̇]ⲟⲥ.

The Dialect is M.E.

XXXVIII Papyrus.   2¾ × 5¾ in.

Fragt. of light-brown colour. The character — cf. that of № XVI (pl. 4), — is clear; it shows the ligature ЄI, as in *R. V, 51.*

Recto: [† ϩⲉ ⲡⲗⲉⲛ ⲙⲡⲛⲟⲩϯ ⲛϣⲁⲣⲡ ⲛϩⲱⲃ ⲛⲓⲙ ⲧⲓⲥϩⲉⲓ ⲉⲓⲱⲓ

        [ⲛⲓ ⲧⲉ.   ]ⲉⲧⲧ ⲉⲣⲉ ⲛⲉⲕⲥⲙⲟⲩ ⲉⲧⲟⲩⲉⲉⲃ

Verso: † ⲥⲩ ⲥⲩ ⲧⲁⲗⲥ ⲡⲁⲓⲱ ⲉⲧⲟⲩⲉⲉⲃ ⲡⲁⲡⲁ

               ⲥⲁⲙⲡⲁ ⲗⲉ ⲡⲛⲟⲩϯ ⲕⲉⲉⲃ

Recto: l.1. ⲉⲓⲱⲓⲛⲓ ; the Particip. is remarkable and seems like a confu-
-ion of the two formula, ⲧⲓ ⲁⲩⲱ ⲧⲓ , and ⲉⲓ ⲉⲓ .
l.2. ⲉⲧⲧ ; v. ad Nº XIV¹.
ⲉⲣⲉ ; one may continue the sentence ; ϣⲱⲡⲓ ⲛⲉⲙⲏⲓ, or ⲉϫⲱⲓ.
Verso: ⲥⲩ for ⲥⲩⲛ, as in *R. V, 54, A.Z. 85, 31,* and Nº XLVIII.
ⲥⲁⲙⲡⲁ ; cf. *Denkschr. (Wien)* XXXVII,129,165,172, ⲟⲇⲙⲃⲁ ; 152, ⲟⲇⲙⲃⲁϛ. One
might however read ⲥⲁⲙⲡⲁⲗⲉ , and cf. the street in Arsinoe,
ψανπαλλιου (so Wessely, *Denkschr. (Wien)* XXXVII, 111 ; but Wilcken,
Zeitschr. d. Ges. f. Erdk. XXII, 80, ψαππαλιου.)
[ⲉ]ⲗⲉ ⲡⲛⲟⲩϯ ⲕⲉⲉⲃ might be ⲥⲁⲙⲡⲁⲗⲉ ⲡⲛⲟⲩϭ ⲓⲡⲉⲥⲃ, for ⲡⲛⲟϭ ⲙⲡⲣⲉⲥⲃ
[ⲩⲧⲉⲣⲟⲥ], though this is improbable. For ⲡⲛⲟⲩϯ ⲕⲉⲉⲃ, v. Nº XV.

The Dialect is M.E.

———

XXXIX Papyrus.   2½ × 8 in.
This has properly no place here, though it is difficult to say to what
class of document it belongs. The irregular and disconnected appearance
of the words upon the Verso suggests that the leaf was used for a writ-
-ing exercise. The fine Boh. uncials employed — cf. *Hyv., Alb.* XXVII, A.D.
957, — may be a further proof of this. The material is of coarse fibre,
the ink quite brown. Above l.1. is a wide margin.
Recto: † ϩⲉⲛ ⲫⲣⲁⲛ ⲙⲡⲉⲛⲟⲥ [ⲓⲏⲥ ⲡⲭⲥ ⲡⲉⲛⲁⲗⲩⲑⲓ[ⲛⲟⲥ]
               ⫽ⲛⲟⲥ ⲛⲛⲟⲩϯ ϩⲉⲛ ⲟⲩ

Verso: ⫽ⲟⲩⲣⲱⲙⲓ ⲉⲡⲉϥⲣⲁⲛ ⲡ⫽

The form of the ϩ, which gives the fragment its interest, is reproduced
on p. 27.
The introductory phrase may be compared with those of *Hyv., Alb.* XXI
and *Mém. de la Miss.*, I, 395.

The Dialect is Boheiric.

XL Papyrus. $4\frac{3}{4} \times 2\frac{1}{2}$ in.

This fragt. has an appearance almost identical with that of N° XIV (pl. 3).
The material is somewhat coarse.

M̊·N +ϢΙN̊Ι   έι ΑΙϬΙΠΕΚϢΙΝΙ Λ

? ΜΠΝ̄Τ̄Κ̄   ϩΚ· ΕΜΑ+ ώΛΙΕ

ϩΜ Π̄Ο̄Ϲ ΤΙΡ̣ΗΝΙ   ΟΥΩΜ· ϩΙ ϹΩ

ΕΝΙϩΛΟΥ ΤΗΡΟ̊Υ   10. ΝΑΚ ΑΜΟΥ ΤΕΝ

5. Κ̄Λ· ΜΠΛΑΠΙ Λ   ϹΙΛ· ΛΥΩ ϢΛΝ

Κ· ϬΙΠΛ· ϢΙΝΙ Μ   ΛΟϹ ΛΥΩ

l.4. ΝΙϩΛΟΥ ΤΗΡΟΥ may belong to the formula <u>R</u>.V,45, ΕΡΕ ΠϪΟΕΙϹ ϩΑΡΕϩ
ΕΝΕϩΟΟΥ ΤΗΡΟΥ ΕΝΕΚΩΝϩ.

l.6. ϬΙΠΛ· ϢΙΝΙ; "make enquiries after me". Probably the dot is of no value.
For the phrase, v. ad N° XVI".

The Dialect is M.E.

XLI Papyrus. $5 \times 9\frac{1}{2}$ in.

Very mutilated; the gap in l.l. 1,2 seems due to burning. The char-
-acter is large and irregular, not unlike that of N° XXVIII (pl. 1.)
Upon the back was a rectangular figure (? cf. N° XIV, Verso, pl. 3.) now
faded, and, perhaps, traces of some large Arabic letters,— all being
burned, as it seems, upon the papyrus. There are remnants of at
least two lines above l.1. Dots represent the missing letters.

ΕΠΝΟΥΤΙ . . . . Β. ϹΑΒΤ ΕΠΑΥ

ΛΟΥ ΝΙΩΤ. . . . . ΝΈΒΟΥΝΕΥ ϩΕ ΠΑΥ

?   ΤΕΒ ΠΕΤΑΒΕΙ ΠΕΚϹΑΙ ΝΕΙ

ΛΙϢΗΝΙ ΕΤΒΗ ΑΠΟΥ ΙΑϩΙΕ ΑΎϪΕΝΟΥΙ ϪΕ ΑΒϱΙ ΜΑΡΑΙΑ ΝΙ

5. ? ΜΑΒΗ ΝΕΚ ϬΕΠΕΒϢΗΝΙ ϩΑΛΛΙ ΚΑΛΩϹ

? ΝΕΚϹΑΝ ΚΑΛΩϹ ΠΟΥϪ̊ . . ϩΕΝ . . ᾹΡ̄Ϲ

l.3. ϹΑΙ = ϹϩΑΙ . Cf. <u>R</u>.V,38, ϹΕΙ .

l.4. ΑΠΟΥ ΙΑϩΙΕ = رجل يشهد . ΙΑϩΙΕ occurs <u>R</u>.V,43,61.
ϪΕΝΟΥΙ ; v. ad N° XXII¹². Perhaps here; "they told me that he had found
Maria."

l.5. ϬΕΠΕΒϢΗΝΙ ; v. ad N° XVI".

l.6. ΟΥϪ[ΕΙ] can hardly be read. I can not complete the second gap.
This line ends the text.

The orthography of this text is remarkably irregular. The Dialect is M.E.

XLII Papyrus. $1\frac{5}{8}$ × $5\frac{7}{8}$ in.

A strip of yellow-gray papyrus. On the back (i.e., the Recto,) there are vestiges of writing.

᷍† ⲧⲉⲓⲥ ⲡⲉⲛⲥⲁⲛ ⲙⲁⲓⲛⲟⲩⲧⲉ (space) ⲟⲓⲉ̄ⲧⲛ ⲭⲁⲏⲗ ?

ⲕⲓⲣⲓ ⲧⲓⲁⲕⲟⲩ ⲭⲁⲏⲗ

To be noted are (1) the elision of (ⲉ =) ⲙ̄ before ⲡⲉⲛ·, of ⲙ̄· before ⲙⲁⲓ·; (2) the ligature ⲟⲧ, in ⲟⲓⲉⲧⲛ; (3) the form ⲧⲓⲁⲕⲟⲩ, for ⲇⲓⲁⲕⲱⲛ, which recurs in Nᵒˢ XLIV and L.

The Dialect is M.E.

XLIII Papyrus. $3\frac{7}{8}$ × $4\frac{1}{4}$ in.

The nature of this fragt. is such as to separate it from the other letters. It is one of those rare texts which employ the Greek instead of the Coptic character. The peculiar Coptic sounds are represented by combinations of the Greek letters. For the similar fragts., v. R. II, 56, 57; V. 41. The character has some resemblance to the cursive colophon, Hyv., Alb. XXI, (written not before A.D. 884), but also to the Greek numerals in Denkschr. (Wien) XXXIII, Taf. 1 (about A.D. 725.) l.1 was the first, but l.8 was not the last.

Recto:

    [ⲟ]ⲩⲧⳗⲁⳍ ⲉⲩⲛⲁⲙⲉ̄ⲣⲓ[ⲧ]

    ⲓⲉˀⲟⲉⲓⲗⲓⲙⲉⲥ ⳍ ⲗⲉϥⲥⲟⲛ

    [ⲟ̄ⲇ]ϫⲓ ⲉⲩⲡⲉⲕⲭⲁⲓ ⲁⲓⲉⲅⲣⲱⲥⲓ ⲧ

    ⲛ̄ⲏⲉ ⳍ ⲧⲓⳗⲉⲛⲁⲣⲓⲕⲓ ⲉⲣⲟⲕ

  5. ⲛⲁⲣⲁⳗⲁ̀ ⲉⲣⲟⲕˀ ⲉⲧⲙⲙⲟⲓ

    ⲡⲓⲡⲓ ⲟⳗⲉⲛⲓ ⲉⲛ

    ⲟⳗⲱⲡⲓ ⲧⲏⲣⲫ ⳍ ⲁⲧ

    ⲓⲁⲕⲏ ⲙⲉⲕⲉⲓⲣⲓ ⲁ̀ⲃ

(Tracing.)

Verso: (in same direction; same ink);
　　1. ⲉⲓⲥ ⲕ̅ⲩ̅ ⲁⲣ̄ ⲯⲱⲧⲓ

Cf. ⲁⲣ̄, N° XII and ⲯⲟⲧⲉ, masc., Zoega, 237.
　　　(in reverse direction; different ink);
　　2. Large, illegible character.
　　3. (Copt.) [ⲙ]ⲁⲣⲕⲟⲥ ⲡϣⲉⲛⲡⲁⲃⲁⲙ ?
　　4.　　　　ⲥⲟⲩ ⲕ̄ⲅ̄ ⲛ̄ⲛ ⲓⲇ

Recto: l.1. ⲟⲩⲇⲁⲓ = ⲟⲩⲇⲁⲓ.
l.3. Cf. R. II, 56, ⲁⲉⲓⲉⲣⲇⲉⲭⲓ ⲛⲉⲕⲥⲩⲇⲉⲓ, and N° XXVII.
ⲉⲣⲩⲁⲉⲓ = ⲣⲱⲉⲓⲛ; v. N° XXVII.
l.4. ⲧⲍⲉⲛⲁⲣⲓⲕⲓ = ⲭⲉⲛⲁⲣⲓⲕⲓ. Its object with ⲉ̄, as Sirach, XIV, 2, XXIX, 6.
l.6. = ⲡⲓⲏⲓ (R. II, 56, ⲏⲉⲓ,) ϣⲓⲛⲓ ⲉⲛ·. Cf. R. V, 27, ⲛⲁⲡⲁⲏⲓ ⲧⲏⲣⲟⲩ ϣⲓⲛⲉ ⲉⲣⲟⲕ.
l.7. ⲟⲍⲱⲡⲓ = ⲱϣⲱⲡⲓ.
l.8. ? ⲕⲩⲣⲓⲁⲕⲏ. But I can not divide the words with certainty.
Verso: l.1. The address of the above letter.
ll. 2–4. The remains of a former text.
l.3. The second name is not ⲃⲁⲙⲟⲩⲗ.
l.4. Before ⲓⲇ may be ⲛⲙ, ⲛⲡ or ⲛⲁⲓ.

The occurrence of ⲋ, l.2, and of ⲋ = ⲁⲩⲱ, places our fragt. beside that in R. II, 57; while, like R. II, 56 and the curs. colophon, Hyv. Alb. XXXII, it employs the ⲭ also. The former letter represents presumably Sah. Boh. ⲋ, the latter, Boh. ⲏ, as in the R. fragts. As in these, too, ⲫ = ⲋ, and ⲟⲍ = ⲱ. As to ⲧⲍ = ⲝ (so Krall in his fragts.) I am not clear. The ⲧ elsewhere has a quite different appearance. Final ⲓ after a vowel, is here -ⲓ, not -ⲉⲓ, as in R. II, 56.

The Dialect, as in the other fragts., is Boh., though ⲙⲉⲣⲓⲧ is a Sah. form.

LISTS and ACCOUNTS.

XLIV Papyrus.　　　　　　　　　　$12\frac{3}{8} \times 8\frac{1}{2}$ in.
Tough material, of yellow-gray colour. The character is large and bold, without any ligatures. The numerals have Greek forms. The colon separates — not always consistently, — the various items.

Missing letters, where calculable, are represented by dots.

ⳁ ⲡⲗⲟⲅⲟⲥ ⲉⲛⲉⲭⲱⲱⲙⲓ · ⲛⲧⲁⲛⲥ†ⲥⲓ ⲙⲙⲁⲩ · ⲟⲩⲧⲣⲉⲟⲩⲁⲅⲅⲉⲗⲓ
   ⲟⲛ ⲙⲡⲉⲧⲁⲗⲟⲛ · ⲁϩⲁ ⲕⲉ ⲍ̄ ⲙⲡⲉⲧⲁⲗⲟⲛ · ⲟⲩⲕⲁⲧⲁⲙⲁⲑⲉⲟⲥ · ⲗⲟⲩⲕⲁⲥ
   ⲃ̄ · ⲙⲁⲣⲕⲟⲥ · ⲟⲩⲡⲣⲁⳉⲓⲥ ⲙⲡⲉⲧⲁⲗⲟⲛ · ⲁϩⲁ ⲕⲉⲟⲩⲉ · ⲟⲩⲁⲡⲟⲥⲧⲟⲗⲟⲥ
   ⲙⲡⲉⲧⲁⲗⲟⲛ · ⲁϩⲁ ⲕⲉⲟⲩⲉ ⲛⲁⲧⲡⲉⲧⲁⲗⲟⲛ · ⲛⲉⲕⲁⲑⲟⲗⲓⲕⲟ[ⲛ] ⲃ̄
5. ⲛⲉⲟⲩⲉⲛⲓⲛ · ⲟⲩⲧⲣⲁⲉⲩⲁⲅⲅⲉⲗⲓⲟⲛ · ⲙⲡⲉⲧⲁⲗⲟⲛ · ⲥⲁϩ̣ . . . . ⲗ
   ⲙⲁⲑⲉⲟⲥ ⲃ̄ · ⲕⲉⲧⲣⲉⲩⲁⲅⲅⲉⲗⲓⲟⲛ · ⲛⲁⲧⲡⲉⲧⲁⲗⲟⲛ · ⲓⲱⲁ̅ⲛ̅ⲏⲥ · ⲗⲟⲩ
   ⲕⲁⲥ · ⲙⲁⲣⲕⲟⲥ · ⲟⲩⲯⲁⲗⲧⲏⲣ[ⲓⲟⲛ] · ⲛⲟⲩⲉⲛⲓⲛ · ⲯⲁⲗⲧⲏⲣⲓⲟⲛ ⲍ̄
   ⲛⲉⲭⲱⲱⲙⲓ ⲛⲱⲱ ⲙⲙⲉϥⲣⲱⲛ ⲓⲃ̄ · ⲛⲁⲡⲉⲥ · ⲛⲉⲃ[ⲉⲣ]ⲓ ⲓⲑ̄ ·
      (space) ⲙⲁⲑⲉⲟ[ⲥ] ⲉ̄ ⲛⲟⲩⲉⲛⲓⲛ · ⲙⲁⲑⲉⲟⲥ ⫽
10. ⲛⲉϩⲗⲟⲩ ⲙⲡⲁⲓⲁⲕⲟⲩ ⲡⲉⲧⲣⲟⲥ ⲉⲗ . . ⲥ̣ϩⲟⲩ · ⲉⲭⲱϥ ·
   ⲛⲉⲭⲱⲱⲙⲓ ⲛⲭⲁⲣⲧⲏⲥ · ⲝ̄ⲑ̄ · [ⲁ]ϩⲁ ⲕ̄[ⲉ] ⲓⲥ̄ ⲛⲁⲡⲉⲥ · ⲛⲉⲭⲱ
   [ⲱ]ⲙⲓ ⲛⲅⲣⲁⲫⲏ ⲭⲁⲣⲧⲏⲥ ⲉ̄ · ⲙⲉϥⲣⲱⲛ ⲓ̄ · ⲛⲉⲕⲁⲛⲕⲟⲩⲓ
   ⲛⲭⲱⲱⲙⲓ · ⲙⲙⲉϥⲣⲱⲛ · ⲛⲁⲡⲉⲥ ⲯ̅ ⲭⲁⲣⲧⲏⲥ ⲍ̄ ⲛⲁⲡⲉⲥ
   ⲟⲩⲙⲓⲥ†ⲕⲟⲛ ⲛⲟⲩⲉⲛⲓⲛ · ⲁϩⲁ ⲟⲩ . . . . . ⲟ̇ⲗ · ⲛⲁⲡⲉⲥ ⲟⲩⲁⲛ†ⲫⲁⲛⲁⲣⲓ
15. ?ⳉ]ⲱⲱⲙⲓ ? ⲫⲁⲛⲧⲁⲩ ⲛⲉⲩ . . . . . . ⲙⲡ ⲥⲟⲩⲣⲓⲁⲛⲏ ⲉ̄
   ? ϩⲟⲩⲛ · ?   ⲡⲉⲧⲁ]ⲗⲟⲛ ? ⲗⲟ]ⲩⲕⲁⲥ ⲙⲛ ⲓⲱⲁⲛⲛⲏⲥ
   ?   ⲟⲥ · ⲃ̄   ?   ⲁⲡⲟ ?   ⲕ]ⲁⲑⲟⲗⲓⲕⲟⲛ ⲃ̄ ·
   ?   ⲃ̄ · ⲉ ?   ⲉⲩⲉⲙ ?   (space)

This is the inventory of part of a library; many points regarding it are unclear to me. The only other which I know is that published Recueil XI, 133 (Bouriant).

The books are not arranged according to their contents, but the text seems to be divided at *ll.* 9, 10. Reckoning only those where the reading is certain, we can count 105 separate works; (Bouriant's list contains eighty;) they are :—

Old Testament (*ll.* 7, 12): Psalters, 8; "The Scripture" (i.e., rest of O.T.) 16.

New Testament (*ll.* 1–7, 9, 16, 17): S. Matthew, 8+?; S. Mark, 2; S. Luke, 4; S. John, 2; "Parts of Gospels", 6; Acts, 2; S. Paul's Epistles, 2; Catholic Epistles, 4.

Liturgical (*ll.* 8, 14): Lectionaries, 44; "Mysticon", 1; Antiphonarium, 1.

Homilies (? *l.* 15): Works (?) of Syrianus, 5.

Of these, 1 Psalter, 5 copies of S. Matthew, 2 of the Cath. Epistles, and the "Mysticon" are in Greek.

l. 1. "The list of the books which we have furnished with ⲥⲟⲩⲅⲙⲁⳃ."

ⲥ†ⲥⲓ = ⲥⲟⲩⳉⲉⲓⲛ, *interpungere*, "to add diacritical marks to a M.S." One of the examples given by *Sophocles* refers to clause-division, the other to metrical punctuation.

ΤΡΕΟΥΑΓΓΕΛΙΟΝ, *l.5,* ΤΡΑΕΥ˙, *l.6,* ΤΡΕΥ˙, *for* ΤΡΕΕΥ˙.

l.l.2–5. ΠΕΤΑΛΟΝ, *l.l.4,6,* ΑΤΠΕΤΑΛΟΝ. πέταλον *is properly a plant's leaf.*
Prof. Wilcken *suggests that these two words may here distinguish the*
Codex *and the* Volumen. *In no instance have we any indication*
of material. The word, as here used, is of no small interest.

l.3. ΑΠΟϹΤΟΛΟϹ; *i.e., S. Paul. (Correct* Bouriant, *N°s 18,19,20.) His Epistles*
usually form but a single book.

l.5. ΟΥΕΝΙΝ; *for Sah.* ΟΥΕΙΝΙΝ, ΟΥΕΕΙΝΙΝ.

ϹΑϩ ⳤc. *I can not fill this gap. It appears to have contained a verb.*

l.8. ϪΩΩΜΙ Ν⳽ⲱϫ. *This term designates three patristic works — narratives*
and anecdotes,— in Hyv. Alb. *XXIV, XXVII, XXVIII. Lectionaries are, in* B'*s*
list, called ΚΑΤΑΜΕΡΟϹ.

ΜΕϬΡⲰΝ = μέμβρανον. *In* B'*s list the form is* ΜΕΒϼ, ΜΕΒΡΑΝΟΝ. *The* Μ
has fallen out as in ΜΗϬΙ, ΜΕΒΕ, Μέμφις, ΚΟϹΤΑΝΤΙΝΕ, Κωνσταντῖ-
νος, ΠΑΤⲰΚΡΑΤⲰΡ (Revill., A. et C. ōz,) παντοκράτωρ, ⳤc.

ΑΠΕϹ = Sah. ΑΠΑϹ. *It occurs four times (l.l. 8,11,13,14). Here it is opposed,*
as in N° XLVII, to ΒΕΡΙ. *Both terms are used of parchment, as well*
as of papyrus, and ΒΕΡΙ *therefore can not be the* (قرطاس)جدبد
by which Prof. Karabacek *understands "paper" (R. IV, 82)* *

l.10. The papyrus is very imperfect here. The lacuna could hold three letters.
The ⲧ *suggests* ⲡⲟⲥ, *but it hardly fits the requirements. The last*
letter of the group was taller than ⲧ.

l.12. ϪⲰⲰⲙⲓ ⲚⲄⲢⲀⲫⲎ; *probably copies of the Old Testament.*

ΚΑΝΚΟΥΙ; *v. ad N^o XVI⁴.*

l.14. ⲘⲓⲤ†ⲓⲔⲟⲚ; *cf.* τὰ μυστικά = μυστήρια, *the sacraments (Sophocl.)*
The lacuna might contain [ⲞⲨⲰⲚϩ ⲈΒ], *"Apocalypse", yet there is hardly*
sufficient space.

ΑΝⲦⲪΑΝΑΡⲓ = Ἀντιφονάριον (Lagarde, Orientalia I, 43, انبفاس.)

l.15. ⲠⲤⲞⲨⲢⲓΑⲚⲎ. *As it stands, this recalls the Neo-platonist,* Syrianus
(† circ. A.D. 400). *But it is, I think, more probably a mistake for*
ϹΕⲨⲎΡⲓΑⲚⲟϹ *of Gabala, whose sermons were in use in Egypt (v.*
Zoega, 120, Woide, Append., [23] ; *and cf.* Migne, Patrol. Gr., LXV.)
Wüstenfeld (Synax., 15) *transcribes his name "*Surianus*", but*
Malan (Calender, Sept. 4,) "Severianus". *(v. also* Ludolf, Ad. Hist.
Æth. Com., 390.)

The Dialect is M.E. *Note the Art. plur.* ⲚⲈ˙ (l.l. 1,4,8,10–12). *Cf. l.5,* ⲚⲈⲞⲨⲈⲚⲓⲚ,
l.8, ⲚⲈΒⲈΡⲓ.

---

* قرطاس جدبد *may be the* ΧΑΡΤΗϹ ΓΕΝΟΥΡ[ΓΟϹ] *which, in* Bouriant's *list, is*
opposed to ΧΑΡΤΗϹ ΠΑΛΛΙΟΝ *or to* ΧΑΡΤΗϹ *alone.*

XLV Papyrus.

$13\tfrac{1}{4} \times 10\tfrac{5}{8}$ in.

Thick but brittle papyrus, of dark yellow-brown colour. The character is not large and has similarity, in some features, with that of Nº XIV (pl. 3). M has a tendency toward the tailed, Greek form; B may be compared with that of Nº XXVI (v. p. 46); λι is a ligature. Dates and numerals are in the Greek script. For the latter, v. "Führer"-Rainer, 1. Th., Taf. V. The margin at the top remains, but the bottom and lower half of the text on one side are lost. I designate the four columns as Ra, Rb, Va and Vb.

Recto

(τυβ) [ΟΥ]ΕΝΑΒΕΡ ΠΕϬΜΗ ΝΤΑΝΩϨΗ δίᵐ α		μ̅ κϝ ΠΛΕϨΤΕ ΠΟΥΛΕΙΑ δίπ	
ϭΙΜΑΧΙ α		ΝΕΑΜΑΥΕΙ ΕʹΠΟΥϹΙϟ αϟ	
ΧΑΗΛ ΠΚΕΡΑΜΕΩϹ α		φαμ̅ α ΠΑΠΑ ΠΕΤΡΟϹ ΠΕϬΜΗ α	
ιϝ ΝΕΡΩΜΕ ΠΑΛΚΕΕΙΩ ϝ		φλ ΜΩΗϹΗϹ ΠΕϬΜΗ α	
5. ιϛ ΟΜ̅ ΝΕΡΩΜΕ ΠΑΛΚΕΕΙΩ β		ΧΑΗΛ ΠΚΕΡΑΜΕΩϲ[ϲ] α 5.	
ιη ΟΜ̅ ΝΕΡΩΜΕ ΠΑΛΚΕΕΙΩ βϟ		ϣΕΝΟΫ ΠΚΕΡΑΜΕΩϲ α	
ιθ [ΟΜ̅ ΝΕΡΩ]ΜΕ ΠΑΛΚΕ[ΕΙΩ] ?		ΒΑϹΙΛΕ ΠΑΛΕϨΩΝΙ β	
? [ΟΜ̅ ΝΕΡΩΜΕ ΠΑΛΚΕ]Ε[Ι]Ω ?ϟ		ΠΕΤΡ̅ ϛ ΚΟϹΜ ΝΕϬΜΑΥΕΙ β	
? [Ο]Μ̅ ΝΕΡΩΜΕ[ΠΑΛ]ΚΕΕΙΩ ?		ΑΒΡΑϨΑΜ ΠΑΜΗ ϛ	
10. ? ΝΕϹΙΜΑΧ[Ι] ΠΩΝΕ β		ε ΚΟϹΜΑ ΠΑΜΡΗ α 10.	
κϝ̅ ΝΕΡΕΜϹΙΜΙϹΤΟΥϹ αϟ		ϛ ΠΔΙΑΚΟⁿΝ ϜΕΩΡϜΙ φαμ̅ ?	
ΜΑΚΑΡΙ ΠΑΤΟΥΤΩΝ α		ΕϨΟΥΝ̅ ϨΑΚ..Ε α	
κϛ ΝΕΡΩΜΕ ΠΑΛΚΕΕΙΩ α		ΠΔΙΑΚΟΝ [Α̅Π̅]Α ΙΟΥΛΙ α	
ΠΑϹΟΝ ΚΛΟΥϬΑ ϨΑ ΜΩϹ̅Ηϲ α		ιη ΝΕΡΩΜΕ [ΠΑ]ΛΚΕΕΙΩ αϟ	
15. [Ν]ΕϹΙΜΑΧΙ ΠΩΝΕ γ		ΝΕϨΑΚΕ ΝΤΑΥϨΑΚΕ β 15.	
[ΠΔ]ΙΑΚΩΝ ϜΕΩΡϜ[Ι] φΑΜϢΗ α		[ΝΕ]ϨΡΑΜΚΥΛΙ ΝϢΑΡΕ α	
ᾱΜϢΗ ΕΥ..ΕϢΗ α		κ Π..Δ.ΥΝ ΑΠΑ ΜΕΡΔΕΙ ι	
? ? α		ΝΕϨΑΜϢΗ ΠΜΟΥΝ̅ α	
Ν[ΕΡΩ]ΜΕ[Π]ΑΛΚ[ΕΕ]ΙΩ β		ΝΕΟΥΙΕ ΕΥΚΑΡΕ ϹΙΜ αϟ	
20. [ΝΕϹΙΜΑΧ[Ι]] ΠΩΝΕ α		ΝΕϨΑΜΚΥΛΙ ΠΙΑΜ θ 20.	
ΛΕ..ΠΟΥ..ΡΕ αϟ		φαμ̅ γ ΠΕΤΡΟϹ ΠΜΑΝϬΑΜΟΥΛ ?	
? ε ? ζ		ΝΕΡΕΜΠΩΛΙϹ ΜΝ̅ΠΝΟΫ ?	
? ε..ϨΕΝΠΕϨ (sic)		ΝΕΡΩΜΕ ΠΑΛΚΕΕΙΩ αϟ	
ΜΟΥϹ α		ΧΑΗΛ ΠΚΕΡΑΜΕΩϲ α	
[ΝΕΡΩΜΕ ΠΑΛΚΕ]ΕΙΩ α		ΝΕΡΕΜϹΙΜΙϹΤΟΥϹ ΕΥ (sic) 25.	
25. ? ε β		ΚΑΡΕ ϹΙΜ αϟ	
? ΕϥΠΑΠΙ α		ΚΟϹΜΑ ΠΑϢΗΝΑΡΩ ϛ	
? ϥϨΕΠΙΦΝΙ α		ΠΕϬϢϢ ΕΠΑΠΑϹ α	
? ΛΙΕΔ αϟ		ΙΩ ΠΑΤΑΝϢΕΕΙ α	
? ΥϹ		ΝΕϬΑΜΟΥΛ ϛ 30.	

30.   ?   ς   α.

            ?   γ

            ?   α

            ?   κοῦ   ς

α fragt.:

        C⸏]Μ⸏]ΧΙ   35.

35. [ΝΕΡⲰΜΕ ΠⲀⲖⲔ[ΕΕⲓⲰ]

                          Verso.

φαρμ̄ ΠⲀⲨⲖ . . . ⲀВⲢⲀⳐⲀΜ	δⲡ̄	β	π̄ ⳑ ιβ	ΕΠΜⲀΝΜΟⲨΕⲓ		?
ιθ [ΝΕΡΕ]Μ̄ΠⲔⲀΝⲰⲀΡΕ		α		ΠⳜΗΝΠΧⲀ . . . ⲚⲀΡⲓ?		α
[ΚΟⳐΜⲀ ΠⲀ]ⳜΗΝⲀΡⲰ		α	ιδ	ΝΕΟⲨⲖⲓΕ		
[ΝΕ]ΡⲰΜΕ ΠⲀⲖⲔΕΕⲓⲰ		ε		ΝΕΡΕΜCⲓΜⲓCΤΟⲨC		β
5. ⲓΟⲨΕ ΝΝΤⲀΒⲰ		ε		ΠⲀⲓⲀⲔΟΝ ⲅΕⲰⲢ̄ ΦⲀΜⲰ[Η]	α	5.
ΕΒⲀΡΜΕCⲓ		?		ΠⲀCΟΝ ΜⲀΡⲔΟC ΝΕⳐⲨΜΕΧ ζ		
[Ν]ΕΟⲨⲖⲓΕ		?		ΦⲰΡΕ ΠⲀⳜⲀΡ?		α
κα ΝΕⲀΜⲦΕⲖⲓ		?		ΕΠΜⲀΝΜΟⲨΕⲓ		β
ΠⲀⲓⲀⲔΟΝ ⲅΕⲰⲢ̄ ΦⲀΜⲰΗ		α	κⳓ	ΟΜ̄ ΠΜⲀΝΜΟⲨΕⲓ		. ζ
10. θΕΟⲀⲢΕ ΠⲖΕⳐΤΕ		ς		ΠΧΟΒΟⲖ ΕΠⳜΕΕⲓ	(sic)	10.
ΟⲨΕΝⲀΒΕΡ ΠΕⳐΜΗ		ς		ΤⲀΚΕΝΗⳜ		ε
ΠⲀⲖ ΗⲖ[ⲓ]Ⲁ ⳐⲨΜΕΧ		θ	κⳓ	ΕΠΜⲀΝΜΟⲨΕⲓ		α
κε ΠΕΤΡΟC [Π]ΕⳐΜΗ ΠCⲀΒΕΤ		α	π̄ⲁ δ	ΠⳜΗΝⲀCΕΜ		β
ΜⲰΗCΗC ΠΟΜΗ ΝΕΠⲓΦ̄		α		ΕΠ[Μ]ⲀΝΜΟ[Ⲩ]Εⲓ	ας	
15. ΝΕΡΕⳐⲖⲀΕⲓC ΕΤΧⲰ̣Ⳝⲟⲡ.		γ		ⲖΕⳐⲰΝⲓ		? 15.
ΕΠΜⲀΝΜΟⲨΕⲓ		κ		ΧⲀΗⲖ ΠⲔΕΡⲀΜΕⲰC		?
[Ν]ΕΟⲨⲓΕ ΠⲰⲀΠⲀΡΜΟⲨΤΕ		ας		ΝΕΟⲨⲖⲓΕ ΠCⲀΒΕΤ		?
κη ΝΕΡⲰΜΕ ΠⲀⲖⲔΕΕⲓⲰ		κα	κⳓ ⲀΠⲀ ⲓΟⲨⲖⲓ ΠⲀΠCⲀΒΕΤ		?
ΠⲀⲓ]ⲀⲔΟΝ [Ⲅ]ΕⲰⲢ̄ ΦⲀΜⲰΗ		ς		ΝΕⲓⲀΤΕ . . ΕΜΟⲨΝ?		?
20. ΝΕⲀΜⲀⲨΕⲓ		ς		(sic) ΝΤⲀⲨΒⲓΤΟⲨ		? 20.
[Π]ⲀCΟΝ ΜⲀΡⲔ ⳐⲨΜΕΧ		γ		ΚΟCΜⲀ ?		?
κθ [ΝΕΡ]ⲰΜΕ ΠⲀⲖⲔΕΕⲓⲰ		κε		ⲚΕΒⲓΤ ?		?
ΝΕΡΕΜΠⲔΟⲨΝⳜⲀΡΕ		α		ΝΕΡⲰΜ[Ε ΠⲀⲖⲔΕΕⲓⲰ]		?
ⲀⲔⲀⲨ ΠⲀΡΗCⲓΜⲀΧⲓ		ας	λ	ΟⲨΕ[ΝⲀΒΕΡ ?		?
25. π̄ γ ΝΕⳐⲀΜⲔⲨⲖⲓ ΠΕⲖⳐⲓCⲰⲔ		γς	επγ β ΠⲀⲨⲖ ?		? 25.
ε ΕΠΜⲀΝΜΟⲨΕⲓ		α	γ ΠΜⲀΝ ?		?
ια Π[ΕΤΡΟ]C ⲥ ΚΟCΜⲀ ΝΕⳐΜⲀⲨ		α	ΝΕ ?		?
? ΕΤ		δ	ΝΕⳐ ?		?
?		δ			
30. ? ⲢΕ		γ			30.

α fragt.:

        ?

        ⲀⲨΕⲓ

    [ΝΕΡΕΜ]ΠⲰⲖⲓC Μ̄Π̄ΠΝΟⲨ[ⳑ]

The measure at the head of the numerical columns is δι (so Wilcken, "sicher", from a tracing,) i.e. διπλοκεράμιον (v. Nº XXX). The text appears therefore to be a wine-merchant's register of sales; though, if so, the amounts entered to the ΡΩΜΕ ΠΑΛΚΕΕΙϢ, who, with " Ibn Asem" (Vb 13), were presumably Moslims, are remarkable. In a list R.V, 45. Kraåll reads the measure δι, i.e. ΔΙΠΙ = Sah. ΟΥΟΙΠΕ, modius. The register covers a period of six months; from January till June. The relative amount of business done in the different months can not be ascertained, owing to the lacuna. It will be observed that the quantities supplied vary continually, even when to the same individual. Among the persons named are the following;

Gardeners; Ra 1, Rb 3, 4, 8, Va 11, 13, 14, 27.
Husbandmen; Rb 19, Va 7, 17, Vb 3, 17.
Herdsmen; Rb 2, 9, Va 20.
Camel herd; Rb 21.
Lion herd? (v. below) Va 16, 26, Vb 1, 8, 9, 12, 14.
Carpenters; Ra 16, 17, Rb 11, 18, Va 9, 19, Vb 5.

Potters; Ra 3, Rb 5, 6, 24, Vb 17.
Smiths; Rb 16, 20, Va 25.
Bakers; Rb 10.
Washermen; Rb 1, Va 10.
Watchmen; Va 15.
Messengers; Ra 2, 10, 20, Va 24.

Besides these, various amounts are repeatedly supplied to the ΡΩΜΕ ΠΑΛΚΕΕΙϢ (Ra 4-9, 13, 19, 24, Rb 14, 23, Va 4, 18, 22, Vb 23; v. ad Nº XXIᵢ¹¹²). At Rb 15, two measures are entered to "The shearers who sheared the sheep." (similar, probably, Rb 12.) At Rb 19, 1½ measures to "The peasants while they cut the grass" (similar Rb 25.) "The outlay for the festival of Takenêsh" amounts to five measures, (Vb 10).

Recto: col. a.
l.1. ΤΑΝΩΓΗ; v. Nº XXXIV.
l.2. ϹΙΜΑΧΙ; cf. R. II, 60, 62, ϹΥΜΜΧ, ib. V, 48, ϹΥΜΜΑΧΙ, and Recueil XI, 148, ϹΥΝΜΑΧϢΙ.
l.3. ΚΕΡΑΜΕΩϹ = κεραμεύς, Kircher, Sc. III, القرمى. Cf. Nº LIII, δαραμε-ΟϹ, Append. P. Bodl., Rec. 25, 31, ϲΕΡΑΜΕΟϹ. For -εος = -ευς, v. G. Meyer, Griech. Gram.², §. 119.
l.5. ΟΜ = ὁμοίως. Cf. Nº L, οϗ, Recueil VII, 144, ΟϘ, ib. XI, 133, 134, ΟΜΛϗ, ΟΜΑϗ.
l.10. ΠΩΝΕ. Obviously a place-name; "The Rock". It may be the native name for the Πέτρα which Quatremère, Mém. I, 470, 472 places in the neighbourhood of the Natron Lakes. The (Ε· =) Nº of the genit. has been absorbed in the preceding vowel, as in l.l. Ra 15, Rb 1, 18, 20, Va 13, 17, 25, Vb 10, 17. (But cf. l.l. Ra 1, Rb 16, Va 14.)
l.11. ϹΙΜΙϹΤΟΥϹ; a (Greek?) place-name, as its praeformative shows.
l.12. ΤΟΥΤΩϩ, تطون, a town in the south of the Fayyum. (v. Schwein-

-furth's map, Zeits. d. Ges. f. Erdk., XV; but the Recencement gives two.) This explains the words, hitherto unclear, which end the M.E. text Quatrem., Rech^s, 249; for the writer signs himself "Son of the late Deacon, Apostolos ΝΤΟΥΤⲰΝ Ⲛ̄ΠΙΑΜ."

l. 14. ⲔⲖⲞⲨϬⲀ = ? Γλαῦκος; but unlikely. Nor is ⲘⲰⲤⲎⲤ for ⲘⲰⲎⲤⲎⲤ, which occurs Rb 4, Va 14, probable. ϨⲀ might be "on behalf of", or we might read ⲔⲖⲞⲨϬ ⲀϨⲀ ⲘⲰⲤⲎⲤ.

l. 26. [ⲣ̄]ⲈϤ̄ⲠⲀⲠⲒ; cf. Va 15.

Recto: col. b.

l. 1, and Va 10, ⲖⲈϨⲦⲈ = Sah.* ⲢⲀϨⲦⲈ, the proper representative of Mariette, Mastab. 70, 90, 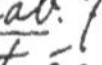, L.D. II, 102, 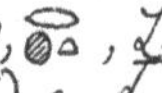. Cf. S. Mark IX, 3 (Mém. de l'Inst. ég., II, ii,) and Fl. Petrie, Hawara, pl. XXII (bottom), ⲖⲈϨⲦ.

ⲠⲞⲨⲖⲈⲒⲆ; also Append., P. Bodl., Rec.[21], ⲠⲞⲨⲖⲈⲒⲦ. It may be compared with several names in Mid. Egypt; Zoega, 24, ⲪⲞⲨⲰⲒⲦ in nome of Ψnes; Abdellat. 685, بوط = Recencem^t; Descript^n, بياض and بويط

l. 2. ⲀⲘⲀⲨⲈⲒ and l. 8, ϬⲘⲀⲨⲈⲒ, = Sah.* ⲀⲘⲞⲞⲨⲈ, *ϬⲘⲞⲞⲨⲈ (v. Stern, §. 214.)

ⲠⲞⲨⲤⲒⲢⲈ; towns of this name occur N° XXIII[7], LII, Append., P. Bodl., Rec. 9, 12, 37, and R. II, 62, 64; V, 31.

l. 4. ⲫⲗ; whether this is ⲠϨⲈⲖ, "the slave" (v. N° XXV), or the abbreviation for Φλαούιος, frequent in the Greek Papyri, I can not determine.

l. 7. ⲖⲈϨⲰⲚⲒ; v. N° XXXIV.

l. 8. ⲔⲞⲤⲘ̄; cf. the abbreviations in N° XIV[9].

l. 12. ⲈϨⲞⲨⲚ = ὑπέρ. v. Append., P. Bodl.

l. 15. ϨⲀⲔⲈ, "Shearer", = Sah. ϨⲰⲔⲈ, ϨⲰⲰⲔⲈ; but the Agent seems always expressed in Sah. by the Relat. ⲈⲦϨⲰⲰⲔⲈ.

l. 16. ϢⲀⲢⲈ; v. ad N° XXII[6]. The localities in Va 2, 23 are presumably not identical with this.

l. 18. ⲘⲞⲨⲚ̄; an abbreviated place-name. I can not identify it.

l. 19, and Va 17, ⲞⲨⲒⲈ is, I suppose, identical with Va 7, Vb 3, 17, ⲞⲨⲀⲒⲈ. The latter would be the legitimate M.E. plur. for Sah. ⲞⲨⲞⲈⲒⲎ, ⲞⲨⲞⲒⲈ (v. Stern, §. 221.)

ⲔⲀⲢⲈ; probably Stat. const. of ⲔⲰⲰⲢⲈ (v. Stern, §. 337), and ⲤⲒⲘ "grass, hay", as e.g. Ps. XXXVII, 2. Yet I can find no example of this verb except applied to cutting down trees or branches. Possibly ⲤⲒⲘ is the sesamum plant, which grows to a few feet in height, and is cultivated for its oil (v. Dulaurier, Journ. As. '43, 448.)

l. 22. recurs V 32 (fragt.). The reading is certain; the mark above Ⲛ (the same as Va 15, ϥ̂,) need not imply abbreviation.

l. 27 ϢⲎⲚⲀⲢⲰ recurs Va 3. Cf. Zoega, 24, ϢⲈⲚⲈⲢⲰ (? in nome of ⲠⲈⲘϪⲈ), Abdellat. and Descript^n, سيررو (in Fayyum); Recencem^t, سنرو

(two in Fayyum); also <u>Champol.</u>, l'Eg. sous les Ph., I, 306, Ψενηρος.

l. 28. ЄΠΑΠΑϹ ?= Ἔπαφος. ΠЄϬⲰϢ is too well established to allow the reading ΠΑΠΑϹ, a frequent name in Egypt.

l. 29. ΤΑΝⲰЄЄΙ; v. ad Nº XXII⁵.

Verso: col. a.

l. 2. ΚΑΝⲰΑΡЄ; cf. l. 23, ΚΟΥΝⲰΑΡЄ. These are probably the same (v. Nº XVI), and appear to be place-names.

ll. 5, 6. ΙΟΥЄ ?= ΙΟΟΥЄ (cf. Peyr., ЄΙⲰΟΥЄ,) plur. of ΙⲰ. For the other words I have no suggestions.

l. 8. ΑΜΤЄⳆΙ. I can not explain this. An error for ΑΜϹΤЄⳆΙ is improb--able, ΑΜ- requiring rather a noun to follow it.

l. 13, and Vᵇ 17, 18, ΠϹΑΒЄΤ; v. Nº XXXV.

l. 14. ЄΠΙΦ; a place-name. The reading is doubtful.

l. 15. ΡЄⳆⳆЄΙϹ; v. Nº XXVI.

l. 16, and l. 26, Vᵇ 1, 8, 9, 12, 14, ΜΟΥЄΙ can not here mean "lion". If it could be shown to mean "wild beast, large game" in general, I would cf. Recueil XI, 148, where (Greek) θηροφύλακες are men-tioned at Achmim. Profr Sayce (Rev. des Éts. grs. '91, 52,) suggests that these huntsmen were employed in stocking a local θηροφυλάκιον.

l. 17. ΠϢⲀΠΑΡΜΟΥΤЄ; ? a place-name; cf. Vᵇ 17. ϢⲀ "festival" is improbable owing to Vᵇ 10, ϢЄЄΙ; nor is ϢⲀΠ, for Sah. ϢⲰΠ "Ἐμπίω", very suggestive.

l. 24. ΑΚΑΥ; this name recurs Nº XLIX. Cf. the frequent ΠΙΑΚΟΥ.
ΑΡΧΗϹΙΜΑΧΙ; v. R. II, 60.

l. 25. ΠЄⳆϬΙϹⲰΚ recurs Append., P. Bodl., Rec.¹⁸, ΠЄⳆϬΙϹΟΟΚ. Cf. Berl. P. 5561, ΠЄⳆϬЄΗϹΙ = Denkschr. (Wien) XXXVII, 107, ΠЄⳆΚЄΗϹΙ; also ib., ΠЄⳆΚ. In Pap. Boulaq II, pl. 4, [hieroglyphs] is a locality in the Fayyum whence Brugsch (Dict. géogr. 197,) derives [Arabic] (v. Abdellat. 686, in Bah--nesa; the Récensem.* gives two in Benisuef.) The names appear to be compounded with those of Sobek and Isis, the grammat--ical relation of their elements being similar to that in the series with ΚЄΡΚЄ· [hieroglyphs] and ΠΙ· [hieroglyphs] (v. Steindorff, Ä. Z. '89, 108.)

Verso: col. b.

l. 7. ΦⲰΡЄ; v. R. II, 60, 62, ΦΟΡЄ.
ϢΑΡ[Є]; probable because of Nº XXII⁶, ϢΑΡЄ.

ll. 10, 11. for Sah. ΠΧΟ ЄΒΟⳆ ЄΠϢΑ ΝΤΑΚЄΝΗϢ. For the Prefᵗ ЄΠ, v. Acts, XXI, 24. In Zoega 540, ΤΑΚΙΝⳆϢ is a hill with a monastery, in or near the Fayyum.

l. 13. = ماقٮ (?) . *Cf. Descriptᵗⁿ* ماقٮ (?) *(in Atfih.)*

l. 18. Perhaps the final word was a distinctive appellation of one of the numerous *Safets (v. Nᵒ XXXV).*

The Dialect here is not wholly M.E. The interchange of ρ and λ is not uniform, neither is that of the vowels λ-ο, ε-λ. The genit. Ñ· is often represented by a vowel only.

———————

XLVI. *Papyrus.*

A. $3\frac{3}{4}$ × $6\frac{3}{4}$ in.
B. $12\frac{3}{4}$ × $6\frac{7}{8}$ in.
C. $7\frac{1}{4}$ × $2\frac{7}{8}$ in.

Fragts. B, C were certainly parts of one document; *fragt. A* probably belonged to them. I can not fit them together, though they must have held, relatively, the positions here given them. The material is of light colour and thick, but soft; the character without ligatures (except ΥΡ in ΚΟΥϨ). λ is angular, as in *Nᵒ XXV;* ϩ has the small projection above, as in *Hyv., Alb. II (both M.SS.).* On the back are traces of a line of large Cufic(?) characters in brown ink. The papyrus was composed of several σελίδϵς; three remain. *Fragt. A* shows an upper margin; *fragt. B,* the complete width. *ll. 7-11* and *29-33* are very illegible.

Fragt. A:

```
       ⳨ ΝⲀϨⲢⲀⲨ ΠϢΗΝ̈ΝⲀϨⲢⲀⲘ ⳽ (space.)
       [ΟΥ]ΕΝⲀϨΕⳑ ΠϢΗΝΝⲀϨⲢⲀⲨ ΠϢΗΝ̇ΤΚΟΥΝϨⲰ ⳽
       [ⲓ̈ΕΡ]ΗΜ[ⲓ̈]ⲀⳜ ⲀΠΟⳑⳑⲰ ΠΕΤΡΕ ⳽ (space.)
       . . . . ΕΜΝⲀΫ⳽Ṁ . . . ΤⲀ̈ⲒΝⲒΝΟΥⲀ̇ ΤⲀⲀΤΟΥ
   5.            ?       .  Ε̇Ρ̇ΓΕⲒ̈ ϨⲒⲰΟ̇Υ ΟΥⲀ̇Ε ⲀΝⲀΝ
                 ?          ?          Ñ⳨ΦⲒⳑⲒⲀ
                                        (space.)
```

Fragt. B: *Fragt. C:*

```
       ⲰⲈⲚ̇        ???ϬΠⲚⲦ           ΝⲀ
       ⲘΟⲚ̇        Γ ? ΝⲦⲘ̄          ϨⲘ
       ?ⲠΘ
   10. Ⲓ̇ΥⲚⲀ̇Ο     (space.)
       Ⲥ̇Ⲓ : ⲘⲚ [Ⲓ̇Ε]ΡΗⲘⲒⲀⳜ : ⲟⲒ̈        
       Π[Ⲁ]ⲒⳑⲒⲔⲟⲚ ⲀⲒ̈ΟΥⳑⲒ : ⲘⲚ λ
       Π?ⲔⲀⲢΠⲀⳜ : ⲘⲚ ΠⲔⲈⲀⲒ̈ΟΥ[ⳑⲒ̇     Ⳝ ΚΟΥϨ
       Ⲓ̇[Ε]ΡΗⲘⲒⲀⳜ ϨⲚⲚ ⲀΠⲀ ⳠⲰⲚ          ΚΟΥϨ
   15.          ΓⲨ ⳧  ΚΟΥϨ ,Ⲃ
```

(space.)

ϯⲩ̈ⲣⲱⲛ:

    ⲛ[ⲓ]ⲗⲁⲙⲙⲱ[ⲛ̄] ⲡⲁⲣⲉⲩ   ⲗⲩ ? ⲱⲱ

    ⲙ[ⲛ̄] ⲃⲓⲕⲧⲱⲣ   ⲕⲟⲩⲃ ⲗⲣⲡⲃ

    ⲛⲉⲛⲧⲁⲩⲙⲉⲅ̇ⲟ̇[ⲩ̇]   ⲛⲱ ⲕⲟⲩⲃ ⲗⲃ

20.   ⲁⲃⲣⲁⲙ : ⲙⲛ ⲓ̈   [ⲁ̄]ⲃⲣⲁⲙ ⲛ̄ⲧⲉϥⲅ̇ⲏ

    (space.) ⲟ̇ⲓⲏ   ⲭ

    ⲛⲉⲕⲟⲩⲓ̈ ⲛ̄ⲧⲁⲩ   ? ⲧ:

(space.)

    ϯⲧⲁⲛⲱϣ̄ⲏ ϩ̈ⲓⲧ[ⲉⲛ   ⲉ ⲕⲟⲩⲃ ⲩ ?

    ⲕⲉⲣⲕⲉⲥⲟⲩϧ ϩ̈[ⲓⲧⲉⲛ

25.   ⲙⲏⲛⲁ : ⲙⲛ ⲛⲁϧ̇[ⲣⲁⲩ   ⲕ]ⲟⲩⲃ   *Fragt. B.*

    ⲁ̈ⲧⲣⲏ ϣ ⲁⲡⲟⲗⲗ[ⲱ   ⲕ]ⲟⲩⲃ ⲭⲓⲁ

                                ϣ ⲕⲉⲣⲁⲙⲓ̈ ⲏ̄:

    (space.)   ⲃⲓⲧⲧⲓⲛⲁ ⲁ

    ϯⲏⲗⲓⲁ ⲡⲁⲣⲉⲩ   ? ϣ ⲕⲟ[ⲩⲃ] ?

30.   ϩ̈ⲁⲧⲣⲏ ⲙ̄ : ⲕⲟⲩ ? ⲟⲩ ?   ⲙⲁ ⲕⲟⲩⲃ ⲃ

    ϯⲡⲁⲡⲁ ⲡⲁⲡⲛⲟⲩϯ[ⲓ:]ⲙ̄ⲛ ⲡⲓⲁⲛⲱ ϩ̈ⲓⲧⲉⲛ ⲁⲡⲁ ⲙⲁ

    ⲕⲁⲣⲓ ?   ⲏⲥ ⲕⲟⲩⲃ   ?ⲇ:

              ⲅⲓ̷ ⲟ̸ ⲟⲙ̇ ϣ̇ ⲕⲟⲩⲃ   ?ⲛⲏ:

    ϯⲁ̈ⲛⲱ ⲛⲉⲛ̄ⲧⲁⲩⲙⲉϧⲟⲩ ϩ̄ⲛ ⲡⲕⲟⲩⲛⲱϩ̇ ⲙⲡⲥⲁⲃⲉⲧ

35.   ⲕⲟⲩⲃ ⲗⲃ ϣ ⲉ̇ ? ⲧ

    ϣ ⲕⲉⲣⲁⲙⲓⲁ : ⲏ : ϣ ⲃⲓⲧⲧⲓⲛⲁ : ⲁ

We have here — at least in fragts. B,C, — various accounts, apparently as to the sale of wine (or oil). The paragraphs, with their initial ϯ, showed the names of the customers and the amounts supplied in each case. The total supplied to a whole group is twice given (ll. 15, 33).

l.l. 1, 2. ⲟϫⲏⲛⲛ· = Sah. ⲟϫⲉⲛ·, ⲟϫⲛ̄·. v. *Steindorf*, Ä.Z. '90, 51; *Stern*, §. 72.

ⲁϭⲣⲁⲙ ; cf. l. 20, ⲁⲃⲣⲁⲙ.

ⲟⲩⲉⲛⲁϧⲉⲗ ; v. *Berl*. P. 5556, ⲟⲩⲉⲛⲁϧⲗ ; *R*. 1, 65, ⲟⲩⲉⲛⲁⲃⲉⲗ. The following names may be those of his father and grandfather.

ⲧⲕⲟⲩⲛϩⲱ ; a new name.

l. 5. ⲟⲩⲁ̈[ⲉ] ⲁⲛⲁⲛ. If this could be read, it would imply that the writer spoke on behalf of the above-named persons.

l. 12. ⲁ̈ⲓ̈ⲟⲩⲗⲓ = Ἰούλιος.

ⲕⲁⲣⲡⲁⲥ ; apparently a proper name.

ⲕⲟⲩⲃ ; v. ad Nº XI[a].

l. 14. ϩⲛⲛ = ϩⲛ̄ ; v. *Stern*, §. 72.

l. 15 and l. 33, ⲅⲓ̷ ⲟ̸ = γίνεται ὁμοῦ ; v. *Stern*, Ä.Z. '84, 150 (cf. Ä.Z. '71, 23,) *Wessely Denkschr. (Wien)* XXXVII, 217 and *Append*, P. Bodl., Rec. 44-46.

l. 17, and *l. 29*, ΠΑΡΕΥ. This name recurs <u>R.</u> V. 53. One might read, ΝΙΛΑΜΜΩ (cf. ΝΙΛΑΜΟΥ <u>R.</u> 1, 65,) S ΠΑΡΕΥ.

l. 19. v. *l. 34*; both are very indistinct.

l. 23. ΤΑΝ ΩℲΗ; v. N° XXXIV.

ϨΙΤΕΝ designates either the consignee, the supplies for ΤΑΝ ΩℲΗ &c. being addressed "to the care of" N.N. (v. *l. 31*), or the person from whom the orders were received. In the former case, cf. ϨΙΤℲΝ, ϨΙΤΟΟΤ· in the Contracts, e. g. Revill., A. et C., ΝΔ, ϬΔ &c.

l. 24. ΚΕΡΚΕϹΟΥΧ; v. <u>A.Z.</u> '83, 162, <u>Denkschr.</u> (<u>Wien</u>) XXXVII, 105, Κερκεσούχων ὄρος.

l. 27. ΚΕΡΑΜΙ[Δ], κεράμια. This measure, with ΒΙΤΤΙΝΔ, is twice added, after the sum of the ΚΟΥϨ has been given.

l. 28. ΒΙΤΤΙΝΔ; possibly = πυτίνη, πιτύνη, a flask covered with plaited work (Stephanus.)

l. 31. ΠΙΑΝΩ. If this is a locality,— more probably a person,— it may be a survival of the ἄνω and κάτω, designating certain subdivisions of the nome (v. Wilcken, Observationes, 25.)

The Dialect is M.E. The resemblance between the proper-names here and in the Memphit. Passports (v. <u>A.Z.</u> '85, 145,) is, no doubt, accidental.

XLVII Papyrus. (v. N° XXI.)   4¼ × 5½ in.

The character of the two texts is very similar, though this is the smaller. The present text follows N° XXI immediately, and is continued upon the Verso in the reverse direction. Some lines between ll. 2; 3 are lost. *l. 12* was the last.

Recto: ϬΛΥΝΕ ˙γ   (space.)
                ΛΛΜΕϢΜΕΛΛΙ ά ΟΥϢΑΡ ΜΗϤΡ ά
Verso: ΟΥϨΩΒϹ ΕϤΧΙϹΤΑΥΡΟϹ   ?
                ΟΥΕΡϢΩΝ ΕϤΧΙϹΤΑΥΡΟϹ   ά
      5.   ΟΥΜΑΠΠΑ ℲΑΛΛΑΕΙ ΝΝΟϬ ά
                ΟΥ[Ϣ]ΤΗΝ ΝℲωκ̈ϟΟϹ   ά
                ΟΥΠΛΛΙΝ ΕΜΕ..ξΙ ΕϤΧΙϹΤΑΥΡΟ[Ϲ] ?
                ΚΑΙΚΟΥΙ ΜΑΠΠΑ ℲΑΛΛΑΝΙ   β
                ΚΑΤΑΠΗΤΗϹ ΟΥΒΕΡΙ ΚΑΙ ΑΠΕϹ ᾱρ̈?
      10.   ϢΤΗΝ ΝΚΛΗΡΙΚΟϹ ά ΚΑΙ ΠΛΛΙΝ
                ΟΥΛΠΠΟΥΜΙϹ   ά
                ΟΥΕ̇ΛΛΕ ΕϤΕϢΕ̇ΕΝΕΛΔ ά

This is a list of clothing, or rather, of ecclesiastical vestments &c.

l.1. = σάκκοι; v. Nº XXII¹², but here it is probably the sleeveless vestment, described by Du Fresne, s.v.

l.2. = ἀλὼ, a mantle, or Dozy, Suppl.ᵗ I, 788, carpet. The absence of the Coptic article is noticeable.

ϣⲁⲣ[ⲙ]ⲙⲏϧ, "a skin of parchment", or, "a dress(?) of skin" (v. Peyr., ϣⲁⲣ.)

l.3. "A covering having the cross (upon it)." The phrase ⲉϥϫⲓⲥⲧⲁⲩⲣⲟⲥ is perhaps of similar meaning to πολυσταύριον (v. Du Fresne, s.v.)

l.5. "A large blue-green coverlet or napkin." ⲙⲁⲡⲡⲁ = خنج, which Tuki, Euchol. II, VII, explains by إبل. v. also Kircher, &c. 118, 121.

ⲅⲁⲗⲗⲁⲉⲓ; probably = l.6, ⲅⲁⲗⲗⲁⲛⲓ. Cf. R. IV, 141, where ⲕⲁⲗⲗⲁⲛⲓ, καλλάϊνος is similarly used.

l.6. ⲅⲱⲕⲅⲟⲥ ? = ⲕⲉⲕⲕⲟⲥ.

l.7. "A ⸺? pallium with the cross (upon it)." ⲡⲁⲗⲗⲓⲛ = παλλίον = Kircher, &c. 120, البلس.

l.8. ⲕⲟⲩⲓ; either for ⲕⲟⲟⲩⲉ or ⲕⲁⲓⲕⲟⲩⲓ = Stern, §. 270, ⲕⲉⲕⲁⲩⲉⲓ.

l.9. = ? ⲕⲁⲧⲁⲡⲉⲧⲁⲥⲙⲁ, the covering for the altar, sacraments, &c., Du Fresne. ⲃⲉⲣⲓ, ⲁⲡⲉⲥ; v. ad Nº XLIV⁸.

l.11. ⲁⲡⲡⲟⲩⲙⲓⲥ; v. Kircher, &c. 117, ⲁⲡⲟⲙⲓⲥ = ἐπωμίς, shoulder cloth, or stole, Du Fresne.

l.12. I can not divide the words here.

The Dialect can scarcely be determined. ϭⲁⲩⲛⲉ and ⲁⲡⲉⲥ are M.E., ⲛⲟϭ is Sahidic.

———

XLVIII Papyrus.   5½ × 10 in.
A much injured fragt. of light colour. The character is large and has features in common both with that of Nº XIV (pl. 3) and of Ä. Z. '85, Taf. I, 1. Margins remain at the top, bottom and left side. ll. 3, 4 are very illegible.

⳨ ⲥⲩ ⲡⲗⲱⲕⲉⲥ ⲛⲉⲥⲟ[̄ ̄]ⲩⲁ
ⲟⲩϣⲏ ⲙⲉ ϣⲙ
ⲛ̅ϩⲁⲉⲓ ϣⲉ ⲙⲉⲃⲧ
ⲛⲉⲣⲧⲁⲃⁱ̈ ⲙⲁϩ ϣⲁⲙⲧⲓ ⲥⲧⲁⲩⲓⲟⲩⲙⲁ
5.   ⲧⲁⲗⲟⲩ̅ⲗⲁⲡ ⲉⲧⲉ ϣⲏⲡⲁⲣⲙⲏⲅ (space.)
ⲙⲏⲧⲁ ⲛⲉⲣⲧⲁⲃ ⲡⲁϫⲗⲉⲓ ⲓⲱⲧ ⲙⲗⲁⲃ ⲙⲉ ⲥⲛⲉ̅ⲩ
ⲛⲉⲣⲧⲁⲃ

A note of quantities of wine; cf. Nº XLIX. I can make little of it.

l.1. ⲗⲱⲕⲉⲥ = λόγος . Cf. M.S. Bodl., a(P.)3, ⲕⲟⲕⲉⲥ = κόκκος, A.Z. 92, 39, ⲉⲓⲧⲏⲥ
   = εῖδος .

l.2. ⲱH =? Sah. ⲱⲓ.

l.5. may begin with an Arabic word.

l.6. ⲙⲏⲧⲁ may be "eleven".

The Dialect is M.E.

———

XLIX. Papyrus. $9\frac{5}{8}$ × $5\frac{1}{2}$ in.

Light-coloured papyrus. The text occupied only part of it, a wide margin above and the strips of fibre below being blank. The character is large; ⲕ resembles that reproduced on p. 52 and ⲙ has a Boh. form. On the back are remnants of a letter which was the earlier text.

          ⳨ ⲡⲗⲟⲅⲟⲥ ⲛⲡⲉⲥⲟⲩⲟ
          ⲁⲕⲁⲩ ⲡⲁⲙⲏ . . . ⲱⲡⲓ   ⲁ
          ⲡⲁⲩⲗⲓ ⲙⲁⲛⲉⲙⲁⲥⲓ ?
          ⲋⲟⲩⲙⲓⲥⲓ ⲙ . . ⲛⲉⲙⲁⲥ[ⲓ]   ⲁ
     5.   ⲡϣⲉⲛⲡⲁⲡⲁ[ⲥ]   ⲓⲁ
          ⲡⲁⲥⲟⲛ ⲁ . . . ⲕⲩⲣ

Likewise a list of the amounts of corn (sold?).

l.2. ⲁⲕⲁⲩ ; v. ad No XLV, Ver.²⁴   The end of the line is quite illegible.

l.3. "Paulos the calf-herd". Cf. Stern, §.173, ⲙⲁⲛⲉⲣⲓⲣ, ⲙⲁⲛⲉⲃⲁⲁⲙⲡⲉ.
     Note the absence of the Article.

l.4. ⲋⲟⲩⲙⲓⲥⲓ ; cf. "Führer"–Rainer, I.Th., 12, "Homeise", a man's name.

The Dialect, with which the character may be said to agree, has Boh. features.

———

L. Papyrus. $8\frac{1}{2}$ × $6\frac{1}{2}$ in.

Fine material, medium colour. The character is free from ligatures. The numerals have Greek forms. The question of "Recto" and "Verso" is decided on the supposition that, above Rec. *l.1*, the name of some measure is lost which should account for the ὁμοίως.

Recto: | ? ο̄μ | ?Ν̄ ζ |
KOCMΑ ο̄μ | ρ̅ι̅ |
?IWM ο̄μ (sic) | αδ |
? ο̄μ | α̅μ̅ |
5. M ο̄μ | αδ ξβ |
ο̄μ | ω̅ν̄ |
ο̄μ | ρ̅ζ̅ |
ΠΙΛΟθ[I] ο̄μ | ππ̅ |
(space) |
KOM.λλδΗ ο̄μ (sic) | μϛ̅ |
10. KOCMΑ EϤΤΑλε πωοι πωλπ |
EI ? ρ̅ι̅ζ̅ π ? ωM ρ̅κ̅γ̅ |
? ΝλϤ ξβ |
?

Verso: (margin, 4½ in.)
ΠΙΛΟθΙ ϬΙΜΗ
EϤΤΙ ΠΑΠΑ ΠΙΛΟθ̄ ο̄μ λ
ΠΑΙΚΟΥ KOCMΑ ο̄μ ι̅ (sic)
ΠΙϤΗΥ ο̄μ (sic)
ΠΙΛΟθΙ ϬΟΠ.Ιω ο̄μ κ̅γ̅ 5.
ΔλΕΙΔ ΒΤΑλΑ ΕΠΙλω̄θΙ ο̄μ μ̅
ϧΟΥΜ[I]C †Ι ΠΙΔΙΑΚΟΥ ?
ΔλΕΙΔ ?

It can not be ascertained to what material this account refers. It was, at all events, dealt with in large quantities.
Recto: ll.3,5. I suppose the 2ⁿᵈ numeral to =200. (v. Wilcken, Observationes, 49.)
l.10. EϤΤΑλε; cf. Ver. 6. Perhaps it means "deliver goods"; v. the example in R.V,44.
ΠωΟΙ; as a name this occurs Zoega 221. Cf. ΠΙωΟΙ, ib. 30.
Verso: l.1. ϬΙΜΗ for ϬΕΜΗ = Sah. ϬΜΕ.
l.4. ΠΙϤΗΥ; v. ad N°XII¹.
l.7. ϧΟΥΜΙC; cf. Zoega 105, ϧωΜΙC, masc.
ΔΙΑΚΟΥ; v. N°XLII.

EΒΤΑλΑ and ϬΙΜΗ indicate the M.E. Dialect.

LI. Papyrus.

A, 8½ × 3½ in.
B, 4½ × 6¼ in.

Two fragts. of the same text. The material is fine and light-coloured, the character regular and somewhat like that of N°XIV (pl. 3.) Fragt. A shows the top and left-hand margins; fragt. B, that on the right hand.

Fragt. A: † πλοκ̄ ΝΕ
Ν̄ΤΑ ϬΑΜΟΥλ̇
ΝΑΠΕϧ CΑ
ΜΠΜΟΝΑCΤ̄ΗΡΙ
5. ΧΙλΙΑ ωΚΤ̄ω

Fragt. B: Υ ϧ Ν̄ ? Κ̇Ο
ΝΠCΑΒΕΤ ΕΙΚΟCΙ
Ε̄ΞΗΚΟΝΤΑ ΓΙ
ω̄ξ CΕΧΡΕωCϤ
ΤΤΑ Ν̄ΤΑΥϪΙ 5.

ΚΟΥΦ ΚΑΜΗ̄	ΟΝΑΦ ΕϩΟΥΝ
Ν̄ΧΟΥΤΕϢΤΗ̄	ΚΟΥϤ ΚΑΜΗΛΙ
ΤΟΥ ΕΠΜΕΝΕ	Χ̄ρΕШϹϯ Ν̄ ῙΛ̄ Ν̄
ΕΠ Β͞Ш͞Ξ Ν̄	ΚᾹΡΠΟϹ Ν̄ΠΕΝΤΗ

10.   Ρ͞Μ ΛΥΩ ϬΛ

     ΤΛϢΧΙΤΟΥ ΕΧ͞Ν

     ῙϚ ΔΕΚΑΤΗ

     ΕΒΛΛ ΝΕϤ Ν̄Τ

     ΝΪϹΛϢΚ Ν

15.   ϢΛ ΠΝΟϬ

     Ν̄ϤΙ ΕΠΜ̄

     ΤΕϤΜΙϹ

     Ν̄ΤΑΝϹΜ

Fragt. A; *l. 1.* λοκ̄ = λόγος, as in *A.Z.* 78, 17.

l. 2. ϭΛΜΟΥΛ; here probably the proper-name.

l. 6. ΚΟΥΦ; v. N° LIV, ΚΟΥΦΟΝ; *Denkschr.* (Wien) XXXVII, 128, κουφων; *ib.* 176, κουφα; *Recueil* VI, 67, 69, κουφαις. *Du Fresne* gives κοῦφα = ἀγγεῖον.
ΚΑΜΗ; recurs perhaps *Fragt. B, l. 7.*

l. 12. ῙϚ = καὶ.

Fragt. B; *l. 2.* ΠϹΛΒΕΤ is doubtful. v. N° XXXV.

l. 8. Ν̄, at the end, introduced the name of the debtor, as in *A.Z.* 78, 18.

This list deals with the affairs of someone spoken of in the 3d pers. (A. 11, 13, 16, 17). The writers too apparently allude to themselves (A. 18), and speak of the debts of certain others (B. 4). The fragts. are interesting from their employment both of the Coptic and Greek numerals (A. 7 and A. 5, 12, B. 2, 3, 9).
ΕΒΛΛ and ΧΟΥΤΕϢΤΗ indicate a M.E. tendency in the Dialect.

LII. Papyrus. $1\frac{1}{8}$ × $7\frac{1}{4}$ in.

This strip of Papyrus shows a character not unlike that of *Hyv.*, *Alb.* XX (colophon).

      Η . . . ΠϢΕΝΚΟΛ   ?

      ΠϢΕΝΚΟΥΜΕϯ ΠΑΠΟΥϹΙΡΙ Χ͞ρ α

ΚΟΥΜΕϯ; cf. the names Κωμητᾶς, Κομήτης.

Χ͞ρ = ?? χευσίον. It could here scarcely be χωρίον. The letter written above has this form ⌐ and need not be ω.

LIII. Papyrus. (from Hawara.)   A, 4 × 4½ in.
                                  B, 2¾ × 5 in.

The material is very brittle, the character irregular and faded.
Fragt. A shows margins at the top and to the right.

Fragt. A: Fragt. B:

ⲁⲣ ⲓⲏ ⳝ ⲡⲁⲣ ⲁⲣ ⲓ   ⲙⲡⲟⲡⲓ ⲡⲓⲃⲁⲣⲁⲙ[ⲉ]ⲟⲥ ⲁⲣ ⲑ

(space) ⲱⲟⲧ ⲁⲣ ⲁ   ⲁⲣ ⲁ ⲗⲗⲉⲉⲧ ⲁⲣ ⲁ ⲡⲁⲣⲁ

ⲛⲗⲡⲧⲁⲣⲓⲭⲓ ⲁⲣ ⲁ   ⲃⲁⲃⲓⲗⲱⲛ ? ⲧⲁⲕⲏ ⲉⲡⲗⲁⲗⲉ[ⲉ]ⲧ

                          ⲡⲟⲁⲧ ⲉⲟⲁⲧⲣⲉ ⲁⲣ ⲋ   ⲗ

              5.   ?ⲡⲕⲗⲱ ⲁⲣ ⲅ

                          (space) ⲙⲟⲩⲥⲁ ⲟⲩⲧ ?

Fragt. A; l.1. ⳝ ; cf. the table of cursive numerals, Stern, s.131. Here
I would suggest ⲉⲏ, for ⲋⲏ = ⳝ + ⳝ, or ⅞.

ⲡⲁⲣ ; v.? ad Nᵒ XII².

l.2. ⲱⲟⲧ ; the dictionaries give "a couch, cushion".

l.3. ⲧⲁⲣⲓⲭⲓ ; "salt fish". It occurs Append., P.Bodl., Ver.ⁱᵃ, Berl. P.5559 (v. ad
    Nᵒ XII¹³) Ä.Z. '68,84, †ⲑⲁⲣⲓⲕⲓ (= ﺳﻤﻚ, ὀψάρεα, Fleischer). Note the gender
    in the last example.

Fragt. B; l.1. ⲃⲁⲣⲁⲙⲉⲟⲥ ; v. ad Nᵒ XLV, Rec.³.

l.2. ⲗⲗⲉⲉⲧ ; perhaps also in l.3.

l.6. ⲙⲟⲩⲥⲁ ; ?= ﻣﻮﺱ .

LIV. Papyrus.   8⅞ × 4 in.

Very dilapidated and brittle, but seems not to have lost much of
its text. ll.1-9 are not in the same ink as ll. 10-14. The character
of these last resembles that of Nᵒ XI (pl.2).

ⲡⲗⲟⲅⲟⲥ ⲛⲉⲕⲟⲩⲫⲟⲛ   10. †ⲛⲇⲉⲓⲙⲱⲥⲓ ⲉⲛⲭⲓⲙⲟⲟⲩ]

    ⲕⲟⲩⲣ   ⲭ̄ⲛ   ⲟⲉⲛ ⲟⲛⲉⲥ ⲥⲟⲩⲗ ⲉⲗⲧⲁⲩ ⲟ

    ⲕⲟⲩⲣ   ⲱ̄ⲝ   ⲥⲟⲩⲗ ⲉⲗⲧⲁⲩ ⲉⲛ†ⲙⲟⲟⲩ

    ⲕⲟⲩⲣ   ⲯ̄?   ⲥⲟⲩⲗ ⲉⲛⲭⲓⲙⲟⲟⲩ ⲛ̄ ⲁ

  5. ⲕⲟⲩⲣ   ⲯ̄ⲡ   ⲛⲉⲧⲛ †ⲙⲟⲟⲩ ⲛ̄ ?

    ⲕⲟⲩⲣ   ⲱ̄ⲕ

    [ⲕⲟⲩⲣ] ⲱ̄ⲛ

[ΚΟΥ]Ϥ   ω̄?
[ΚΟ]ΥϤ   (sic)
      (space)

The first text is a wine-account; the second relates to the collection or payment of taxes.

l.1. ΚΟΥϤΟΝ; v. N⁰ LI. A similar reckoning in ΚΟΥϤ, <u>Wien. Stud.</u> XII,87.

l.10. ΔΕΙΜΩϹΙ = δημόσιον.

l.11. ϦΝΕϹ ? = ϦΝΗϹ, Herakleopolis. Other occurrences of it cited, <u>R.</u> I,64, II,58. ϹΟΥΑ ΕΛΤΑϥ = Sah. ϹΟΥΟ ΕΡΤΩΒ. Cf. N⁰ XLVIII, ΕΡΤΑΒ.

l.13. extremely uncertain.

The Dialect is M.E.

———————

LV. Papyrus.   7½ × 3 in.

A strip of thin papyrus, showing the left-hand margin only, and bearing a regular character, somewhat like that of N⁰ XIV (pl.3).

	ΝϷ.ΝΑϷ		ΕΛΚΟΥ ΝΩϦϹ
	ϹΙϤ.ΚΑ	10.	ΚΕΛΕΒΙΝ ΝΑ
	ΩΝ.ΒΩ		ϦΑΡΤΙ ΠΕΝΙΠ[Ι
	ΚΑΚΕΛΙ ΒΑϷΩ[Τ		ΤΩΒΕΤΑΒΕΤΕΒΝ̇
5.	ΚΑΚΕΛΙ ΠΕΝΙΠΙ		ΤΡΑΠ ϬΑΝΝΑϹΑ?
	ΤΙΚΑΝΙ ΠΕΝΙΠΙ		ΜΕϹΩΒΙ ϬΑΝΝΑϬ
	ϹΟΥΠΛΙΝ ΠΕΝΙ[Π]Ι	15.	ϹΟΥΜΑΡΙ Ν̇
	ϬΙϹΛΑΚ ΒΑϷᵒ̇Τ		ϤΑΛ

A list of various objects in metal. The identifications are merely tentative.

l.4. ΚΑΚΕΛΙ; for κάγκελος; "a bronze grating(?)." ΚΕΛΙ, for Sah. Ⲕⲗ̄ⲗⲉ, is improbable, owing to the ΚΑ-.

l.5. The same object in iron.

l.6. ΤΙΚΑΝΙ; for τήγανον; "an iron crucible, pan."

l.7. ϹΟΥΠΛΙΝ; for σουβλίον; "an iron awl."

l.8. ϬΙϹΛΑΚ; for Sah. *ϬΙϹΛΟΚ; "(a vessel holding) half a κοτύλη". Cf. ϬΙϹΚΙΤΕ.

l.9. ΕΛΚΟΥ, "a jar, pitcher" (<u>Peyr.</u>) would leave ωϦϹ unexplained.

l.10. "an ax of —?"

l.11. ϦΑΡΤΙ = Sah. ϦΟΡΤΕ; "an iron knife".

l.12. unintelligible to me.

l.13. ΤΡΑΠ ; *cf. Peyr.,* ΤΡΑΠС, "*an awl.*"

ϬΑΝΝΑϹΑ *seems to be a loan-word.*

l.14. ΜΕϹωΒΙ ; *cf. Kircher, Sc. 132,* ЄΜϹΟΒΙ, "*shoemaker's needle*".

l.15. ϹΟΥΜΑΡΙ ; *cf. Freytag,* اِبْرِيق *Vas, urna.*

The absence throughout of the genit. Ν- (*v. esp. ll. 8,13*) *might make it preferable to translate, "a grating,—bronze," "a crucible,—iron", &c.* ϬΑΡΤΙ *shows the Dialect to be M.E.*

APPENDIX.

Pap. Bodleian., a (P.) 4.   21 × 7 *in.*
brought from Sheik Hammad, near Sohag.

Of a grey-brown colour, this papyrus bears a clear character, similar to that of No XIV (pl. 3). Many lines are faded. It is complete in width, but l.1 was not the first. The numerals are Greek and much like those in the Arabic papyrus Denkschr. (Wien) XXXIII, Taf. 1 (circ. A.D. 725). Some of them are uncertain and lacunæ make their control impossible. Greek cursive characters recur also in several places through the text. The data do not determine which side of the sheet is the Recto, for the same months are found upon both. I designate therefore as "Recto" that side upon which the text lies at right-angles to the fibres. (v. the remarks in the Preface, p. vii.)

	Recto.				Verso.			
?	ПΚϪΥΜΑΡΙΤΕϹ		·α		ΙΑΚω[Β]⸱Νϣω ΕϱΟΝ	?		
?	?	⸱ic	·ϛ		ΙωϹΗΦ ΠΟΤΑΜΙΤΕϹ ΕϱΟΝ	?		
?	?	λ	·ιβ̄		ΑΒΑΕΛΛΑ ϛ ΑΜΡΟϹ⸱ ΤΑ	?		
?	?		·α		ΟΥΕΝΑΒ[Ε]Ρ	?		
5.	?	?	ϲ	ϛ	ϱΙ ΠΙΑ͞Κ ΜΗΝΑ ϛ Κ?	?		5.
	?	ωΗ ϛ ΟΥϣωϹ	κ̄β̄		ΓΕωϱ ΠϣΑϹΒΑΜΠΕ ϩ	?		
ΠΑϹΑΝ ΒΑϹΙΛΙ ΕϱΟΝ ΝΕΠΑΛΛΙΝ			?		[ΠΑϹΑΝ] ΒΙΚ ΕϱΟΥΝ ΟΥΑϱ?	?		
τ̄ κα ΠΑΥΛΕ ΦΑΜϣΗ		⸱ic	·α		ϹΕΥΗΡΟϹ ΠΤΑΙΜΑΥ	Χ Η͞Ι͞Ε		κ̄ϛ̄
ϹΕΡΙΝΗ ΠΑΠΟΥϹΙΡΙ			·α		?Κβ ΠΑΙΑ͞Κ θωΜΑϹ ΕϱΟΝ ΟΥϱ ϛ		·α	
10.	? ωΤΙ ΤΑΤΑΝϣΕΕΙ		α		ΒΑΡΑΧ ΕϱΟΝ ΝΕΤΑΡΙΧΙ...Β̄Τ		ι͞ϛ	10.
ΠΑΠΟϹΤΟΛΟϹ ΠϹΑΝ ΝΑΒ̄ρ			ᾱ		ΠΙΑ͞Κ ΠΕΤΡΟϹ ΕϱΟΝ ΠΕϥΒΙΚΗ	?		
ΠΑΠΑ ΒΑϹΙΛΙ ΠΑΠΟΥϹΙΡΙ			ϛ		[ΠΑ]ϹΑΝ ΖΑΧΑΡΙΑϹ ΕϱΟΝ ῑ ΠΑΡΕϹ α			

	ⲭⲁⲏⲗ ⲡⲁⲗⲉⲣⲱⲛⲓ	ⲅ̄	⳿.ⲛⲕⲏⲛⲓ̈ⲥ ⲣⲉ ⲧⲡⲟⲗⲓⲥ	ⲏ̄
	ⲥⲉⲣⲓⲛⲏ ⲋ ⲑⲉⲱⲁⲱⲣ̄ ⲛⲁⲗⲉⲣⲱⲛⲓ ·ⲃ		ⲕⲟⲥ ?	?
15.	ⲓⲱⲣⲁⲛⲛⲏⲥ ⲡⲗⲉⲙⲙⲁⲣⲏⲥ ⳽ ⲡⲉⲩ̂ ⲕⲍ̄ⲕⲇ̄		ⲡⲁⲡⲁ ⲟ̣ⲓ.. ⲉⲣⲟⲛ ⲡⲉⲩ̂ⲣ̂ⲱⲕ	? 15.
	ⲓⲱⲣⲁⲛⲛⲏⲥ ⲡⲕⲱⲙⲁⲣⲓ̂ ⲉⲣⲟⲛ ⲛⲉⲱ̈ⲉ̄ⲃ ·ⲁ		? ⲕⲉⲗⲉ̂ ⲋ ⲁⲡⲁⲧ ⲣ̄ⲙⲃ̄	
	ⲡⲓⲥⲓⲛⲑⲓ° ⲡⲁⲛⲉⲡⲁⲓⲉⲧ	ⲋ̄	ⲟⲩⲉⲛⲁⲃⲉⲣ ⲉⲣⲟⲛ ⲡⲣⲱⲕ ⲡⲁⲡⲁⲣⲓ̣ ·ⲃ̄	
	ⲧⲥⲓⲙⲓ ⲛ̄ⲑⲉⲱ̂ ⲡⲁⲡⲉⲗⲟ̇ⲓⲥⲟⲟⲕ	ⲋ̄	ⲉⲣⲟⲛ ⲣⲣⲏ ⲛⲉⲃⲁⲙⲡⲓ ⲣⲉ ⲧⲭⲉⲓⲗⲓ ·ⲁ	
	ⲑⲓⲟⲫⲓⲗⲉ ⲡⲱⲟⲥ ⲉⲣⲟⲛ ⲕ̄ ⲛⲉⲥⲁⲩ̂	ⲍ̄	ⲅⲓⲣⲁⲥⲉⲓ ⲉⲣⲟⲛ ⲕⲋ̄·ⲁ	ⲅ̄
20.	ⲡⲉⲧⲣⲉ ⲡⲛⲏⲏⲃ ⲉⲣⲟⲛ ⲡⲱⲟ̇ⲃⲁⲣ ⲥ̄ⲕⲇ̄		ⲁⲛⲟⲩ̂ⲓ̇[ⲏ̇] ⲡⲗⲉⲩⳉ... ⲉⲡⲟⲩⲱⲉⲡ ·ⲅ̄ 20.	
	ⲡⲗⲉⲙⲡⲟⲩⲗⲉⲓⲧ ⲡⲉⲃ̇ⲱⲱ ·ⲩ̄ⲃ̄		ⲓⲥⲁⲁⲕ ⲫⲁⲙⲱⲏ	
	ⲓⲱ̄ ⲉⲣⲟⲛ ⲧⲭⲏⲣⲉ ⲙⲓⲥⲁⲏⲗ ·ⲁ		ⲥ̄ⲕⲃ̄ ⲡⲁⲓⲁ̈ⲕ̄ ⲙⲏⲛⲁ ⲉⲣⲟⲛ ⲡⲙⲁⲛⲙⲓⲛⲓⲧⲉⲛ̈·ⲃ̄	
ⲙ̄ ⲩ̄ⲃ̄	ⲡⲱⲏⲛⲁⲡⲟⲩ ⲇⲁⲟⲩⲇ ⳽ⲟⲩⲱⲁⲣ̂ⲱ ·ⲋ̄		ⲓⲱⲣⲁⲛⲛⲏⲥ ⲉⲣⲟⲩ̄ⲛ ⲁⲣⲁⲕⲁ ·ⲩ̄	
	ⲙⲱⲩⲥⲏⲥ ⲉⲣⲟⲛ ⳿.̄·ⲧ̇ⲉⲗⲛⲟⲩⲣⲓ ·ⲁ		ⲉⲣⲟⲩⲛ ⲧⲏⲃⲉⲧ [ⲛⲉ]ⲥⲛⲏⲟⲩ ·ⲩ̄	
25.	ⲁ[ⲃⲣⲁ]ⲣⲁⲙ ⲡⲅⲉⲣⲁⲙⲉⲟⲥ ⲟⲩⲉⲛⲏ ⲥ̄ⲏ̄		ⲡⲉⲧⲣ̄ ⲉⲣⲟⲛ ⲡⲙⲁⲛⲙ̈ⲁⲛⲓⲛⲉⲃⲁ[ⲙⲡⲓ] ·ⲏ̄ 25.	
	ⲅⲉⲱ[ⲣ̄] ⲡⲁⲛⲉⲡⲁⲓⲉⲧ	·ⲏ̄	ⲉⲣⲟⲩⲛ ⲙⲟⲥⲭⲁⲧⲱⲛ ⲉⲧ ⲕ̄ⲕ̄	ⲋ̄
·ⲏ̄	ⲣⲁⲥⲥⲁⲛ ⲉⲣⲟⲛ ⲡⲙⲉⲥⲓ ⲛⲧⲁⲃⲉⲗⲟⲩ ·ⲁ̄ⲃ̄		ⲫⲁⲣⲓ̈ ⲉⲣⲟⲛ ⲁⲣⲱⲓⲛ ⲋ ⲁⲣⲁⲕⲁ ·ⲥ̄ⲏ̄	
ⲫⲁⲣ̈ⲙ̄ⲃ̄	ⲥⲁⲙⲟⲩⲏ̂ ⲡⲁⲧⲉⲱ̇ⲙⲟⲩⲛⲓ ·ⲁ		ⲉⲣⲟⲩⲛ ⲓⲱ̄ ⲛⲉⲩⲣⲱⲟⲣ ⲥⲓⲥ ⲥ̄ⲕ̄ⲃ̄	
	ⲗ.... ⲓ ⲡⲱⲱⲥ ⳽ ⲟⲩⲡⲁⲗⲗⲓⲛ ·ⲋ̄		ⲡⲁⲥⲁⲛ ⲥⲉⲩⲏⲣⲟⲥ ⲉⲣⲟⲛ ⲟⲩⲡ ?	?
30.	ⲧ̇ⲙⲉ̇ ? ⲏ̄ ⲓ̈·ⲥ̄ ·ⲁ		? ⲉⲣ[ⲟⲛ] ·ⲁ 30.	
	ⲅⲉⲱⲣ̄ ⲡⲅⲉⲣⲁⲙⲉⲟⲥ ·ⲅ̄ⲃ̄		ⲉⲣⲟⲩⲛ ⲃ̄ ⲕⲟⲗⲗⲁⲑⲓ ⲛⲗⲉⲥⲓ ⲥ̄ⲕⲇ̄	
	ⲫⲓⲗⲓ̄ⲑⲉⲟⲥ ⲋ ⲑⲉⲱ̂ ⲉⲣⲟⲛ ⲥⲁⲣⲉⲧ_ ·ⲃ̄		ⲡⲁⲥⲁⲛ ⲡⲁⲡⲛⲟⲩ̂ ⲉⲣⲟⲛ ⲟⲗⲁ̈ⲛⲣⲣⲏ ·ⲅ̄	
	ⲓⲥⲁⲕ ⲡⲱⲏⲛⲁⲃⲣⲁⲣⲁⲙ ⲡⲱ̇ⲃⲁⲣ ·ⲁ̄		ⲓⲱⲣⲁⲛⲛⲏⲥ ⲫⲉⲗⲁ ⳽ ⲟⲙⲓⲟⲥ ·ⲋ̄	
	ⲥⲁ̂ⲙⲟⲩ̂ⲏⲗ ⲉⲣⲟⲛ] ⲡⲱ̇ⲃⲁⲣ ⲙⲡⲏⲓ ·ⲋ̄		ⲓⲱⲣⲁⲛⲛⲏⲥ ⲡⲗⲉⲙⲥⲁⲭⲏ ⲉⲣⲟⲛ ? ·ⲅ̄	
35.	ⲅⲉⲱⲣ̄ ⲡⲁⲧⲁⲛⲱⲉⲉⲓ _ ·ⲩ̄		ⲕ ⲑⲉⲱⲫⲓⲗⲉ ⲡⲱⲟⲥ ⲉⲣⲟⲛⲉⲕⲧⲏⲏⲙ ·ⲁ 35.	
	ⲓⲱ̄...ⲏⲑ _ _ ·ⲁ		ⲑⲉⲱⲫⲓⲗ̈ ⲡⲱⲟⲥ ⲉⲣⲟⲛ ⲡⲉⲩ ?	?
	ⲱⲉ[ⲛⲟⲩⲧ]ⲓ ⲡⲁⲡⲟⲩⲥⲓⲣⲓ ·ⲅ̄		ⲡⲁⲡⲟⲥⲧⲟ̇ ⲋ ⲡⲓⲥⲓⲛⲧⲓ ⳽ ⲁⲣ̄ ⲉⲕ̄] ·ⲁ	
	ⲑⲉⲩ̇ⲧ̇[ⲱ]ⲥⲓ ⲫⲁⲙ ⲉⲣⲟⲛ ⲟⲩⲃⲉⲣⲥ̂ ·ⲁ		ⲫⲁⲣ̈ⲙ̄ ⲉⲣⲟⲛ ⲁⲣⲱⲓⲛ ⲋ ⲁⲣⲁⲕⲁ ⳽ⲭ	
	..ⲁⲣ̄.ⲛⲟⲩ ⲧⲁⲧⲓⲕⲉⲙⲏⲛ ·ⲅ̄		ⲕⲟⲥⲙⲁ ⲡⲁⲙⲏ ⲋ ⲟⲩⲉⲛⲁⲃⲉⲣ ·ⲁ *	
40.	ⲧⲥⲓⲙⲓ̂ ⲛⲁ̈ⲑⲁⲛⲁⲥⲓ ⲧⲁⲛⲉⲡⲁⲓⲉ̄ ·ⲁ		[same line, at *, ⲉⲣⲟⲛ ⲡ̄ⲣⲃ̄ⲧⲕ̄ ⲥⲓⲥ	
	ⲑ...ⲡⲱⲟⲥ ⳽ ⲁⲣ̄ ·ⲁ ·ⲃ̄		ⲭⲁⲏ ⲡⲱⲏⲛⲝⲏⲑ ⲉⲣⲟⲩⲛ ⲏ ? ·ⲃ̄ⲩ̄ⲃ̄ 40.	
	ⲡ[ⲁ̄ⲡ̄ⲁ̄]ⲫⲓⲃⲁ̈ⲙ ⲉⲣⲟⲛ ⲁⲣ̄ ·ⲩ̄ⲃ̄ ·ⲋ̄		ⲉⲣⲟⲛ ⲃ̄ ⲡⲁⲣⲉⲥ ⲉⲡⲙⲁⲛ̄ ? ·ⲩ̄	
	? ⲁⲙⲙⲱⲛⲓ ⲡⲗⲉⲃ̇ⲱⲱ ⳽ ⲁⲣ̄ ·ⲩ̄ⲃ̄ ·ⲁ̄ⲋ̄		ⲛⲉⲗⲉⲩⲭⲓ ⲁⲅⲁⲡⲏ ? ? ?	
			ⲉⲣⲟⲩⲛ ⲡⲓⲛⲓⲡⲓ _ ⲥⲓⲥ ?	
			ⲉⲣⲟⲛ ⲧⲏⲃⲉⲧ ⲛⲉⲥⲛⲏⲟⲩ ·ⲩ̄	
	ⲅⲓ ⲛ̄ ⲣⲃⲩ		ⲡⲁⲥⲁⲛ ⲡⲁⲩⲗⲉ ⳽ ⲡⲉⲃⲃⲓⲕ̄ⲏ ? ·ⲩ̄ 45.	
45.	ⲋ ⲉⲣⲟⲛ ⲛⲉⲏⲣⲡ · ⲟⲋ̄		ⲡⲓⲁⲝ̄ ⲁⲙ̄ⲙ̄ ⲡⲗⲉⲃⲱⲱ ⳽ ⲟⲩ? ·ⲁ̄ⲋ̄	
	ⲑ̄ · ⲣⲛⲃⲉⲅ̄		ⲡⲁⲥⲁⲛ ⲫⲓⲃⲁⲙⲟⲩ ⲉⲩⲧⲓⲁⲕⲱ? ⲥ̄ⲏ̄	
			? ⲣ̄ⲅⲩ̄ⲙⲓ̈ⲏ̄	
			ⲛⲃ̄	

We have here a statement of expenditure during four (perhaps more) months —from about January till April. Among those who receive payment are

Shepherds (Rec. ll. 19, 29, 41, Ver. 35, 36), Goat-herds (Ver. 6), Agricultural labour-
-ers (Ver. 39), Vine-dressers (Rec. 1, 16), Water-men (? Ver. 2), Carpenters (Rec. 8,
Ver. 21), Potters (Rec. 25, 31), Sailors (Rec. 20). But payment is often made
—to women as well as men,—where the services rendered are not stated.
The accounts are reckoned in νομίσματα (ϩΟΛΟΚΩΤϹΙ), as is clear from
Rec. 44 (whence it is also evident that the dot preceding each sum is to
be read νόμισμα*) The fractions therefore are κεράτια. From the appear-
-ance, upon both faces, of the same months (cf. esp. Rec. 8, Tybi 21, and Ver. 22,
Tybi 22,) and the probability of Ver. 48, 49 being, like Rec. 44, 46, the
total of the amounts on that face, I think the papyrus must bear two
independent accounts.

Recto:

l. 1. ΚΟΥΜΑΡΙΤΕϹ ; v. l. 16, ΚΩΜΑΡΙ .

l. 3. The numeral here is ιβ̄, i.e. ιβ = $\frac{1}{12}$. This is clear from Rec. 41, 42, 43, where
the figure of the amounts paid is, in each case, double that of the
quantity of the material bought.

l. 6. The two letters in the numeral here have but one stroke above. (The
same in ll. 15, 20 and Ver. 28.) They stand, I think, for $\frac{1}{24}$ (? one κερ-
-άτιον).

l. 7. ΕϩΟΝ; here sometimes ΕϩΟΥΝ. The Brit. Mᵐ. Pap. XCV (dated A.D. 777,)
repeatedly writes Ο for ΟΥ, but indicates the omission by a stroke
above the syllable. (v. also Stern, §. 45). A comparison of Rec. 7 with
Rec. 29, of Rec. 41, 43, Ver. 37 with Ver. 45, shows that ⟨ is used as its
abbreviation; i.e., it = ὑπέρ.

ΠΑΛΛΙΝ; also l. 29. v. Nᵒ XLVII.

l. 10. ΤΑΝϢΕΕΙ ; v. ad Nᵒ XXII⁵.

l. 11. ends with an abbreviation for ΑΒΡΑϩΑΜ.

l. 15. ΛΕΜΜΑΡΗϹ ; v. R. II, 51, ΛΕΜΑΡΗϹ.

l. 16. The mark above the final word may be γ. Probably some product of
the vineyard is intended.

l. 17, and ll. 25, 40, ΝΕΠΛΙΕΤ ; Lybia (? the Lybian nome) or its inhabitants
v. Peyr. 266. Cf. Ä.Z. '65, 51, ΦΑΙΑΤ = لبية.

l. 18. ΠΕΛϬΙϹΟΟΚ; v. ad Nᵒ XLV, Ver.²⁵.

l. 19. At this rate, one sheep should cost 8·4 kerats, i.e., a little more
than a τρεμήσιον.

l. 20. ϢϬΑϷ; v. l. 34, where it seems that the meaning is "rent, hire".
In Ä.Z. '84, 157, ΤΙ ΕΠϢΚΑϷ is to "let (land)."

* Perhaps the development of this abbreviation may be traced as
follows; Ν, passim = Berl., P. 5561, ℓ′ = Brit. Mᵐ. Pap. XXXII (v. Wessely in
Wien. Stud. '87, 242,) and ib., Orient. 1028, ϩ, θ = •, as here. v. also ad Nᵒ XXIII⁷.

l.21. ΠΟΥΛΕΙΤ; *v. ad* N⁰ XLV, Rec.¹ .

ΠΕϬΩϢ, from its position, is probably "the Æthiopian".

l.22. ΤΧΗΡΕ [Μ]ΜΙΣΛΗΛ; "the threshing-floor of Misael, Μισάηλ.".

l.23. = أبو الله .

ϢΛΡΩΤ. The form of this word scarcely allows a comparison with *Zoega* 529, ϢΟΡΤ, "mask(?)". Perhaps شروط is as probable.

l.24. ΤΕΛΝΟΥϤΙ; ? "branch of sycomore." Cf. S. Matth. XIII, 32 (*Mém. de l'Instit. égypt.*, II, ii,) ΤΕΛ = Boh. ϪΛΧ.

l.25. ΓΕΡΛΜΕΟϹ; *v. ad* N⁰ XLV, Rec.³ .

ΟΥΕΝΗ; ? for ΟΥΕΝΙΝ (*v.* N⁰ XLIV,) = Sah. ΟΥΕΙΝΙΝ. Cf. the position of ΠΕϬΩϢ, *l.21.*

l.27. "Hassan, for the calf that was sick(?)", for Sah. ρ̄ϭωΒ.

l.28. ΤΕϢΜΟΥΝΙ; the name of this locality, "The Eight," forms a parallel to that of ϢΜΟΥΝ.

l.33. ϢΛΡ̄; cf. N⁰ XLV, Ver.⁷, ϢΛϤ?

l.34. v. l. 20, above.

l.38. ΘΕΥΤΩϹΙ; *v. ad* N⁰ XXIII⁹.

ΦΛΜ, for ΦΛΜΕ = ΠϨΛΜΕ, is unlikely, because of Ver. 39, ΠΛΜΗ.

ΒΕΡϹΛ; for βύρσα.

l.39. ΤΚΕΜΗΝ; a locality, probably in the Herakleopolite nome; *v. Champollion, l'Ég. sous les Phar.* I, 318.

l.41. This line and *ll.42,43,* Ver. 37, show the groups ⲁρ̄ᵗ, ⲁρ̄ᵗ, ⲁρ̄ᵗ, ⲁρ̄ᵗ. The 3ᵈ letter looks like ϥ or ν, but may merely indicate abbreviation.

l.43, and Ver. 46, ΛΕΒϢΩϢ = Sah. ρΕϤϢΩϢ, ἀναγνώστης. R. II, 47, ΛΕΒΠϢΩϢ is probably intended for this.

ll. 44—46. ΓΙ Ṅ = γενέσθαι νομίσματα, and ⳝ = ὁμοῦ (*v. ad* N⁰ XLVI ¹⁵). ϥ = ⅔ (*v. Stern*, s. 131, Taf.), and thus the total ($82\frac{2}{3} + 70\frac{1}{4} =$) $152\frac{2}{7}$ is correct.

Verso:

l.2. ΠΟΤΛΜΙΤΕϹ; ποταμίτης, a rare word, occurs *Denkschr. (Wien)* XXXVII, 184. Note the absence of the Article before π.

l.3. ΛΒΛΕΛΛΛ recurs R. I, 23; ΛΜΡΟϹ = زمر ; cf. R. V, 38, ΛΜΒΡΟϹ.

l.5. The date here is written ϧⳫⲃ. ΠΙΛϾ and *l.11,* ΠΙΛϾ, = ΠΙΛΚΟΥ.

l.6. ϢΛϹΒΛΜΠΕ; a case of "Annexion" similar to those in *Stern*, §. 192. From *l.18* one would expect ΒΛΜΠΙ.

l.8. ΠΤΛΙΜΛΥ; ? "The irrigator." Cf. ΤΛΙΚΒΛ and *v. Peyr.* in ΜΟΟΥ.

l.9. The date has the form ϧⲫⲕⲍ. The final word is ϧⲣⲧ.

l.10. ΒΛΡΛΧ; cf. Ä.Z. '85, 35, R. V, 53, ΒΛΡΛϬ, الرب . The gap might contain [ΝΤΗ], and the words be translated, "for salted fish". ΤΛΡΙΧΙ = τάριχος, τάριχιον; *v.* N⁰ LIII.

l.12 and *l.41.* ΠΛΡΕϹ; apparently also in N⁰ XXVI. Cf.? *Zoega* 352, ΠΟΡϹ, something hung up as a substitute for a door.

l.16. ? for Sah. ⲕⲉⲗⲱⲗ ⲋ ⲁⲡⲟⲧ.
One would expect the numeral to read ιβ μη.

l.17. ⲡⲁⲡⲁϥⲓ cf. Zoega 365, ⲡⲁⲡⲟϥⲉ, ? "cow-stall keeper." ⲣⲱⲕ here suggests "ox-driver."

l.18. ⲧϫⲉⲓⲗⲓ. I can only suggest that this is for Sah. ⲧⲱⲁⲓⲣⲉ, "fold," and would translate "Good for the stall-fed goats." For ϫ = ⲧⲱ, cf. Revill., *A. et C.*, ϙ̄ⲃ, ϫⲉⲣⲉ = ib., ϙ̄ⲏᴮ, ⲧⲱϣⲉⲣⲉ, and *R. V.*, 34, ϫⲱϫⲟⲙⲧⲉ = ϫⲟⲩⲧⲱϣ-ⲙⲧⲉ.

l.19. ϥⲓⲣⲁⲥⲉⲓ; a foreign name, which I can not find elsewhere. The abbreviation may be for κέραμος, or some such word, "a thousand tiles." Cf. the prices of bricks Denkschr. (Wien) XXXVII, 113.

l.20. ⲉⲡⲟⲩⲁϫⲉⲡ; for Sah. ⲉⲡⲟⲩⲱϫⲁⲡ, "for the loan."

l.23. and *ll.* 27, 38, ⲁⲣⲁⲕⲁ; اراق, ʼaraq; probably here the plant or its fruit, rather than the liquor.

l.24. v. l. 44, ⲛⲉⲥⲛⲏⲟⲩ for ⲉⲛⲉⲥⲛⲏⲟⲩ; "fish for the brethren."

l.26. ⲙⲟⲥⲭⲁⲧⲱⲛ; the price makes, I think, μοσχάς -αδος, "heifer," improbable.

l.27. ⲁⲣϣⲓⲛ = Kircher, Sc. 193, العدس, φακός, lentil.

l.28. "Grain for the dogs" is too improbable to be correct.

l.31. ⲕⲟⲗⲗⲁⲑⲓ = κόλλαθον, κόλαθος. It recurs in this form in Berl. P. 5559; in Pap. Bodl., a. 1, ⲕⲟⲗⲗⲁⲑ; in Pap. Bodl., a. 2, ⲕⲟⲩⲗⲁⲑⲉ; in R. V., 32, ⲕⲟⲩ-ⲗⲁⲑⲉ, ⲕⲟⲗⲗⲁⲑⲓ; v. also A. Z. '71, 121.

ⲗⲉⲥⲓ; v. ad Nᵒ XVI¹⁰.

l.33. φελα; cf. Nᵒ XXII¹¹,¹³, ϧⲉⲗⲁ.

ⲟⲙⲓⲟⲥ; probably = ὁμοίως.

l.34. ⲥⲁⲭⲏ seems to be a place-name.

l.35. ⲕⲧⲏⲏⲙ. One is tempted to read ⲕⲧⲏⲏⲣ.

l.37. The ratios between amounts bought and sums paid in the parallel cases (ll. Rec. 41—43) suggests ⲋ here. The sign following the numeral resembles that given in Denkschr. (Wien) XXXIII, 218, as half a kerat.

l.39. ⲡϥⲃⲓⲕⲏ would seem to be an error for ⲡⲉⲩⲃⲓⲕⲏ.

l.40. ⲍⲏⲑ ? for Σηθ.

l.42. "Those who partake of the ἀγάπη," or charitable repasts following certain of the sacraments (Vansleb, Hist. de l'Egl. d'Alex., 112.)

l.46. ⲁⲙ̄ⲙ̄ = l. Rec. 43, ⲁⲙⲙⲱⲛⲓ. An analogous abbreviation is ⲉ̄ⲧ̄ⲧ̄, for ⲉⲧⲧⲁⲓⲏⲩ; v. Nᵒ XIV¹.

ll. 48, 49. The fragts. of which these lines are composed are not accurately joined, and the text therefore is unclear. In l. 49, ⲡ may have preceded the figures.

The Dialect of this text is clearly M.E. (ⲥⲁⲛ, ⲉⲥⲁⲩ, ⲗⲉⲙ·, ⲗⲉϥ·, ⲉⲗ·, &c.)

The number of Greek words is considerable.

ADDITIONS and CORRECTIONS.

Page 1, line 8; for colon, read double-colon.
In the text it should be inserted on Recto, after ϩοϲι, ογωм

4, l.l. 1,14; for ⲱⲓⲏ, ⲱⲓⲑ, read ⲥⲓⲏ, ⲥⲓⲑ (as corrected on p. 3,) My error was pointed out to me by the Rev. G. Horner.

10, line 37; for ⲗⲁϩ ⲛⲁⲃⲉⲗ, read ⲗⲁ ϩⲛ [ⲛ]ⲁⲃⲉⲗ, "thy tears have not ceased from my eyes." *sic*

11, last line of text; read ⲉⲣⲛⲗⲁϣⲧ[ⲉ], "— thy prayers protect —".

14, line 20; cancel ⲃⲉⲣⲉⲃⲱⲟⲩⲧⲉⲥ.

15, 29; Probably [ⲁⲡⲁ] ⲙⲁⲕⲁⲣ[ⲓ⸱] ⲙⲉⲛ ⲡ]ⲉⲛⲓⲱⲧ ⲁⲡⲁ ⲡⲓⲥⲉⲛϯ.

21, 33; ⲙⲟⲩⲥⲑⲁⲣⲓ = Μυσθαρίων, in the newly-published "Aegyptische Urkunden a.d. königl. Mus⸗ zu Berlin", 1. Heft, s.5.

25, 15; Add; The Dialect is M.E., though ρ is not replaced by λ.

30, 30; Add; Brit. M⸗, Pap. 100 (Rankin I, C, a,) ⲗⲁϣⲁϣ, = ⲗⲁϣⲁⲛⲉ.

32, 27; Add; ⲕⲁⲛⲁϩⲓ, pl., № XVII.

36, 27; for ⲧⲟⲩⲟⲩ, read ⲧⲟⲩϩⲟⲩ.

39, 13; for ϥⲗ ⲁⲡ-, read ϥⲗⲁ ⲡ·. (Cf. Append., P. Bodl., Ver. 33.)

43, 2; ⲉⲓ is more probably the verb, and not ⲏ.

49, 27; Cf. Lagarde, Aegypt. 238, ⲅⲉⲱⲣⲅⲓⲟⲥ ⲫⲁⲕⲟⲥⲙⲁ.

50, 24; It is the writer's sister who is referred to.

60, 2; for ⲯⲱⲧⲓ, read ⲛⲯⲱⲧⲓ.

61, 12; ϣⲱⲱⲙⲓ ⲛⲭⲁⲣⲧⲏⲥ. In Sah. Jerem. XXXVI, 2, 4, (Erman, Bruch-stücke,) this = χαρτιον (χαρτην) βιβλιον, = Boh. ⲧⲟⲙⲟⲥ ⲛ̄ϫⲱⲙ (Tattam).

65, 39; Cf. ⲡⲓⲥⲓⲙⲓⲧⲟⲩⲥ, quoted by Stern from a Berlin fragt., A.Z. '85, 31.

69, 2; for ?ⲩⲣⲱⲛ, read probably [ⲥ]ⲩⲣⲱⲛ, a locality found several times in the Greek papyri; v. Denkschr. (Wien) XXXVII, 108.

74, 21; for debtor, read creditor.

INDICES.

N.B. The figures refer to the numbers of the M.SS.
R.= Recto,   V.= Verso.

i. PROPER NAMES.

ΠΑΠΟϹΤΟΛΟϹ. Ἀρ.	ΠΟΙΜΗΝ. 13.	ϹΟΥΡΙΑΝΗ.44.	Ψ
ΠΑΡΕΥ. 46.	ΠΙΜΗΝ.22.	ϹΤΕΦΑΝ.14.	ΨΑΤΙ.36.
ΠΑΥΛΙ.45, 49, Ἀρ.R.	ΠΡΑΥ. 25.	Τ	?ΠΨωΤΙ.43.
ΠΕΤΡΟϹ.5, 13,17,19,23,	?ΠΨωΤΙ.43.	ΤΑΙΛΙΑ.6.	ω
44,45, Ἀρ.V.	ΠωΟΙ.50.	ΤΑΝΙΕΛ.37.	ωΕΝΟΥΤ.45 R.
ΠΕΤΡ. 45 R., Ἀρ.V.	Ρ	ΤΕΛΕΜΗ.28.	ωΕΝΤ.22.
ΠΕΤΡΕ. 46, Ἀρ.R.	ΡΜΙΗΛ. 15.	?ΤΚΟΥΝϩω.46.	ϩ
ΠΙΑ̅Κ̅, Ἀρ.V.	Ϲ	Φ	ϩΑϹϹΑΝ. Ἀρ.R.
?ΠΙΑΝω.46.	ϹΑΜΟΥΗΛ.22, Ἀρ.R.	ΦΙΒΑΜΟΥ. Ἀρ.V.	ϩΑΤΡΕ.28,53.
ΠΙΛΟΘΙ.50.	ϹΑΜΠΑϹ.38.	ΦΙΒΑΜ. Ἀρ.R.	ϩΑθΡ?.27.
ΠΙΛωΘΙ.50.	ϹΕΜΕωΝ.24.	ΦΙΛΪΘΕΟϹ. Ἀρ.R.	ϩΑΤΡΗ.46.
ΠΙΛωΤΙ.36.	ϹΥΜΕωΝ.27.	ΦΙΛωΘ.12.(l.29.)	ΑΤΡΗ.46.
ΠΙϹΕΝ† 7V.	ϹΕΝΟΘ.27.	ΦΙΛΟΘ.20,22.	ϩΟΥΜΙϹΙ.49.
ΠΙϹΙΝΘΙ. Ἀρ.R.	ϹΕΡΙΝΗ. Ἀρ.R.	ΦΟΙΛΟΘ.13.	ϩΟΥΜΙϹ.50.
ΠΙϹΙΝΤΙ. Ἀρ.V.	ϹΕΥΗΡΟϹ. Ἀρ.V.	ΦωΡΕ.45V.	Χ
ΠΙϹΥΝΤΙ.12.	ϹΕΥΗΡ°.24.	Χ	?ΧΕΒΗΡ.31.
ΠΙϩΗΥ. 12,50.	ϹΙϹΙΝΝ?.36.	ΧΑΗΛ.13,20,42,45,Ἀρ.	
		ϭ	
	ϭΑΙΛ.15,	?ϭΑΜΟΥΛ.51.	

ii. GEOGRAPHICAL NAMES.

Β	Π	?ΠωϪΑΠΑΡΜΟΥΤΕ.45V.	ΤΚΕΜΗΝ. Ἀρ.R.
[Β]ΑΒΙΛωΝ.53.	ΠΕλϭΙϹΟΟΚ. Ἀρ.R.	Ρ	ΤΟΥΤωΝ.45R.
ΠΑΒΥΛωΝ.22.	ΠΕλϭΙϹωΚ.45V.	ΡΑΚΟΤΕ.5.	?ΤΟΥϩΟΥ.19.
Ε	ΠΙΑΜ.25?, 45R.	Ϲ	ω
ΕΔωΜ.7R.	?ΠΙΑΝω.46.	?ϹΑΧΗ. Ἀρ.V.	ωϪΑΡΕ.22,45R.
Κ	ΠΚΑΝωϪΑΡΕ and	ϹΙΜΙϹΤΟΥϹ.45(v.p.83)	ωϪΡ. Ἀρ.R.
ΚΕΡΚΕϹΟΥΧ.46.	ΠΚΟΥΝωϪΑΡΕ.45V.	ϹΙωΝ.8.	ωϪΡ?.45V.
ΚΗΜΕ.5,23.	ΠΜΟΥΝ̄.45R.	[Ϲ]ΥΡωΝ.46(v.p.83.)	ωΗΝΑΡω.45R.
λ	ΠΟΥλΕΙΔ.45R.	Τ	ωΜΟΥΝ.11?.
λΕϩωΝΕ.34.	ΠΟΥλΕΙΤ. Ἀρ.R.	ΤΑΒω.45V.	ϩ
λΕϩωΝΙ.45, Ἀρ.R.	ΠΟΥϹΙΡΕ.23,45R.	ΤΑΚΕΝΗω.45V.	?ϩΕΠΙΦΝΙ.45R. (cf.45V.
Μ	ΠΟΥϹΙΡΙ.52, Ἀρ.R.	ΤΑΝωϩΗ.34,45R,46.	ΕΠΙϕ.)
ΜΑΡΗϹ.5,23, Ἀρ.R.	ΠϹΑΒΕΤ.35,45R,46,	ΤΑΝωΕΕΙ.22,45R,	ϩΝΕϹ.54.
Ν	51.	Ἀρ.R.	ϩΡωΜΗ.5.
ΝΕΠΑΙΕΤ. Ἀρ.R.	ΠωΝΕ.45.	ΤΕωϪΜΟΥΝΙ. Ἀρ.R.	

iii. GREEK WORDS.

ΑΓΑΘΟΝ, ἀγαθος, 28,29.
  ἀκαθως, 6.
ΑΓΑΠΗ, 24,27, Ἀρ.V.
ΑΓΓΕΛΙΚΟΝ, 5
ΑΓΓΕΛΟC, 3.
  ΑΝΓΕΛΟC, 15.
ΑΓΙΟΝ, 33.
  ΑΓΙΩΝ, 12.
  ϙΑΓΙΑ, 22.
ϙΡΕΤΙΚΩC, αἱρετικος, 6.
ΕΧΜΑΛΩCΙΑ, αἰχμαλωσια, 8.
ΔΙΩΝ, 13.
ΑΚΡΙΒΙΑ, ακριβεια, 11.
ΑΛΛΑ, 3.
ΑΛΥΘΙΝΟC, αληθινος, 39.
?ΑΜΑ, 16.
ΑΝΑΓΓΕ, αναγκη, 27.
ΑΝΑΚΑCΕ, αναγκαζειν, 11.
ΑΝΑΓΝΩCΤΗC, 5.
ΑΝΕΧΕ, ανεχειν, 4.
ΑΝΤΦΑΝΑΡΙ, αντιφοναριον, 44.
ΑΠΑ, 7V, 12,13,22,25,29,37,38,45R,
    46, 50, Ἀρ.R.
  ΑΠ, 20.
  ΠΠ, 15.
ΑΠΑΝΤΑ, απαντᾶν, 5.
ΑΠΟΚΡΙCΙC, 22,25.
  ΑΠΟΚΡ, 24.
  ΑΠΩΚΡΕCΙC, 12.
  ΑΠΩΚΡΗC, 30.
ΑΠΟCΤΟΛΟC, 2,10,44.
ΑΡΕΤΗ, 23.
ἀρθ, 53. (v. Stern, Ä.Z.'85, 157.)
ΑΡΧΗΜΑΝΤΡΙΤΗC, αρχιμαν-
  -δριτης, 25.
ΑΡΧΙCΙΜΑΧΙ, αρχισυμμαχος,
  45 V.   [-ηγος, 10.
ΑΡΧΗCΤΡΑΤΙΚΟ[C], αρχιστρατ-

ΑΡΧ[ΩΝ], 7R, 12, 53.
ἀρ?, Ἀρ.(v. ad l.Rec.41.)
ΑCΠΑΖΕ, ασπαζειν, 12,13,14,20,
  21, 23, 25.
ΑCΥCΤΡΟΦΟC, 34.
ΑΦΩΡΙΖΕ, αφοριζειν, 24.

ΒΕΡCΑ, βυρσα, Ἀρ.R.
ΒΙΤΤΙΝΑ, ?πυτινη, 46.
ΒΟΗΘΟC, 7R.
ΒΩΙΘΙΑ, βοηθεια, 23.

ΓΑΛΛΑΝΙ, καλλαινος?, 47.
  ΓΑΛΛΑΕΙ, ditto?, 47.
ΓΑΡ, 1,3, 7R, 11, 34.
ΓΕΡΑΜΕΟC, κεραμευς, Ἀρ.
ΓΗC, 8.
ΓΙ, 46, ΓΙ, 51, γινεται.
?ΓΟΚΡΟC, κοκκος, 47.
ΚΡΑΜΜΑ, γραμμα, 18.
ΓΡΑΦΗ (ΧΩΩΜΙΝ·), 44.

ΔΕ, 1,2,27. ΔΗ, 8.
ΔΕΙΜΩCΙ, δημοσιον, 54.
ΔΕΚΑΤΗ, δεκατης, 51.
  ΔΕΚ, 35.
ΔΕΚΙ, δεχεσθαι, 27.
  δεχι, 43.
ΔΕΥΤΕ, 8.
ΔΙΑΚΟΝΟC, 5. ΔΙΑΚΟΝ, 45.
  ΔΙΑΚ, 13,14,22, Ἀρ.V.
  ΔΙΑΚΟΥ, 44,50. ΔΙΑΚΩΝ,
  45. ΔΙ, 12,15,23,24,27.
  Δ, 19. ΤΙΑΚΟΥ, 42.
ΔΙΚΑΙΟΝ, 14.
δι, διπλο[κεραμιον], 30,45.
ΔΟΓΜΑΤΙΟΝ, ?δογματικος, 13.
ΔΟCΙ, δοκειν, 4.

ΕΓΕΙΡΕCΘΑΙ, εγειρεσθε, 8.
ΕΘΝΟC, 7R. ϙεθνος, 3.
?ΕΙΔΟC, v. ΗΤΕC.
ΕΙΔΩΛΟΝ, 5.
ΕΙΚΟCΙ, 51.
ΕΙΜΗ, ει μη, 6.
ΕΙΡΗΝΗ, 13. ΙΡΗΝΗ, 19,30,40.
  ΗΡΗΝΙ, 12,16.
ΕΚΚΛΗCΙΑ, 13. ΕΚΛΗCΙΑ, 28.
  ΕΚΛΕCΙΑ, 30.
ΕΛΑΧΙC, ελαχιστος, 12.
  ΕΛΑΧΥC, 23. ΕΛΑΧ, 13.
ΕΛΠΙC, 8.
ΕΝ, εν, 17,27.
ΕΝΔ, ενδοξοτατος, 12.
ΕΞΗΚΟΝΤΑ, 51.
ΕΞΟΥCΙ, ?εξουσια, 21.
ΕΠΑΚΟΥCΟΝ, 8.
ΕΠΙΘΥΜΙΑ, 2.
ΕΠΙCΚΟΠΟC, 11,12. ΕΠΙCΚ, 23.
ΕΠΙCΤΟΛΗ, 11.
ΕΠΙΤΑ, επειτα, 23,27.
ΑΠΠΟΥΜΙC, επωμις, 47.
?ΕCΧΑΤ, εσχατον, 11.
ΕΥΑΓΓΕΛΙΟΝ, 44.
  ΕΟΥΑΓΓΕΛΙΟΝ, 44.
ΕΥΓΕΝΗC, 4.
ΕΥΛΟΓΕΙΤΕ, 8.
ΕΥΧΑΡΙCΤ, ευχαριστειν, 12.
ΕΥΧ, ευχη, 23.
Η, ειη, 9.
Ι, η, 8.
ϙΗΓΕΜΩΝ, ηγεμων, 7R.
ϙΗΓΟΥΜΕΝΟC, ηγουμενος, 35.
ϙΗΜΕΡΟC, ημερος, 4.
ΗΜΩΝ, ημων, 8.
ΗΤΕC, ?ειδος, 24.

ΘΗΡΙΩΝ, θηριον, 6.
ΘΥCΙΑ, 1.

Ι, ή, 8.
ΙΔΟΥ, 8.
ΙΗC, Ιησους, 23,39. ΙC, 2,12.
ϱΙΛΑCΤΗΡΙ, ιλαστηριον, 11.
ΙΚΟΥΜΕΝΗ, οικουμενη, 5.
ΙΝΔ, ινδικτιωνος (genit.) 35.
ΙΟΥΔΑΙ and ΙΟΥΤΑΙ, 6.
ϱΙCΤΩΡ[ΙΑ], ιστορια, 5.

ΚΑΔΟΥC, καδος, 34.
ΚΑΘΑΡΩΝ, καθαρος, 12.
ΚΑΘΕΔΡΑ, 5.
ΚΑΘΟΛΙΚΟΝ, καθολικος, 44.
ΚΑΙ, 35?, 35,47. Κϛ, 51.
ΚΑΚΟC, κακως. ΚΑΚΗ(†), 11.
ΚΛΚΕΛΙ, καγκελος, 55.
ΚΑΛΩC, 15,16,22,41. καλος, 12, 13,14,22.
ΚΑΜΑCΙ, καμασιον, 25.
ΚΑΝ, 4, 23.
ΚΑΡΠΟC, 51.
ΚΑΤΑ, 2,11,12,13,14,23,24,25,36, 37,44. ΚΑΤΑΡΑ', 15. ΚΑΤΑΛΛΑ, 24.
ΚΑΤΑΞΙΟΝ?, 8.
ΚΑΤΑΠΗΤΗC,? καταπητασ-μα, 47. [11.
ΚΑΤΑΦΡΟΝΙ, καταφρονειν.
ΚΑΤΕΧΕ, κατεχειν, 14. ΚΑΤΕΧΙ, 26.
ΚΑΥCΩΝ, 7ℛ.
ΚΕΛΕΥΕ, κελευειν, 25. ΚΕΛΕΥ, 26,28.
ΚΕΡΑΜΕΩC, κεραμευς,45. ΓΕΡΑΜΕΟC, αβ. βαραμεος, 53. βαρα?37.
ΚΕΡΑΜΙΑ, 46.
ΚΕϱ, ? κεραμος, αβV.

ΚΛΗΡΙΚΟC, 47.
ΚΛΗΡΟΝΟΜ[ΕΙ], κληρονομειν,5.
?ϱΟΚϱΟC, κοκκος, 47.
ΚΟΛΛΑΘΙ, κολαθος, κ., αβV.
ΚΟΥΜΑΡΙΤΕC, αβR.
ΚΩΜΑΡΙ, αβR.
?ΚΟΥΠΛΙ, 14.
ΚΟΥϱ, κουρι, κ, 11,46,51,54.
ΚΟΥΦΟΝ, 54. ΚΟΥΦ, 51.
ΚΡΑΜΜΑ, γραμμα, 18.
ΚΡΙΝΕ, κρινειν, 11.
ΚΡΙΤΗC, 2,3.
ΚΥΡΙΑΚΗ, 22.
ΚΥΡΙΕ (sic), 8. ΚΥΡΙΟΝ (sic), 8.
ΚΥΡΟ, κυριος, 20. ΚΥΡΩ, 22,23. ΚΥ, 12. ΚΙΡΙ, 42.
ΚΙΡΩ,15. ΚΩ, κυριω, 12 (l.29), 17,27.
ΚΩCΜΙΚΩΝ, κοσμικος, 24.

ΛΑΟC, 7ℛ, 25.
ΛΟΓΟC, 44,49,54. λοκ, 51. ΛΩΚΕC, 48.
ΛΟΙΠΟΝ, 14,22,25. λοιπο, 18. ΛΙΠΟΝ, 24. λιπ, 15,24. λιπ, 20?, 30.

ΜΑΘΕΤΗC, μαθητης, 1.
ΜΑΛΛΩΝ, μαλλον, 23.
ΜΛΠΠΑ, 47.
ΜΕΝ, 13,14. ΜΝ, 17, 25.
ΜΕϱΡΩΝ, μεμβρανον, 44. ΜΗϱΡ, 49.
ΜΙCΤΙΚΟΝ,? μυστικος, 44.
ΜΟΛΒΙΤΗC, 7ℛ.
ΜΟΝΑCΤΗΡΙΟΝ, 35. ΜΟΝΑCΤΗΡΙ, 11,51.
ΜΟΝΟΧΟC, μοναχος, 17. [αβ.
ΜΟCΧΑΤΩΝ,? μοσχατ-αδος,
Ν, νομισμα, 51,54. •/8, 23,36, αβ.

ΝΟΜΟΘΕΤΗC, 2.
ΝΟΙ, νοειν, 34. ΝΩΕΙΝ, 27. ΝΩΕΙ, 43. Νωι, 12.

Ο, ω, 8.
ΩΚΤΩ, οκτω, 51.
ϱΟΜΙΛΙ, ομιλειν, 4.
ΟΜΙΟC, ομοιως, αβV. ομ,45. ομ, 50.
θ, ομου, 46. θ, αβR.
ΟΡΘΟΔΟϟΟC, 25.
ΟΡΘΟΔΩϟΗΙΑ, ορθοδοξια, 6.
ΟΥΔΕ, 11.
ΟΥΚΟΥΝ, 3.
ΟΥΝ, 34.

ΠΑΛΛΙΝ, παλλιον, 47, αβR.
ΠΑΡΑ, 24.
ΠΑΡΑΒΛΑ?, 11.
ΠΑΡΑΓΕ, παραγειν, 5.
ΠΑΡΘΕΝΟC, 22. ΠΑΡΘΕΝΩC, 30. ΠΑΡΘ, 23.
ΠΑΡΟΥ?, παρουσια?, 32.
ΠΑΡϱΗCΙΑ, παρρησια, 15.
ΠΕΝΤΗ, πεντε, 51.
ΠΕΡΑΤΩΝ, 8. [44.
ΠΕΤΑΛΟΝ and ΑΠΕΤΑΛΟΝ
ΠΙΘΕ, πειθειν, 5. ΠΙΘΙ, 22.
ΠΙCΤΕΥΕ, πιστευειν, 4.
ΠΙCΤΙC, 2.
ΠΙΤΑΓΙ,? πιττακιον, 37.
ΠΛΗΝ, 11.
ΠΝΕΥΜΑ, 20,29. ΠΝΑ, 2,11, 12,23,33.
ΠΝΕΥΜΑΤΚΟC, 21. ΠΝΙΚ, 17. ΠΝΙΚ, 23, 40. ΠΚ, 12.
ΠΟΛΕΜΙ, πολεμειν, 4.
ΠΩΛΙΜΟC, πολεμος, 6.
ΠΟΛΙC, 2, αβV. πωλιc, 23, 24, 45ℛ.
ΠΟΝΗΡΙΑ, 3.

ΠΟΤΑΜΙΤΕϹ, ποταμιτης, ap.V.
ΠΡΑΞΙϹ, 44.
ΠΡΕϹΒΥΤΕΡΟϹ, 5.
   πρε, 17. πρ, 27.
ΠΡΟΕΦΘΑϹΑΝ, 8.
ΠΡΟΚΡΗΜΑΤΙΖΕ, προκρι-
  -ατιζειν, 11.
ΠΡΟϹ, 11.
ΠΡΟϹΚΥΝΕ, προσκυνειν, 23.
  ΠΡΟϹΚΥΝΙ, 29. προσ-
  -ΚΗΝϹΟΜΕΝ, προσκυ-
  -ησομεν, 8.
ΠΡΟϹΤΑΤΗϹ, 25.
ΠΡΩΦΗΤΗϹ, προφητης, 7R.

ϹΑΒΒΑΤΟΝ, 1. ϹΑΒΑΤΟΝ, 22.
?ϹΑΧΑ, 17.
ϹΗΜΑΝΕ, σημαινειν, 27.
ϹΙΜΑΧΙ, συμμαχος, 45.
?σιρ, ap.V.
ϹΚΕΠΑΖΕ, σκεπαζειν, 23.
ϹΟΝ, 8.
ϹΟΥΠΛΙΝ, σουβλιον, 55.
ϹΤΑΥΡΟϹ, 47.

ϹΤΑΥΡΟΥ, σταυρουν, 6.
ϹΤϹΙ, στιζειν, 44.
ϹΤΥΧΕ, στοιχειν, 28.
ϹΥ, ?σε, 8.
ϹΥΝΑΓΕ, συναγειν, 29.
ϹΩΜΑ, 11, 23.

ΤΑΝΙ, ? δανειον, 15.
ΤΑΡΙΧΙ, ταριχιον, 53, ap.V.
ΤΗϹ, 8.
ΤΙΚΑΝΙ, τηγανον, 55.
ΤΙΜΩΡΙΑ, 3.
?ΦΙΛΙΑ, 46.
ΤΟΛΜΑ, τολμαν, 28.
ΤΟΝ, 8.
ΤΟΠΟϹ, 22.
ΤΟΤΕ, 1, 7R.
ΤΩΝ, 8.

ΥΙΟΙ, 8. Υ, 36.
ΥΠΠ, υποποδιον, 23.

ΦΑΡΙϹΕΟϹ, 1.
ΦΥΛΙϹΤΙΜ, 7R.
ΦΩΤΟϹ, 8.

ΧΑΡΙϹ, 15.
ΧΑΡΤΗϹ, 44.
ΧΕΡΕ, χαιρε, 10.
ΧΙΛΙΑΔΕϹ, χιλιαδης, 51.
ΧΙΩΝ, 7V.
ΧΡΕΩϹ, χρεωστειν, 51. [5.
ΧΡΗϹΤΙΑΝΟϹ, χριστιανος,
ΧΡΙΑ(ΕΡ-), χρεια, 12, 16.
ΧϹ, Χριστος, 2, 12, 23, 32, 39.

ΨΑΛΤΗΡΙΟΝ, 44.
ΨΥΧΗ, 11, 13. ΨΥΧ, 23. ΨΧΗ, 16.

ω, 6.
ο, ω̃, 8.
ῳΩΔΗ, ωδη, 7R.
ΩΚΤΩ, οκτω, 51.
ῳΩϹΔΕ, ωδε, 1.

?δΑΝΝΑϹΑ, 55.
δΑΡΑΜΕΟϹ, κεραμευς, 37, 53.

---

iv. ARABIC WORDS.

ΚΕΕΙῳ(αλ-), 45; ΚΕΕῳ(αλ-), 26; ΚΕΗῳ(αλ-), 18, 23; ΚΗ-Ηῳ(αλ-), 18, الجيش .

ΜΕῳΜΕΛΑΙ(αλ-), المشلا, 47;
?ϹΟΥΜΑΡΙ, ? سمار, 55.
?δΟΥΛΑΠ(αλ-), fem., 48.

ΤΕΡϱΛΑΜ, درجة, 18.
ΤΕΡϱΛΑΜ, 16.

---

v. COPTIC WORDS.
(a selection only.)
The forms referred to for comparison are the Sahidic.

ⲁ, verb. prefix?, 4.
ⲁ = ⲉ-, preposition, 2, 22.
ⲁⲗ- = ⲁ- (ⲛⲧⲁⲗ-), 25.
ⲁⲗ- = ⲁ, perf., 1.

ⲁⲗⲁⲗⲓ (ⲕⲁⲛ-), 20.
ⲁⲗⲉⲩ = ⲁⲗⲏⲩ, 15. [45].
?ⲁⲙ (ⲁⲙⲧⲉⲗⲓ) = ϩⲁⲙ?

ⲁⲙⲁϱⲉ, 11. ⲁⲙⲁϱⲧⲓ, 6.
ⲁⲙⲏ, 45R., 49, ap.V.
ⲁⲙⲁⲩⲉⲓ, 45.

ⲁⲙⲟⲩ, imperat., 19, 34, 40.
ⲁⲙⲣⲏ, 45R.
ⲁⲛ = ⲟⲛ, 11, 18.
ⲁⲛ ?= ϩⲁⲛ (ⲛⲟⲩϱ), 26.

ⲀⲚⲀⲨ, 14?.
ⲀⲞⲨⲈⲒⲚ, 30.
ⲀⲠⲀⲦ, ap.V.
ⲀⲠⲈⲤ, 44, 47.
ⲀⲢⲀⲒⲔⲀ, ap.V.
ⲀⲢⲒⲔⲈ, 11,12. ⲁⲣⲓⲕⲓ, 43.
ⲀⲢⲰⲒⲚ, ap.V.
?ⲀⲤⲀⲦⲈⲢ, 26.
ⲀⲢ(ⲢⲈⲔ)=?ⲁⲣⲓ, 24.
ⲀⲢⲀ, 14,19,24,21,37,44.
ⲀⲢⲒ(ⲔⲀⲚ-), 17, ap.V.?

ⲂⲀⲞ ⲈⲂⲀⲞ, 18.
ⲂⲀⲢⲞⲦ, ⲂⲀⲢⲰⲦ, 55.
ⲂⲀⲘⲠⲒ, ap.V. [45V.
?ⲂⲀⲢⲘⲈⲤⲒ, or ⲂⲀⲢ ⲘⲈⲤⲒ
ⲂⲈⲢⲒ, 44,47.
ⲂⲒⲔⲎ, ap.V.
?ⲂⲰⲰⲒ, 14.

Ⲉ-, preposition :-
ⲈⲢⲞ-, 6,11,13,14,21.
ⲈⲢⲀ- 6,12,15,23.
ⲢⲀ- 24. ⲈⲖⲀ-,1,6,25
26. ⲖⲀ-,22.
Ⲉ-= Ⲙ, 5,15,17,19,26.
ⲈⲤⲀ=ⲚⲤⲀ,6.
omitted; 20,22,26,30,
38,42.
ⲈⲈ-= Ⲉ-, 27.
ⲈⲂⲀⲞ ⲢⲒ, 12,26. ⲈⲂⲀⲞ
ⲢⲒⲦⲈⲚ,24,29.
ⲂⲀⲞ, 24. ⲂⲀⲞ-,18.
-ⲂⲞⲞ,45V.
ⲈⲒ,vb. 12,14,15,18,22,23,
1, 1,11,18, 23,24, 57.
Ⲓ ⲦⲀⲀⲦ-,36.
ⲈⲒⲘⲈ, 11,14. ⲒⲘⲈ,11.
ⲈⲒⲢⲈ and vars, 1,5,12,43
ⲈⲢ-, 11,13,27,43.
ⲈⲞ-,24,25,29, ap.R.

Ⲣ, 12,34.
ⲀⲀ-, 11. ⲈⲒⲦ-,24.
ⲀⲞⲈ,11.
ⲈⲒⲤ, interject., 11,15.
ⲈⲒⲰⲦ,ⲒⲰⲦ, passim.
ⲒⲞⲦⲈ, 13. ⲒⲰⲦ,7V.
ⲈⲔⲰⲦ, 17.
ⲞⲈ=ⲈⲞⲈ, ⲈⲢⲈ, 38.
ⲈⲞⲔⲞⲨ, 55.
ⲈⲞⲠⲎⲒ, 1.
ⲈⲘⲀⲦ, 40.
ⲈⲚ,vb. 11. ⲈⲚⲦ-,14,23,
24,28. Ⲛ̄Ⲧ-,11.
ⲈⲠ-(ⲢⲰⲘⲈ), 23.
ⲈⲠⲬⲒⲚⲬⲎ,11.
ⲈⲢⲦⲀⲂ,48. ⲈⲞⲦⲀⲞ,54
ⲈⲢⲰⲀⲚ,4,28.
ⲈⲢⲰⲰⲚ,47.
ⲈⲤⲀⲨ,1,45R., ap.R.
ⲈⲦⲀ-, part.perf.absol,1.
ⲈⲦⲀ-, relat.perf,2,27.
ⲈⲦⲂⲎ (v.Stern,§.558)
22.
ⲈⲰⲞⲨ,7R.(cf.ⲰⲞⲨ,i)
ⲈⲰⲰⲠⲈ,14,28.
ⲈⲰⲰⲠⲒ,11.
ⲈⲢⲎⲦ, 23.
ⲈⲢⲞⲚ=ⲈⲢⲞⲨⲚ, ap.
ⲢⲞⲨⲚ,30,37.
ⲈⲂⲰⲰⲬ(Ⲡ-),45R.,ap.R.

ⲎⲒ, ap.R. ⲎⲒ,43.
ⲎⲢⲠ,11,15,19,24.ⲈⲢⲠ,30.
ⲐⲎⲦ,vb.,13.

?Ⲓ, ap.R.
ⲒⲈ,11.
ⲒⲰ,11. ?ⲒⲞⲨⲈ,45V.
ⲒⲰⲦ,?barley,48,ap.V.?
ⲒⲰⲢⲒ(ⲤⲒⲦ-),36.

?ⲔⲀⲘⲎ?,57(cf.ⲔⲀⲘⲎⲞⲒ,i?)
ⲔⲀⲢⲈ,vb.,45R.
ⲔⲀⲦ, build,17.
ⲔⲀⲦ ?=ⲚⲔⲀⲦ, 28.
ⲔⲀⲰ, 27?,53?. [46.
ⲔⲈ, 11,13,18,23,24,29,44.
ⲔⲈⲖⲈⲂⲒⲚ,55.
ⲔⲈⲖⲈ, ap.V.
?ⲔⲈⲚ,24.
ⲔⲈⲢⲒ,24.
?Ⲕ̄Ⲕ̄(ⲈⲦ),ap.V.
ⲔⲞⲨⲒ,6,11,13,26,30,44,46,
47. ⲔⲞⲨⲚ-(v.p.32)29.
45V.,46?. ⲔⲞⲚ-(v.p.
32,)17. ⲔⲀⲚ-(v.p.32)
17,20,44,45V.
?ⲔⲦⲎⲎⲘ, ap.V.
ⲔⲨⲖⲒ(ⲢⲀⲘ-),45.
ⲔⲰ ⲚⲢⲦⲎ-,8.
ⲔⲀⲀ-,15. ⲔⲀ-,24.
ⲔⲈ,23. ⲔⲈⲈ-,22,23,
30,38. ?ⲔⲀ,23.
ⲔⲰⲦ,8,27?

Ⲗ. For M.E. initial Ⲗ; v.
at ⲣ.
ⲖⲀ, cease,6. (v.p.83.)
ⲖⲀⲀⲨ,11,25. ⲖⲀⲨ,16.
ⲖⲞⲨ,14?,23.
ⲖⲀⲔ=ⲖⲞⲔ,(ⲈⲒⲤ-),55.
?ⲖⲀⲖⲈⲈⲦ,53.
ⲖⲀⲤ,6.
ⲖⲈⲔⲰⲦⲤⲒ &c., v. ⲢⲞⲖⲞ-
-ⲔⲞⲦⲦⲒⲚⲞⲤ.
ⲖⲈⲤⲒ, 16,ap.V.

ⲘⲀ, imperat., 14?.
ⲘⲀⲀⲢⲈ =ⲘⲞⲞⲰⲈ, 2.
ⲘⲀⲒ(ⲚⲞⲨⲦⲈ),11,12,16,17,
20,21,24,34,42.
ⲘⲀⲔ-, aor.neg., 11.

ⲘⲀⲚ-, herd, 45. [ap.V.
ⲘⲀⲚⲈ-,49. ⲘⲀⲚⲒ-,
ⲘⲀⲢ,? optat.,14.
ⲘⲀⲞ-,11,24.
ⲘⲀⲤⲒ,49. ⲘⲈⲤⲒ, ap.R.
ⲘⲈ =Ⲙ̄Ⲛ, 18,23,24,30,
36,37,48.
ⲘⲈ (ⲠⲰⲰⲤ Ⲉ-), 5.
ⲘⲈⲢⲒⲦ,14,15,33,43.
ⲘⲈⲢⲎⲦ,6. ⲘⲈⲖⲒⲦ,22.
ⲘⲢⲢⲈⲦⲈ,2.
ⲘⲈⲨⲈ,ⲘⲈⲨⲒ,13.
ⲘⲈⲢⲒ,20. ⲘⲈⲢ-,46?.
ⲘⲀⲢ-,22,48.
ⲘⲈⲢⲦ.6.
ⲘⲚⲎⲰⲈ,14. ⲘⲚⲰⲈ,13.
ⲘⲎⲚⲈⲘⲀⲚ=Ⲙ̄ⲘⲒⲚⲘ̄
-ⲘⲞⲚ,11.
ⲘⲘⲞ-,11,12,27,54?.
ⲘⲞ-,11. ⲘⲘⲀ-,15,24,
25,28,44. ⲘⲀ-,6,11,
12,16,23,24,26,28,30.
ⲘⲚⲚⲤⲀ, v. ⲚⲤⲀ.
ⲘⲚⲦ-,2,11,17. ⲘⲈⲦ-,5,
6,16,20,21,22,24,25,30
ⲘⲞⲈⲒⲦ,23.
ⲘⲞⲨ,vb.,28.
ⲘⲞⲨⲈⲒ,45.
ⲘⲠⲀⲦⲈ,11,28.
ⲘⲠⲈ-,6,11,12,14,23.
ⲚⲠⲈ-,24. [11.
ⲘⲠⲈⲢ-,6,12,14. ⲘⲠⲈⲞ
ⲠⲈⲞ-,26. ⲚⲠⲈⲢ-,24.
ⲚⲠⲈⲞ-24.
ⲘⲠⲰⲀ,2.
ⲘⲦⲞⲚ,ⲘⲦⲀⲚ,vars,6,12,
13,20,33. [ap.V.
ⲘⲀⲨ(ⲦⲀⲒ-)?=ⲘⲞⲞⲨ,

Ⲛ,Dative:-ⲚⲀⲒ,11,12,21,
24,27; ⲚⲈⲒ,16,19,26,

29,41; ΝΗΙ, 14,25;
ΝΔΚ, 12,15,18,23,34,
40; ΝΕΚ, 16,19,26;
ΝΗΚ, 6,11,25; ΝΕ,4,
ΝΔϥ,11,24; ΝΗϥ,1.
11; ΝΕΒ,11; ΝΔΝ,15,
18,23; ΝΗΤΝ,11;
ΝΛΥ,11; ΝΗΟΥ,1.
ΝΛ´, possess. art., Ap.R.
ΝΛ, pity, 12. ΝΛΙ,6,22
ΝΕΕΙ,1.
ΝΛΙ, demonstr., 12,17,
23,24; ΝΕΙ,17,19,20,
30; ΝΗ,27; ΝΙ,13,
21².
ΝΛΝΟΥϥ, 25. ΝΛΝΟΥΒ
6. ΝΛΝΟΥС,22.
ΝΕΥ, hour, 6².
ΝΛϣΤ[Ε] (ep.),6.
ΝΕ, copul., 2,11,12,20.
ΝΕ, artic., 44,45,54,Ap.
  ΝΙ,40.   [22,30.
ΜΕΝΕ´ = ΝΜΜΛ, 19,24
? ΝΕΤ (or ΠΑΝΕΤ),22.
ΝΕϨΙ, vb., 1.
ΝΗΗΒ, Ap.R.
ΝΗΥ, 23: ΝΗΟΥ,14.
ΝΙΒΕΝ, 13,31. ΝΙΒΙ,25,26.
ΝΙΜ, 6,11,21,23,29,33,37,38.
ΝΝ´= Ν´, before vowel,
1,7R, 25,46.
ΝΛΒΕ,11. ΝΛΒΙ,1.
ΝΟΥΝ, 11².
ΝΟΥ =ΝΟΥΤΕ,12,17,18,19,
20,23,24,30.
ϥϮ, 13,27.
ΝΟΥϥ,?gold, 24.
? ΝΟΥϥ(Π´),45.
ΝΛϨΜ,23.
?ΝΟΥϨΙ, Ap.R.   [26.
ΝΟ6, 13,32,47,51. ΝΛ6,

ΝСΛΒΛΛ´,34.
ΜΝΝСΛ,17,24.
  ΜΝΝΕСΛ,19.   [30?
ΜΕΝΕСΛ,12,18,20,26,
ΝΤΛΛ´, perf., 25.
ΝΤΕ, genit., 17. ΕΝΤΕ
24, ΝΤΕΚ,17.ΝΤΗΜ
11.?ΝΤΝ,17. ΝΤΕ-
-ΤΕΥΤΝ,11.ΝΤΛΟΥ
16.
ΝΤΕ, conjunctive:—
ΤΕ,13,23. ΤΛ´,11,12,
14,16. ?ΤΛΙ´,22.
ΝΚ´,14. Νϥ´,11,23,
51. ΕΝϥ´,12. ΝΒ?
19,29. ΕΝΒ´,12.
ΝΕΒ´,18. ΝΤΕΒ´,
26. ΤΕΒ´,17. ΝΤΕΝ
28. ΝСΕ,11. ΤΟΥ´,
12,23,30.
ΝΤΟΟΤ´,5. ΝΤΛΛΤ´,14,
ΝΤϨ,8.
ΕΝϣΛ´, aor.part.,12.
? ΝΧΙ, 5.

ΟΥΕ =ΟΥΛ, 23,44.
ΠΟΥΛ ΠΟΥΛ,13.
ΟΥΛΛΒΕ, 2. ΟΛΛΒ,
15. ΟΥΕΕΒ,38.
ΟΥΕΒ, 22.
ΟΥΛΙΕ, 11,45V.
ΟΥΙΕ,45.
? ΟΥΛΧΗΡ, vb., 15.
ΟΥΛΧ, 11,23.
ΟΥΕΝΙΝ,44.
? ΟΥΕΝΗ, Ap.R.
? ΟΥΕСΛωϨ, vb., 15.
ΟΥΕϨ´,12. ΟΥΗϨ,5.
ΟΥΛΕΙω,6.
ΟΥΟΝ, 31,33. ΟΥΛΝ,1,6,
10,23,26.

ΟΥω,11,20.
ΟΥωΜ,40.
ΟΥΟΡΠ´,13. ΟΥΛΡΠ´,23.
ΟΥωΤΕΒ, 35.
ΟΥωϮ,23. ΟΥΛΛΤΕ,
18,23. ΟΥΛΤΕ,14,26.
ΟΥΛΛΤ´, 12,18.
Ο̊ΛΤ´,16.
ΟΥωϣ,12, 17,19, 20, 26,
27,28. ΟΥΕϣ,1.
ΟΥωϣΕΠ, Ap.V.
ΟΥωϣΗ,8.
ΟΥϨωωρ, Ap.V.
ΟΥΧΛΙ,6,12,13,14,15,17,18,
27,31,33. ουτϟ̇δι,43.
ΟΥΧΕΙ, 16,20,22,25,
30.

ΠΛ´, poss. art., 22,45,52,
Ap.R.
ΠΛΛΠΙ, 40.
ΠΛΙ, demonstr., 4, 23.
ΠΕΙ, 17, 22,24.
?ΠΛΛ, noun, 24.
?ΠΛΠΙ, 45R.   [Ap.V.
ΠΛΡΕС (or ?Greek),26,
ΠΛΡΜΟΥΤΕ (Πωλ),
45V.
ΠΛϨΛΥ(ϨΕ´),12.
ΠΕ, copul., 1,6,11,14,19,
25,31,34,36,37. [Ap.V.
ΠΕΝΙΠΙ,55. ΠΙΝΙΠΙ,
ΠΙ, artic., 11,13,18,26.
ΠωΤ, 6,23,24. ΠΟΤ,22.
ΠωϨ, 6,23.

ΛΛΕΙС, 26, 45V.
ΛΛΙС, 22.
ρΛΤ, foot:— ρΛϥ,6.
?ρΕ´, 24.   [Ap.
ρΕΜ´, 23,45. ΛΕΜ´,28,

ρΕΜΙΛΥΙ,6.
ΛΕΝ,30. ΛΝ,22.
ΛΕϥ´,Ap.V. ΛΕΒ´,22,26,
Ap.R.
ΛΕϨΤΕ,45.
ρΗΜΗ,6.
ρω,11.
ρωϣΕ,11.?Λωϣι,26.
СΛΒΛΛ,37.
СΛΒΤΙ (ΚΟΝ´),17.
СΛΙΗ, 15,24.
СΛΝ, artifex, 17, 23.
СΛΠωϣΙ,13.
СΛΡΕΤ, Ap.R.
СΛΥ=СΟΟΥ, 21.
?СΛΥΒΟΥ´,11.
СΛϨ[Τ´],22.
СΛ6 (ep´),11.
СΒω (Ϯ),11.
?СΕΚ,14.   [V.
СΕΤ´,11. СΕΤΕϥΡΗΧ,
СΕΤ ΕϨΟΥΝ,19.
СΙΤΙωϨΙ,36.
СΕϥΤωΤ,25.
СΗΗΠΕ,14,29?
СΙΜ,45R.
СΜΛΤ,11.
СΜΟΥ,15,21,38.
СΝΛΥ,23? СΝΕΥ,25,26,
СΝΟΥΤΙ,22.
СΟΝ, СΛΝ,passim.
Ĉ,23. СΝΗΥ,13,14,
23. СΝΗΟΥ,29,Ap.V.
СΟΟΥΝ,11,34.
СΛΟΥΝ,1,29.
СΟΠ,11,13,32. СΛΠ,6,14,
18,24, 29.
СΟΥΟ,49. СΟΥΛ,48,54.
СΟΥΤωΝ,6.
СΟΥωΝΤ,6.

?ⲤⲢⲂⲈ =?ⲤⲢϤⲈ, 34.	ⲦⲈⲒ, demonstr., 22, 24.	ⲦⲰⲱ, vb., 11. Ⲧⲗⲱ, 11.	ⲱⲦⲈⲔⲗ, 6.
?ⲤⲦⲀ, 24.	?ⲦⲈⲗ = ?ⲂⲟⲖ. ⲭⲁⲗ, Ⴃр?	ϕ = ϥ in ⲡⲉϕ, ⲧⲏϥϕ, 43	ⲱⲦⲎⲚ, 47.
ⲤⲦⲈⲢⲦⲈⲢ, 7.ℛ.	ⲦⲈⲗ = ⲦⲎⲢ, 30. [25.		ⲱⲦⲰⲢⲒ, 23.
ⲤⲰ, 20.	ⲦⲈⲚⲚⲗⲞⲨ, 6. ⲦⲚⲀⲨ	ⲱⲱ, read, 44, Ⴃр.ℛ.	ⲱⲱⲤ, 28. ⲱⲟⲤ, Ⴃр.
ⲤⲰⲚⲒ, 6, 29.	ⲦⲈϤⲚⲞⲞⲨⲈ, 17.	?ⲱⲢⲤ, 55.	ⲱⲗⲤ, Ⴃр.ⅴ.
ⲤⲰⲞⲨⲉ, 12.	?ⲦⲈϤⲚⲀⲨⲈⲒ, ib.		ⲱϪⲰⲦ(ⲤⲀⲚ), 17.
ⲤⲰⲞⲨⲀϩ ⲈϩⲞⲨⲚ, 3	ⲦⲎⲂⲈⲦ, Ⴃр.ⅴ.		ⲱⲟⲁⲢ, Ⴃр.
ⲤϩⲀⲒ, 11, 12, 13, 18, 23, 27, 28, 33. ⲤⲭⲀⲒ, 43. ⲤϩⲈⲒ 26, 29, 37, 38. ⲤϩⲈ, 26. ⲤⲀⲒ, 41. ⲤⲈⲒ, 22. ⲤϩⲎⲦ, 23. ⲤϩⲈⲦ, 26. ⲤϩⲎⲦ 31.	ⲦⲒ, for †, prefx. 1 sg., 12, 13, 14, 16, 17, 20, 22, 23, 26, 28, 29, 30, 33, 38, 43. for †, vb., 12, 18, 20, 22, 23, 24, 50. also in ⲚⲞⲨⲦⲒ, 16, 26, 37, 38, 41; ⲠⲈⲦⲒ-18; ⲠⲒⲗⲰⲦⲒ, 36; ⲠⲒ-ⲤⲒⲚⲦⲒ, 12; ⲠⲮ-ⲰⲦⲒ, 43; ⲤⲚⲞⲨ-ⲦⲒ, 22; ⲦⲒⲢⲎⲚⲎ 19; ⲦⲒⲔⲀⲚⲒ, 55.	ⲱⲗ, prefn., 15, 26, 27, ⲱⲗ ⲉ-, 13. ⲱⲗⲒⲱ, 25. ⲱⲗⲘⲦⲒ, 48. ⲱⲗⲚⲦⲈ, 11, 12, 22. [13. ⲱⲗⲚⲦⲒ, 14. ⲱⲗⲦⲉ, ⲱⲗⲡ, 15. [45ⅴ. ?ⲱⲗⲡⲀⲢⲘⲞⲨⲦⲈ (ⲡ), ⲱⲗⲢ, 47. [25 ⲱⲗⲢⲈ, aor., 11, 14, 22, 24, ?ⲱⲗⲢⲰⲦ, Ⴃр.ℛ. [25.	ϩⲒⲦ, 11. ⲂⲒⲦ, 22, 45ⅴ. ϩ in ⲤϩⲎⲦ, 31; ϩⲗⲒⲎ, 13; ϩⲈⲘ, 31; ϩⲈⲚ, 39 ϩⲗⲉⲒ = ϩⲗⲎ, 2. ϩⲗⲢⲠ = ϩⲱⲢⲠ, 2. ϩⲉϥⲦ = ⲱⲗϥⲦⲈ, 2. ϩⲘ, 2. ϩⲚ, ib. ϩⲰⲠⲈ = ⲱⲱⲠⲈ, 2.
ⲤϩⲒⲘⲈ, 11. ⲤϩⲒⲘⲎ, 6. ⲤⲒⲘⲒ, Ⴃр.ℛ.		ⲱⲗⲨ(ⲉⲢ-), 11. ⲱⲉⲨ, ⲱⲉⲉⲒ = ⲱⲗ, 45ⅴ. ⲱⲉⲱⲂ = Ⲥⲗⲱϥ, 28. ?ⲱⲉⲃ̄, Ⴃр.ℛ. ⲱⲉⲘⲗ, 24. ?ⲱⲉⲢⲡ (ϩⲱⲂ), 11. ⲱⲎ =? ⲱⲒ, 48. ⲱⲎⲚ, 22, 45ⅴ, 46, Ⴃрℛ ⲱⲉⲚ, 49, 52.	ϩⲗ, prefn., 18, 23. ϩⲗⲗ, 16, 22, 41. ϩⲗⲂⲗⲗ, 11. ϩⲗⲔⲈ, 45ℛ. ?ϕⲗⲘ, Ⴃр.ℛ. ϩⲗⲘⲔⲨⲗⲒ, 45ℛ. ϩⲗⲘⲱⲈ, 34. ϩⲗⲘⲱⲎ, 45, Ⴃр. ϩⲗⲘϩⲈⲘ, 7ℛ. ϩⲗⲢⲉϩ, 11, 21. ϩⲗⲦ, 27, 53?
ⲦⲀ, poss. art., Ⴃр.ℛ. ⲦⲀⲀⲦ, 18, 22, 24, 36. ?ⲦⲀⲂⲰ, 45ⅴ. ⲦⲀⲒ = ⲚⲦⲀⲒ, rel. pers? 36, 37. ⲦⲀⲒⲀ, 10, 12. ⲈⲦⲦⲀⲒⲎⲞⲨ, 11, 29. ⲈⲦⲦⲀⲒⲎⲞⲨⲦ, 30. ⲈⲦⲦⲀⲒⲎ?, 21. ⲈⲦⲦ, 14, 22, 26, 38. ⲈⲦⲀⲈⲒⲞⲨⲦ, 16. ⲈⲦ^ᴧ, 12, 20, 23.	†, vb., 11, 13, 15, 34, 54. ?ⲦⲎ, 22. ⲦⲀⲗ, 12 ⲦⲀ, 12, 23. ⲦⲀⲒⲦ, 30. ⲦⲈⲒⲦ, 14, 24. ?ⲦⲀⲒ, Ⴃр.ⅴ. ?†ⲈⲗⲒ, 45ⅴ. In address; ⲦⲀⲀⲤ, 11, 34, 36, 38. ⲦⲈⲈⲒⲦⲤ, 22. ⲦⲈⲒⲤ, 16, 25, 42. ⲦⲞⲚ(ⲦⲒ), 22. [23.	ⲱⲒⲚⲈ, 11, 13, 14, 17, 21, 23, 28. ⲱⲒⲚⲒ, 12, 13, 15, 16, 20, 22, 24-27, 30, 38, 40. ⲟϫⲓⲛⲓ, 43. ⲱⲒⲚⲈⲒ, 33. ⲱⲎⲚⲒ, 41. ⲱⲎⲗ = ⲱⲗⲎⲗ, 6. ⲱⲟⲡⲒ = ⲱⲱⲠⲈ, 22. ⲱⲟⲟⲠ, 35. ⲱⲟⲠ, 22. ⲟϫⲱⲡⲓ, 43.	ϩⲗⲦⲈϩ, 25. ϩⲗⲐⲎ, 12, 22, 23. ϩⲗⲑⲈ, 11. ϩⲗϩⲦⲎ, 28. ϩⲗⲦⲎ, 14, 24, 34.
ⲦⲀⲔⲀ, 24. ⲦⲀⲗⲀ, 11, 50. ⲦⲀⲗⲈ, 50. ⲦⲀⲘⲞ, 31. ⲦⲀⲘⲰ, 27. ⲦⲀⲘⲀ, 6, 11, 16, 20, 23, 24, 26, 28, 29, 30. ⲦⲀⲘⲦ, 24. [11. ⲦⲀⲢⲈ, ⲦⲀⲗⲈ, conj. fut. ⲦⲗⲞⲨⲀ, 16, 17, 19. ⲦⲀⲨⲀ, 11. ⲦⲈ, copul., 1, 36? ⲦⲈ, ⲦⲀ, ⲧⲟ, conjunct, v. ⲚⲦⲈ.	ⲦⲞⲩ, nome, 35. ⲦⲀⲩ ⲦⲟⲃⲈ (ⲗⲈⲘ), 28. ⲦⲢⲗⲠ, 55. [ib. ⲦⲢⲈ, part, 44. ⲦⲢⲀ ⲦⲤⲖⲒⲈⲱⲗϪⲈ, 4. ?ⲦⲰⲂⲈⲦⲀⲂⲈⲦⲈⲂ?, 55. ⲦⲀⲨ = ⲦⲞⲞⲨ, 8. ⲦⲰⲦ, 20. ⲦⲰⲦ ⲘⲈⲚ 31, 37. ?ⲦⲀⲦ, 24.	ⲱⲟⲢⲠ and vars., 13, 14, 17, 33, 36, 37, 38, 50. ⲱⲟⲦ, 53. ⲱⲦⲀⲘ, 6.	ϩⲈ = ϩⲘ, 16, 19, 20, 22, 23. ϩⲈⲚⲚ, 7ℛ. ϩⲚⲚ, 41. ϩⲈ, manner, 34. ϩⲎ, 12, 23, 24, 25, 37. ϩⲈⲒ, interjecta., 1, 12, 16, 19, 23, 26, 30. ϩⲈ, 24.

ϩⲉⲗ,25. ?ⲫⲗ,45.
ϩⲉⲗⲁ(ⲡ·), ap.V.
?ϩⲗⲁ,22.
ϩⲉⲙⲥ, corn-ear, 1.
ϩⲉⲛ, indef. art.,17,26,
ϩⲁⲛⲛ,7R.
ϩⲉⲛⲉⲟⲩ = ?ϩⲛⲁⲁⲩ,30.
ϩⲏⲙⲉⲭ,12. ϩⲩⲙⲉⲭ,
45V.
ϩⲏⲧ, heart, 13,20,23,24,
ϩⲧⲏ′,8.
ϩⲓ, prep.tn., 6,11,15,26,
32. ϩⲓⲱⲱ′,24.
ϩⲉ,12.
ϩⲓ, vb.;, 41. ϩⲓ ⲧⲁⲗⲧ,1.
ϩⲓⲣ(ⲡ′),14.
ϩⲓⲥⲉ,34. ϩⲓⲥⲓ,24.
ϩⲓⲧⲛ,ϩⲓⲧⲉⲛ,13,22,
23,24,29,46.
ϩⲓⲉⲧⲛ,42.
In address;11,16.
ϩⲓⲭⲟ sic = ϩⲓⲭⲛ,18.
ϩⲓⲭⲱ sic,23.

ϩⲙⲁⲁⲥ,23.
ϩⲙⲏ, forty,22.
ϩⲟ(†),13.
ϩⲟⲗⲟⲕⲟⲧⲧⲓⲛⲟⲥ,35.
ⲗⲉⲕⲱⲧⲥⲓ,15.
ⲗⲟⲩⲓⲕⲧ,18.
ϩⲟⲙⲧ,?31.
ϩⲟⲩⲁⲧⲉ,12,23.
ϩⲟⲩⲁ,20.
ϩⲣⲁⲱ,24.   [ap.V.
ϩⲣⲉ, food, 19?. ϩⲣⲏ,11,
ϩⲣⲟⲕ,4.
ϩⲱⲃⲥ, covering,47.
ϩⲱⲕ,11, ap.V. ϩⲁⲕ·,11.
ϩⲱⲛⲧ ⲉϩⲟⲩⲛ,23.
ϩⲱⲭ,22.

ⲭ = ϭ in ϭⲁⲣⲉⲭ,6;
?ⲛⲭⲓ,5.
ⲭ′=ⲭⲉ, 6,24,28,29.
ⲭⲁⲗⲉ vb.,20.
?ⲭⲉⲓⲗⲓ, ap.V.
ⲭⲁⲗ, v. ⲧⲉⲗ.

ⲧϫⲉⲛ(ⲁⲣⲓⲕⲓ),43.
ⲭⲏⲣⲉ, ap.R.
ⲭⲏϭⲧ,6.
ⲭⲓ, 15,21,22,23,47,54, ap.R.
ⲭⲓⲧ′, 14,16,25,28,57.
ⲭⲓ ⲥϩⲁⲓ,11.
ⲭⲓⲛ, prep.tn.;
ⲉⲭⲓⲛ,11,30. ⲉⲭⲛ,2.
ϭⲓⲛⲉ′,13.
ⲭⲓⲛ′=ϭⲓⲛ′,6.
ⲭⲛⲟⲩ′,22. ⲭⲉⲛⲟⲩ′,44.
ⲭⲟ[ⲉ]ⲃⲟⲗ,45V.
ⲭⲟⲕ ⲉⲃⲟⲗ,13. ⲭⲏⲕ
ⲉⲃⲁⲗ,23.
ⲭⲟⲩⲧⲉϥⲧⲏ,57.
ⲭⲣⲭⲣⲉ = Sah. ⲭⲏⲣ,2.
ⲭⲱⲱⲙⲉ,12.
ⲭⲱⲱⲙⲓ,44.

ϭ=ⲕ in ⲁⲟϭⲓ,4;
ϭⲁⲣⲁⲙⲉⲟⲥ,53,37?.
?ϭⲁⲓⲉ,5. ϭⲁⲓⲏ,24.
ϭⲁⲗ=Boh.ⲭⲟⲗ,7R.

ϭⲁⲗⲗⲩⲭ,25.
ϭⲁⲗⲓⲗ,34.
ϭⲁⲙⲟⲩⲗ,45.
?ϭⲁⲛ, vb., 14,37?, ap.V.?
ϭⲁⲡ′,12,16.
ϭⲁⲣⲉⲭ,6.
ϭⲁⲣⲧⲓ,55.
ϭⲁⲩⲛⲉ,47. ϭⲁⲩⲛⲓ,22.
ϭⲓⲛ, v. ⲭⲓⲛ.
ϭⲓⲛⲉ;
ϭⲛ′,11. ϭⲙ′,12.
ϭⲛⲧ′,11.
ϭⲓⲡⲱⲓⲛⲓ,16,40.
ϭⲏ———,22.
ϭⲉ———,30,41.
ϭⲓⲥⲗⲁⲕ,55.
ϭⲙⲏ,45. ϭⲓⲙⲏ,50.
ϭⲙⲁⲩⲉⲓ,45. [R.
ϭⲟϥ(ⲉⲗ),?=ϭⲱⲃ,ap.
ϭⲱ,14.

Pl. 1.

NO. XXVIII. SLIGHTLY REDUCED.

NO. II,   DITTO.

Pl. 2.

NO. XI. SLIGHTLY REDUCED

Pl. 3.

NO. XIV, (RECTO AND VERSO), SLIGHTLY REDUCED.

NO. XV,   DITTO.

Pl. 4.

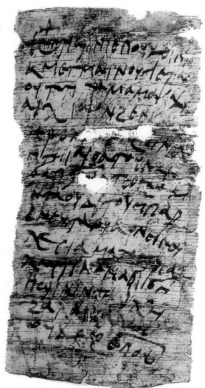

NO. XVI, SLIGHTLY REDUCED.

NO. XVIII.   DITTO.

ImTheStory.com

Personalized Classic Books in many genre's

Unique gift for kids, partners, friends, colleagues

Customize:

- Character Names
- Upload your own front/back cover images (optional)
- Inscribe a personal message/dedication on the inside page (optional)

Customize many titles Including
- Alice in Wonderland
- Romeo and Juliet
- The Wizard of Oz
- A Christmas Carol
- Dracula
- Dr. Jekyll & Mr. Hyde
- And more...

Lightning Source UK Ltd.
Milton Keynes UK
UKHW020950130720
366454UK00017B/1685